DATE DUE

MEANINGFUL PLAY, PLAYFUL MEANING

Gary Alan Fine, PhD
Editor
University of Minnesota

Human Kinetics Publishers, Inc.
Champaign, Illinois

Proceedings of the 11th Annual Meeting of The Association for the Anthropological Study of Play (TAASP) held March 14–17, 1985 at Washington, DC.

Library of Congress Cataloging-in-Publication Data

Association for the Anthropological Study of Play.
  Meeting (11th : 1985 : Washington, D.C.)
  Meaningful play, playful meaning.

  (The Association for the Anthropological Study
of Play ; vol. 11)
  ''Proceedings of the 11th Annual Meeting of the
Association for the Anthropological Study of Play
(TAASP) held March 14–17, 1985 at Washington, D.C.''
—T.P. verso
  Bibliography: p.
  1. Amusements—Social aspects—Congresses.
2. Play—Social aspects—Congresses. 3. Games—
Congresses. I. Fine, Gary Alan. II. Title.
III. Series: Association for the Anthropological Study of
Play (Series) ; v. 11.
GV14.45.A87 1985   306'.48   86-21513
ISBN 0-87322-087-0

Developmental Editor: Laura E. Larson
Production Director: Ernie Noa
Assistant Production Director: Lezli Harris
Copy Editor: Ann Bruehler
Typesetter: Brad Colson
Proofreader: Linda Purcell
Text Layout: Denise Peters
Cover Design: Jack Davis
Printed By: Braun-Brumfield, Inc.

ISBN: 0-87322-087-0
ISSN: 0885-8764

Printed in the United States of America

10 9 8 7 6 5 4 3 2 1

Human Kinetics Publishers, Inc.
Box 5076, Champaign, IL 61820

To
Gloria DeWolfe

Contents

Contributors   vii

Preface   ix

Part I. Theoretical Issues in Play Research

Callois Revisited: A Developmental Classification of Games   3
Patrick Biesty

Part II. How Americans Play

Mind Games: Imaginary Social Relationships in American Sports   19
John Caughey

How They Play in Peoria: Models of Adult Leisure   35
John R. Kelly

The Manliness Paradox in Ernest Thompson Seton's Ideology   45
of Play and Games
Jay Mechling

Making Work Play   61
John R. Bowman

Part III. Children's Play Under Constraint

Playing Around: Children's Play Under Constraint   75
Caroline Zinsser

Researching Play in Schools   85
Nancy R. King

The Effects of Traditional Playground Equipment on Preschool   101
Children's Dyadic Play Interaction
Chris J. Boyatzis

The Strains of Idioculture: External Threat and Internal Crisis   111
on a Little League Baseball Team
Gary Alan Fine

Coping in Adversity: Children's Play in the Holocaust   129
George Eisen

Part IV. Play and Social Identity

Revival, Survival, and Revisal: Ethnic Identity Through   145
"Traditional Games"
Alyce Taylor Cheska

Play, the Development of *Kakada'*, and Social Change Among   155
the Bulusu' of East Kalimantan
Laura P. Appell-Warren

The Rugby Tour: Construction and Enactment of Social Roles   173
in a Play Setting
Dan C. Hilliard

Contra Dance in New York: Longways for as Many as Will   193
Judy Levine

Part V. Play and Modern Technology

Social Impact of Video Game Play   209
Steven B. Silvern, Mary K. Lang, and Peter A. Williamson

Will Video Games Alter the Relationship Between Play   219
and Cognitive Development?
David F. Lancy

A New Environment for Communication Play: On-Line Play   231
David Myers

Contributors

Ms. Laura P. Appell-Warren
Milton Academy
Milton, MA 02186

Prof. Patrick Biesty
Dept. of Sociology
County College of Morris
Route 10 & Center Grove Road
Randolph, NJ 07869

Prof. John Bowman
Dept. of Sociology
Pembroke State University
Pembroke, NC 28372

Mr. Chris J. Boyatzis
Psychology Department
Brandeis University
Brown 125
Waltham, MA 02254

Prof. John L. Caughey
Dept. of American Studies
University of Maryland
Room 2140 Taliaferro Hall
College Park, MD 20742

Prof. Alyce Cheska
Dept. of Physical Education
University of Illinois
Urbana, IL 61801

Prof. George Eisen
California State Polytechnic
   University
3801 West Temple Avenud
Pomona, CA 91768

Prof. Gary Alan Fine
Dept. of Sociology
University of Minnesota
Minneapolis, MN 55455

Prof. Dan C. Hilliard
Dept. of Sociology
Southwestern University
Georgetown, TX 78626

Prof. John R. Kelly
Dept. of Leisure Studies
University of Illinois
Urbana, IL 61801

Prof. Nancy R. King
Dept. of Education Policy,
   Planning, and Administration
College of Education
University of Maryland
College Park, MD 20742

Prof. David F. Lancy
Dept. of Elementary Education
Utah State University
Logan, UT 84322

Ms. Judy Levine
510 East 20th Street, #4A
New York, NY 10009

Prof. Jay Mechling
American Studies
University of California
Davis, CA 95616

Prof. David Myers
Dept. of Communications
Loyola University
6363 St. Charles Avenue
New Orleans, LA 70118

Prof. Steven B. Silvern
Auburn University
Curriculum and Teaching
Auburn, AL 36849

Ms. Carline Zinsser
45 East 62nd Street
New York, NY 10021

Preface

Every title deserves an explanation. In the case of this volume, *Meaningful Play, Playful Meaning* was chosen to represent two sides of play theory and research. The first side recognizes that play is significant in and of itself. Play stands for something, and the very purpose of organizations like The Anthropological Association for the Study of Play is to recognize in their existence that play is meaningful. We can learn much by breaking through what Brian Sutton-Smith has playfully termed "The Triviality Barrier." Through play we can see values, norms, expectations, symbols, and organizations reflected in a fractured and distorted mirror, but reflected nonetheless. Play affects players and presents them to others and to themselves. Even if we do not agree on what the connection between play and "the real world" is to be, we recognize that the dynamics of play are the dynamics of human life.

The second half of the title pays heed to another set of themes in play theory. The world of work is not devoid of play. "Slop" exists in all systems. Rarely, if ever, do we find a social system that lacks some leeway for playful, unserious activity. One cannot exclude play from any social world. Through the world we can see play, and we can see the need for play to grease the iron wheels of the mundane. Play affects workers just as players, and permits them to present themselves to others and to themselves.

This set of papers addresses both of these concerns using methodologies including experiments, surveys, interviews, participant observation, observation, and historical analysis. The settings of play range from the Yukon to Indonesia, from Poland to Peoria. Play includes rugby, baseball, daydreaming, computer hacking, and seal skinning. Surely play researchers have no lack of topics to examine and no lack of methodologies with which to examine them. Sex, aggression, cognitive development, aging, and identity each contribute to the models that those who have contributed to this volume have chosen to emphasize. Further, the papers are both meaningful and playful in turn. They range from Hilliard's exuberant account of the macho world of rugby players to Eisen's mournful and moving account of Jewish children's play during the Holocaust. Mechling presents an unexpected account of the androgynous themes in the life and work of one of the founders of the supposedly masculine Boy Scouts of America, whereas Caughey demonstrates that virtually all Americans develop close personal ties to media sport figures.

Many of these papers were first presented at the Eleventh Annual Meeting of The Anthropological Association for the Study of Play, held March 14–

17, 1985, in Washington, DC. This volume is not, however, a proceedings, but an annual. All papers were subject to review and evaluation, and some papers not presented at the conference were included for publication. As editor, I wish to thank referees who helped maintain the quality of this volume: Maria Allison, Wanni Anderson, Jan Beran, Kendall Blanchard, John Bowman, Alyce Cheska, Garry Chick, George Eisen, Marjorie Goodwin, Ann Marie Guilmette, Janet Harris, Nand Hart-Nibbrig, Dan Hilliard, Sandra Hoffman, Linda Hughes, John Kelly, Diana Kelly-Byrne, Roberta Lavenda, John Loy, Frank Manning, Jay Mechling, Bernard Mergen, Andrew Miracle, Richard Mitchell, Anna Nardo, Roberta Park, Stuart Reifel, and James Weatherly.

Gary Alan Fine

PART I

Theoretical Issues in Play Research

Caillois Revisited: A Developmental Classification of Games

Patrick Biesty

Caillois's discussion of play in *Man, Play, and Games* (1961) is appealing for many reasons, not least of which is his expansive approach to the concept. Although his theory is fundamentally sociological, Caillois blends philosophy in his definition of play, psychology in relating types of games to "essential and irreducible impulses" (1961:14), and cultural history in his discussion of the interdependence of a society's typical games and its culture. He is particularly suggestive in his discussion of the game types he believes underlie the cultural organization of preliterate and historical (civilized) societies.

Each of these levels of human activity is related to the others by partaking of the four modes of play that make up the classification of games. This contention of continuity across the animal kingdom, across cultures, and across age is at the heart of Caillois's objection to considering the development of capacities as the main function of play. In effect, Caillois is saying if the play forms are *a priori* impulses they are not carried out for purpose other than themselves.

His perspective equates the leaping play of an African springbok with the highly refined skill of a downhill skier and the play-making agility of basketball players. Although it retains a pristine purity for human play, the approach slights the distinctive ways that humans are self-conscious. By overlooking the self-conscious element of play, Caillois's system lacks an important differentiating tool. Nowhere is the lack of differentiation more obvious than in systematic avoidance of developmental functions.

That Caillois's objection to a developmental function for play distorted his presentation of the classification system and that a reappraisal of the system shows a compatibility with one or more developmental perspectives as they relate to play is the argument of this paper.

Caillois's perspective on development can be partially traced to the distinctions he makes between himself ahd Huizinga (1955). Caillois makes two major points. One, that although play approaches the mysterious, it exposes and expends it. Play to Caillois is fundamentally profane. "It is a fact that the ideas of the free and the profane are expressed by the same word in many languages . . . play, free activity par excellence (sic), is the pure profane" (Caillois, 1980:160). Secondly, in contrast to Huizinga, who left them out, Caillois argues for the inclusion of games of chance in any discussion of play.

Caillois's emphasis on games of chance is particularly important theoretically, for it helps explain his objection to linking play to development in a causal relationship. Although he admits that play often develops capacities, he states "the proper function of play is never to develop capacities. Play is an end in itself" (1980:167). He supports this position with the contention that "pure games of chance do not develop any physical or mental aptitude in the player" (1980:167). Thus his most distinguishing and controversial ideas are linked theoretically: Play is profane activity, games of chance are play, and play's function is not development.

Caillois's perspective can be summarized as: (a) Although play is often coincidental with the development of capacities, play's proper function is to be an end in itself; (b) because games of chance develop no physical or mental capacities because of the passive nature of the player's role, the nondevelopmental function of play is demonstrated; (c) play is a universal expression of a shared human nature that through interaction is socialized into unique cultural expressions; (d) although varying in specifics, play takes on four forms in games: vertigo, mimicry, competition, and chance; and (e) as an expression of human nature, play should be understood as irreducible impulses that are also present in animals.

The Concept of Development

By claiming that play's function is not development, Caillois poses rather than resolves a dilemma. He does not marshal empirical evidence against development; he argues against it deductively. Furthermore, he leaves important questions unanswered. What is play's relationship to individual development? More precisely, what relationship of play to development might be consistent with his conceptions? A further critical question arises from the description of play as an end in itself. To be done for itself implies that an action is conducted with some awareness and assessment of oneself. Is play then a means of displaying oneself (developmentally and otherwise) to oneself, and does the act of self-display facilitate development in, or come as a result of, the display?

Caillois does not deny a relationship between play and development; he denies play's subservience to any nonplay end, whether that end is religion, culture, or development. His discussion of play and the sacred can be taken as a model of the relationship to nonplay goals, for here Caillois spells out his objection to nonplay purposes.

> Without doubt, secrecy, mystery, and even travesty can be transformed into play activity, but it must be immediately pointed out that this transformation is necessarily to the detriment of the secret and the mysterious, which play exposes, publishes, and somehow *expends*. In a word, play tends to remove the nature of the

mysterious. On the other hand, when the secret, the mask, or the costume fulfills a sacramental function one can be sure that not play, but an institution is involved. All that is mysterious or make-believe by nature approaches play: moreover, it must be that the function of fiction or diversion is to remove the mystery; i.e., the mystery may no longer be awesome, and the counterfeit may not be a beginning or symptom of metamorphosis and possession. (Caillois, 1961:4–5)

Play's relation to the sacred is to "expose, publish, and expend" it; in other words, play removes the sacred's motive force by being wise to it. The self-consciousness of the sacred in play is its manufactured or constructed nature for the ongoing play. In play, self-consciousness is from the internal reality of its constructed nature and has no necessary effect on the sacred in the social world. *Homo ludens* is in essence *Homo sapiens* without sapient consequences.

One can be mysterious without the consequences of religious awe. Outside of the play one need not believe. Likewise, being wise to the sacred does not mean debunking it because that too would be a nonplay purpose. Rather, play's function relative to the sacred is to be aware of the operation of the sacred in an activity. Play provides a store of knowledge, the door of which may or may not be opened for use in understanding the sacred in its own sphere of operations. Play can teach one about the sacred, but one does not have to pay attention or give credence to the lesson. Play that deals with mystery is an end in itself in the sense of making a mysterious display of oneself to oneself. As it is said that there is a measure of play in a rope, play with the mysterious is the looseness of the mysterious.

By substituting development for the sacred, Caillois's criticism of the developmental orientation of Chateau and Piaget can be seen as, in essence, the same as his criticism of Huizinga. To Caillois both the sacred and development are overinterpretations of play. By extending Caillois's argument to this point, his dismissal of the developmental function of play becomes clearer. In addition, by following the logic of his critique, a relationship of play to development emerges. Play makes one wise to development in the sense of making one aware of what capacities one has, without there being a subsequent or necessary use or application for that *in situ* awareness. Although development may often be a function of play, it is the freedom that is the play. The awareness of the developmental skill or capacity is the essential function.

Another explanation of Caillois's objection to a developmental interpretation of play is his focus. Although it is true that he begins his discussion with a definition of play, his main focus is on game activities, that is, on socially structured activities in which play can take place. This shift of focus from play to play in games may account for his insistence on the absence of developmental goals. Certainly, games of chance, Caillois's prime focus, are the least interesting form of game play to young children, whose play seems always to have some developmental function (Garvey, 1977). The relative absence of games of chance among modern children may be strongly influenced by our concept of childhood and its appropriate activities (Aries, 1962). Caillois's relative indifference to the distinction between pregame play and game play reflects his assertion that play crosses species and age differences.

Thus Caillois apparently was presenting inappropriate data in support of his antidevelopmental argument, especially as it applies to children. He drew on the social activities of adolescents and adults to argue against developmental theories that were mainly concerned with young children. Although the error of that type of argument is clear, the argument emphasizes one of Caillois's commanding assumptions: Activities are shared in their essential character by infrahuman animals and humans as well as by children and adults. This assumption is at the heart of his application of data from one play level (games) to another (childhood play) and underlines the profane character of play.

Caillois's emphasis on the profane nature of play serves as the key to resolving the dilemma of a developmental function for play. Play's function as an end in itself is argued to be an expression of the player's knowledge of his profane condition, whether that condition is an experienced development, stasis, an alternative condition, or a decline in capacities. After all, games of vertigo are essentially experiences of the loss of control; games such as blind man's bluff and pin the tail on the donkey likewise make sense only as ways of having fun by observing oneself fail to accomplish tasks; and in games of chance, Caillois's main focus, almost all players lose and know beforehand that they probably will. Each of these games in one way or another belies the contention that the proper function of play is to foster skill development. Each, however, is fun by virtue of the self-reflection it involves.[1]

In addition, many researchers have found that theories of unilineal development, such as Piaget's cognitive theory, do not account for actual games played by children and adults. Adolescents, such as the Manus children studied by Mead (1930) play mainly sensory-motor games of running and chasing supposedly appropriate to younger children. Eifermann (1970, 1971a, 1971b) found that the social context of children's lives—that is, social class and educational settings—influence the choice of games. For example, symbolic play is rare in Israeli upper middle-class children, aged 6 to 8, and common among lower class children. These and other studies (El'Konin, 1971; Singer, 1966) lend support to Caillois's stance.

A Revised Definition of Play

Addressing the issue of what is (are) the relationship(s) between play and development is still necessary. By defining play here as a profane self-expression that is self-revelatory, free, uncertain, separate, unproductive but rule-governed, and/or of a make-believe nature, Caillois's break with developmental interpretations is reinterpreted.[2] Play is often developmental. When it is not, play has a developmental potential by virtue of the self-awareness it encompasses. Caillois's aversion to developmental interpretations of play seems to have led him to overreact to the point of unnecessarily confusing his classification system. To correct this exclusion a compatible relationship of play to development is being suggested. Play will be seen as related to development in an interactive manner. Play displays the self's profane condition in a celebratory self-regard, and this display may itself be an act of developmental change and further display. Whatever the outcome of play, some potential developmental change is present due to the self-regard inherent in the action.

The concept of development will be used here to mean any increase or addition in skill or capacity that allows the subject to handle the tasks that confront it. This broad definition overlaps various developmental perspectives that focus on the development of one type of capacity, for example, motor skills, cognitive skills, emotional skills, moral understanding, and so forth. The definition does not imply or deny an integration of one level of skill with a later level. Although the formulation accepts a sequence of stages that can build on earlier stages, an evaluation of one stage being "higher" or "lower" is not implied (cf Langness, 1974). This formulation also allows for the inclusion of apparent regressive directions in skills when the subject has the compensating ability to deal with that regression or stasis by some other skill. If I fail at blind man's bluff but gain an acceptance of myself and others with greater emotional and social skill, I have developed.

Caillois's Classification System

Because he rejects outright anything other than a coincidental developmental function for play, Caillois's explanatory table of game types suffers from an imposed simplicity (see Table 1). Therefore, before attempting to go beyond this system it is worthwhile to examine the table to understand what it communicates and fails to communicate about play and games.

In the unlabeled left-hand column Caillois places examples of one-person play on a continuum from *paidia* or frenzy to *ludus* or ordered play. Although an obvious progression in degree of control to this continuum exists, Caillois does not note it as developmental, and from the examples given no developmental relationship is apparent.

The top row labels the subsequent four columns as types of games, but they are presented in no particular order. In each column games progress from the least to the most ordered of that type. However, as one reads across the table, the level of placement is not related from one column to the next. For example, athletics, heads or tails, masks, disguises, and waltzing are all at the same level. Some curious inclusions require, but do not receive, explanation. Traveling carnivals and theater productions are work for the "players." An alternate interpretation is that the audience are to be considered players. The reader is left to interpret the answer.

Table 1 Caillois's Classification of Games

	agon (competition)	alea (chance)	mimicry (simulation)	ilinx (vertigo)
Paidia	Racing, wrestling	Counting-out rhymes	Children's initi-actions, games	"Whirling" Horseback
Tumult		Heads or tails	of illusion	Swinging
Agitation			Tag, arms	Waltzing
Immoderate laughter			Mask	
Kite flying	Boxing, billiards	Betting		Valador
Solitaire	Fencing, chess	Roulette		Traveling
Patience	Contests, sport		Theater	carnivals
Crosswords	in general	Lotteries	Spectacles	Tightrope walking
Ludus				

Why these varied and complex social events are classified as games is not specified, but they certainly partake of the play spirit. As a number of writers citing Caillois have suggested (Manning, 1983; Turner, 1983), carnivals, especially grand, national events, engulf all the game categories. However, Caillois in *Man and the Sacred* (1980) regards festivals as social events of much larger significance than a mixture of game types would suggest.

From a classificatory perspective the integration of multiple game types in mass celebrations, such as Brazilian carnivals and the American Super Bowl, would be better understood as entertainments or festivals rather than as games. They reflect social affiliations and communal identity more powerfully than individual identity. Furthermore, festivals appear to serve functions outside themselves such as social unity and religious rejuvenation that alter a purely play function (Caillois, 1980; Cox, 1969). Although the play element in festivals is relevant, their inclusion as a class of games seems misleading. Their proper classification as some supragame type, related to cultural development, is called for but beyond the scope of this paper.

Despite its deficiencies, Table 1 does illustrate the four types of games and levels of individual control at which these game types can be played. The table also serves as a heuristic prod by its very incongruity of parts. On what is the order from *paida* to *ludus* based? Is that order in any way related to development? Can the games be equated across the table in some meaningful way? Is an implicit order to this table hidden by its apparent simplicity?

The order to the table is developmental, which is not to say that a developmental function exists in each of these games. Rather, it illustrates

Caillois's determination to resist reducing play to a purposeful role outside itself. He also did not misinterpret the relationship because the developmental thesis presented here is taken directly from his classification system.

A Developmental Sequence

Any of a number of developmental theories might be applied to Caillois's scheme to gauge a good fit.[3] Each in its own way might enlighten our understanding of the transformation of play from a frenzied to an ordered manner. Each might also provide some relational structure to the types of games. For a number of reasons George Herbert Mead's (1934) concepts of infancy, play at roles, and game playing will be used. Most important is the fact that Mead's "stages" are really modes of interaction that grow out of and continue within social life. These modes of interaction become means of self-reflection and self-definition, thus facilitating the definition of activity as play.

As Mead's focus was not so much on development as on how interactive patterns are internalized and then externalized as expressions of the self, his perspective is compatible with Caillois's thesis that development ought not be considered the function of play. Mead does not contend that the child's play at roles is for the purpose of adapting to society, although that is its likely outcome. In addition, Mead's "stages" can be seen as a sequence of social activities that a player may integrate in varying ways as the interactive process of self-reflection, but not all selves develop alike. By being an interactive model, each stage provides a distinct means of self-awareness. These distinctive modes will be shown to be the defining characteristics of game types.

In addition, like Caillois, Mead was interested in the distinction between make-believe and rule-governed play. To Mead that distinction was related to the development of linguistic skills and the character of the dialogues between the "I" and the "me." In addition, Mead's concept of the generalized other included the larger social world in the concepts of play and games. Caillois's speculation on the connection between game types and cultural epochs would benefit from a Meadian analysis, and Mead's concept of generalized other would benefit from a formulation as combined game organizations. This analysis, however, will focus solely on the polar dimensions of play and the classification of games.

Although he distinguished between play and the game, Mead referred to the life spaces and activities that precede and follow them. Prior to the acquisition of language the child is dependent on physical and vocal gestures to communicate. Thus Mead implicitly posits infancy and gestural communication as a first stage. The early use of language develops concurrently with play at roles or what might be called the pretend stage. Game playing develops later as the child acquires the ability to see him- or herself as others see him or her. The child does this by taking the role of the other in rule-governed interactions; this is the third or game stage. Adult life is much like the game stage except that it is not play. Actually,

Table 2   Stages of Communication and Types of Play

Stage	Forms of communication	Typical play
Infant	Physical and verbal gestures	Almost all activity
Pretender	Language, roles, fantasy	Imitation, imaginary scenarios
Game player	Reciprocal rules, role-taking interaction structures	Competitions, cooperative games
Adult-like	Abstract calculation, generalized role taking	Creating, constructing, re-creating

game play and tasks develop concurrently. Mead is clearly not talking about playful games when he discusses ways in which people develop narrow or full selves. To consider his discussion of adult behavior as more than an alternative to playful games is justified. Adult behavior is ideally the behavior of serious social beings interacting in some harmony of self and community interests. In the adult stage one is most often concurrently taking the role of the generalized other as one interacts in a game-like fashion. The adult communicates not just as a role player the way a baseball player does but also communicates as an embodiment of the collectivity.

Each "stage" has its distinguishing features as Table 2 illustrates. Although the order is developmental, that is, increasingly complex, the forms of communication and the types of play are available to anyone who has completed the sequence of socialization. Thus one can play in a manner—for example, in the physical-gestural mode—that no longer has developmental consequences.

The order from paidia to ludus can now be represented as follows:

Paidia

     Gestural: tumult, agitation
     Linguistic: immoderate laughter (as at comic distortions)
     Interactive: kite flying, solitaire, patience
     Abstracted: crosswords (re-creating a fixed pattern)

Ludus

The sequence of developmental competencies is clear in this reformulation of Caillois's continuum of solitary play, and the interactive modes can now be applied across the category of games so that a horizontal correlation is established. The game types are social forms that require role play at various levels of communication. Thus a game can be played at any of the levels indicated.

Game Categories

The developmental sequence also has relevance for the categorization of games. The four game types closely resemble the developmental stages, or more precisely, the interactive forms. In Table 3 the games have been arranged from left to right in the order suggested by the developmental sequence. Games of vertigo are placed first because they rely on physiological communications that depend on an internalized sense of gravity. No matter how complicated the activity, games of vertigo are self-displays of one's physical competencies and/or incompetencies.

Simulations are placed second because they involve constructions of symbolic irrealities. On each of the levels of communication the self-display is as an object other than the taken-for-granted "me" of everyday life.

Games of competition are third because they depend on a tension between equal and unequal ordering of statuses. The clear distinction between mimicry and competition/cooperation is that the self-display in the latter is not as an object; the self-display is as another subject, that is, as a person whose actions are not under control. Taking on and displaying oneself as the subjectivity of another is the heart of agon and can be played at each of the levels. In a strict Meadian sense a game requires more than taking on the gestures and presented roles of others; a game requires taking the role of the other as the other is subjectively (Biesty, 1986).

Games of chance are last because they are based on a fixed order of the universe in which they operate. In the development of abstracted communication, play reaches the point where the player creates and risks the definition of reality (e.g., in a death-defying tightrope walk or an overidentification with the character one is playing). In alea, however, the player risks only a portion, a part, or a token. The created reality remains unchallenged. The roulette wheel will spin again, giving the player another chance. If the player falls from the high wire, the player risks all. The two vectors meet at the bottom right-hand corner of the chart. The creator-founder-operator of a football pool takes a chance on losing his money. He also risks losing his whole operation.

Each game is consciously entered into as a role-playing/role-taking interaction. Nevertheless, the game itself may require that the players enact a role with one or another means of communication. Thus games of vertigo may be simple gestural interactions such as rolling down hills; they may require alterations of reality as in whirling to create visual distortions and dizziness; they may require skilled role taking of the other as in dancing or horseback riding; or they may require abstract formulation of the balance of forces that impose ultimate meaning on a situation as in tightrope walking or any other so-called "death-defying" activity. A highly skilled player could include each level: A downhill skier, for example, could tumble with abandon in deep powder snow, whirl in somersaults, make carefully crafted herringbone patterns with other skiers, and make death-defying leaps from precipices high above ground.

Table 3 A Developmental Classification of Games

Play	Ilinx (vertigo)	Mimicry (simulation)	Agon (competition)	Alea (chance)
Paidia Gestural communication (Pure Play)	rolling, rocking bouncing, swinging	imitating animals, practical jokes	mutual tickling, lovers "wrestling"	hide-and-go-seek, peek-a-boo
Linguistic communication (Make-Believe Play)	children whirling, staring at the sun, holding one's breath, roller coasters, rides in general	"house," trick or treat, parades	turn-taking games, tag, billiards, shooting galleries, Johnny-on-the-pony	counting-out rhymes (e.g., "eenie, meenie, minie, moe"), heads or tails
Interactive role communication (Game Play)	social dancing, skiing, horseback riding	playing theater, masquerades, performing on stage	baseball, boxing, sport in general	board games (e.g., Monopoly), card games, video games (e.g., Asteroids)
Abstracted communication (Serious Play)	tightrope walking, automobile racing	playing Santa Claus to children, story-telling	coaching a team, arguing	gambling, charting horses
Ludus				

Remember that the means of communication in games are not always discreet entities, but they overlap on other communications. The levels are therefore separated by dotted lines to represent the openness of the borders. Nevertheless, each level can be examined on its own terms. To this end I have labeled each level to describe the essence of the mode of play.

The first row is pure play—activities that are most clearly done for their own bodily pleasure. The second row is labeled make-believe play to characterize their alteration of the definition of social reality. The third, game play, denotes the quality of rule-governed interactions. The last is serious play and borders on purposeful intentions outside itself.

Caillois's contention that play is an irreducible impulse that crosses species lines is retained by naming the first row ''pure play.'' Although the developmental sequence, representing greater levels of self-abstraction, is used to organize the increased complexity of a type of activity and its social meaning, the same four categories of communication organize play on the horizontal level. The essential quality of each of the game types is found in animals, infants, and socialized humans.

If Gregory Bateson (1956) is correct, river otters engage in solitary tumbling (ilinx), interpreting a piece of paper as ''food'' (mimicry), play wresting (agon), and hiding and chasing (alea). Human infants rock (ilinx), imitate adults (mimicry), wrestle adults as equals (agon), and play peek-a-boo (alea). The implication is that some self-signaling system is operating in each case of pure play.[4]

Row 4, serious play, is governed by abstract communications and by actions representing oneself as a generalized other. These actions border so closely on the serious that their inclusion in the table might be questioned. However, they share the common element of risking the very definition of play in which they operate. Maintenance of the definition of the activity as play is the play, the freedom or looseness from extraneous purpose.

Certainly tightrope walking and automobile racing risk the physical life of the players. Other examples of vertiginous play, such as skiing and diving, may enter this category when pushed to their limits. In games of mimicry such as enacting Santa or story telling, didactic and/or moral goals may intrude. Similarly, coaching a team stretches the coach's ability to maintain a playful consciousness. Lastly, serious gambling risks fortune and property. How then does one play at a serious game? Probably by insuring the play's freedom from serious consequences.

Conclusions

In his classification system Caillois took an adamant stance against considering play's function to be anything other than itself. The shallowness of this approach was a too-restrictive interpretation of what the relationship of play and development might be. An analysis of the relationship from Caillois's own work has resulted in a restatement. Play's proper function as an end in itself is a self-reflection that celebrates the profane condition of the self in development, stasis, and exhibit current capacities and failings. Play also develops capacities.

Whether or not it develops skills, play is organized around developed capacities, especially communicative skills. Thus the classification of games reveals a developmental order despite Caillois's clear intention not to organize his system that way.

The revised classification system depends upon the inclusion of a celebratory self-consciousness in play that is shared by humans and ''lower'' animals. The classification system implies that animals and humans can and do signal a posture, or image, of themselves to themselves and to others in the four ways that one can play.

What the irreducible impulses are can only be suggested here. The four signals somehow represent a distance of the actor from the action itself. That distance from self is represented in the quality by which we categorize the same types. Ilinx, or vertigo, is typically a direct physical signal of self to self. Mimicry, or simulation, is a signal of equation of another thing or person with the self. Alea, or chance, is a signal that self and the regarded order of things are in tune. The unique ability of humans to use language has resulted in the development of these signaling devices to complex levels.

At the heart of Caillois's classification system is a paradox: Play has developmental functions; yet, play is a fundamental expression of what an animal is, whether or not it develops. Thus the developmental classification system is in fact a matrix of communication modes within which types of play and games develop and are transformed.

The developmental classification system offered here is not intended to be restrictive or all-inclusive. Some games such as card games and board games overlap game categories because they have elements of chance and competition in them. The very concept of competition might be reconsidered as competitive-cooperative games to account for their true character and to include noncompetitive games. Schwartzman (1978) reviews several examples of games of equivalence in which play continues until the scores are equal. In addition, the Chinese concept of *wan* that Caillois describes as an appreciative, self-affecting involvement with one's activity is not discussed.

However, this developmental classification of games is based in the distinctively human capacity to create social meanings through communication. It therefore represents fundamental patterns of interaction in and out of play. The classification lends itself to further elaboration, especially as a tool for examining the connections between games and culture and games and festivals. It also suggests avenues for understanding the links between human and other animal behavior. Hopefully, the revised classification system also maintains the expansive scope of Caillois's original.

Notes

1. This contention is in accord with Goffman's (1961) contention in ''Fun

in Games'' that it is the framing activity that surrounds games that provides their fun.

2. This definition emphasizes the profane quality of play. As noted, the purpose is to emphasize the related but not subservient role of play to development. An alternative to profane, which is always contrasted with the sacred, is mundane or ''as is.'' Both terms specify the focus of play as within itself.

3. The only work to relate Caillois's game categories to a developmental scheme that I know of is an effort by Mauricio Abadi (1967) entitled ''Psychoanalysis of Playing.'' Abadi sees games as means of working through psychic conflicts. In his interpretation competitive games are related to oedipal struggles; chance is related to concern over one's own death; mimicry is a way of finding one's personality; and ilinx is a symbolic reproduction of sexual orgasm.

4. Milton Singer (1980) provides an excellent survey of the value of a semiotic approach to the concept of self. The three sign types (icon, index, and symbol) have been hypothesized to be found among both animals and humans.

References

Abadi, M. (1967). Psychoanalysis of playing. *Psychotherapy and Psychosomatics, 15*, 85–93.

Aries, P. (1962). *Centuries of childhood*. New York: Vintage Books–Alfred A. Knopf.

Bateson, G. (1956). The message ''this is play.'' In B. Schatfner (Ed.), *Group processes: Transactions of the second conference* (pp. 145-242). New York: Josiah Macy, Jr., Foundation.

Biesty, P. (1986). If it's fun, is it play? In B. Mergen (Ed.), *Cultural dimensions of play, games, and sport* (pp. 61–72). Champaign, IL: Human Kinetics.

Caillois, R. (1961). *Man, play, and games*. New York: The Free Press.

Caillois, R. (1980). *Man and the sacred*. Westport, CT: Greenwood Press.

Cox, H. (1969). *The feast of fools*. Cambridge, MA: Harvard University Press.

Eifermann, R. (1970). Cooperation and egalitarianism in Kibbutz children's games. *Human Relations, 23*, 579–587.

Eifermann, R. (1971a). *Determinants of children's games styles*. Jerusalem: Israeli Academy of Arts and Sciences.

Eifermann, R. (1971b). Social play in childhood. In R. Herron & B. Sutton-Smith (Eds.), *Child's play* (pp. 220–297). New York: John Wiley.

El'Konin, D. (1971). Symbolics and its functions in the play of children. In R. Herron & B. Sutton-Smith (Eds.), *Child's play* (pp. 221–230). New York: John Wiley.

Garvey, C. (1977). *Play*. Cambridge, MA: Harvard University Press.

Goffman, E. (1961). *Encounters: Two studies in the sociology of interaction*. New York: Bobbs Merrill.

Langness, L.L. (1974). *The study of culture*. San Francisco: Chandler and Sharp.

Manning, F.E. (1983). Get some money for your honey: Gambling on the wages of sin. In F.E. Manning (Ed.), *The celebration of society* (pp. 80–99). Bowling Green, OH: Bowling Green University Popular Press.

Mead, G.H. (1934). *Mind, self, and society*. Chicago: University of Chicago Press.

Mead, M. (1930). *Growing up in New Guinea*. New York: Morrow.

Schwartzman, H. (1978). *Transformations*. New York: Plenum Press.

Singer, J.L. (1966). *Daydreaming: An introduction to the experimental study of inner experience*. New York: Random House.

Singer, M. (1980). Signs of the self: An exploration in semiotic anthropology. *American Anthropologist*, **82**, 485–507.

Turner, V. (1983). Carnival in Rio: Dionysian drama in an industrializing society. In F.E. Manning (Ed.), *The celebration of society*. Bowling Green, OH: Bowling Green University Press.

PART II

How Americans Play

Mind Games: Imaginary Social Relationships in American Sport

John Caughey

Outside the Baltimore Orioles' spring training camp last year, on the back of a white convertible, the following bumper sticker was displayed: "I love baseball. Don't mess with my reality." In this essay I would like to ignore that warning in order to explore an important but neglected aspect of American sport. But I want to do so in a way that partially honors the bumper sticker sentiment. No doubt many important ways exist in which play and everyday life interpenetrate and overlap, but in terms of individual experience it is sometimes useful to conceive of sport as an alternative reality, a series of psychological zones partially outside the experience of ordinary life. I am particularly interested in vicarious dimensions of sport and the ways in which people subjectively connect to and experience these psychological zones. I will also consider some of the effects these imaginary experiences seem to have on actual identities and social roles.[1]

Although the bumper sticker's anonymous author may not know this, the phrasing is consistent with the work of phenomenological sociologists such as Schutz (1962) and Berger (1970). One aspect of their argument goes like this: In any society, people's consciousness is dominated by the cultural knowledge and rules associated with the taken-for-granted reality of everyday life, particularly the "paramount reality" we experience by acting out the routine social roles of kinship and work (cf Berger & Luckmann, 1966:23). However, as Schutz observes, the individual also experiences certain "interruptions" in his ordinary life. These include

> the shock of falling asleep as the leap into the world of dreams; the inner transformation we endure if the curtain in the theater rises as the transition into the world of a stageplay; the radical change in our attitude if, before a painting, we permit our visual field to be limited by what is within the frame as the passage into the pictorial world. (1962:234)

Such interruptions take the individual into states of mind that are to a greater or lesser degree outside the ordinary paramount reality. These writers mention a variety of imaginary processes that have this quality, and I will turn to these in a moment. But they also discuss certain actual activities that take the individual away from the consciousness of ordinary social reality. Among their examples are boxing and, by implication, the actual playing of any sport. In sport, typically, one physically leaves home and work settings and enters a separate ritual arena such as a tennis court, first going through a transitional area such as the locker room. Here the dress of ordinary life is discarded as one dons the uniform of sport play. This symbolizes the psychological leaving-behind of outside social roles. But sport, too, is social. One leaves behind the outside reality and feels a sense of "escape"—but one enters and experiences the new physical and psychological reality by taking on and playing out the social roles around which the game is structured. One assumes the role of "pitcher" to someone else's "batter." Having said this, I want to leave behind the actual playing of sport and consider some of its vicarious or imaginary dimensions. But I will suggest that the manner in which we make the transition outside of ordinary reality and connect to vicarious sport parallels the social sequence I have just described. However, this transition often involves a drastic shift, not only in social roles but in personal identity as well.

In examining vicarious dimensions of American sport, I will occasionally draw on published reports, but I will mainly rely on information from my own informants. This information includes material drawn from my earlier general study of imaginary experience that involved some 500 subjects (Caughey, 1984). It also includes data from 48 individuals who were asked about their vicarious sport experiences during the winter of 1985. Most of these people were students at a large university in the eastern United States. To obtain descriptions of imaginary or vicarious sport experiences, I asked informants to monitor their daydreams and spectatorship. I then analyzed their reports for patterns characteristic of the informants' "other world" experiences. Although undoubtedly variation exists across the complex cultures of contemporary America and further research is needed to explore this, my impression—from my own research, from media reports, and from other studies—is that the patterns described below are widespread in "mainstream" American experience.

Sport Knowledge and Emotional Orientations

Before considering vicarious experience, we must examine the sport knowledge of an American fan. Stored in such an American mind is a fund of knowledge about the rules of many games. But we also find an incredible amount of information about particular people, most of whom the individual has never actually met. The average fan knows about hundreds of unmet sport figures: all the baseball, football, hockey, golf, Olympic, soccer, racing car, and even bowling figures that are "familiar" to him or her. Add to this the number of sport announcers, coaches, and writers, as well as various fictional sport figures such as "Rocky," and the sheer number of unmet sport figures is peculiar and impressive indeed. An

American is also expected to possess extensive information about these sport figures. Even an average fan does not merely know a baseball player's name; he also knows about his team, uniform number, position, past accomplishments (e.g., batting average), salary, appearance, personality, medical history, and off-the-field conduct. In the fall of 1980, for example, millions of Americans knew about George Brett's hemorrhoids and Terry Bradshaw's marital difficulties. To an interesting extent, such information is socially necessary because a significant number of American conversations revolve around the doings of various sport figures. As one woman said, her unusual lack of interest in sport often makes her feel "like an outsider in my own society."

But sport knowledge is turned to personal uses as well. Despite the complete lack of real face-to-face contact, an American fan *feels* strongly about sport figures. Indifferent to a few, he or she likes or dislikes others, and toward some feels truly powerful emotions. In discussing their feelings, my informants sometimes used terminology associated with the evaluation of sport performance; the person "hustles," is a "great streak shooter," and so on, but more commonly they evaluate sport beings personally. Those they dislike are characterized as "conceited," a "big mouth," a "male chauvinist," and so forth. Those they like are said to be "attractive," a "total person," a "great personality," and so forth. In short, people characterized sport figures as if they knew them personally and were intimately involved with them—and in a sense they are. To assess the importance of sport in American society, it is necessary to explore the fact that many Americans not only know about and feel strongly toward unmet sport figures, they also engage in imaginary social interactions with them.

Imaginary Social Relationships

Berger and Luckmann suggest that theater provides a paradigmatic example of our experience with alternative realities. In attending the theater a spectator is psychologically drawn out of his or her actual social world into the realm of the play. At one moment the play-goer is talking with his or her companion in the next seat. At the next moment both are absorbed in the fictional doings of an 18th-century drama.

> The transition between realities is marked by the rising and falling of the curtain. As the curtain rises, the spectator is "transported to another world," with its own meanings and an order that may or may not have much to do with the order of everyday life. As the curtain falls, the spectator "returns to reality," that is, to the paramount reality of everyday life. (1966:25)

The analogy with sport is clear, the transition between realities often being marked, significantly, by the playing of our national anthem. Every time an American attends a game or turns on a television sport program, he or she slips mentally out of the ordinary social world and connects to a vicarious experience.[2] Sometimes people may watch the actions of sport figures as outside observers, but often they assume some social role that links them psychologically to the participants in the game. By this means the individual vicariously enters the "other world." To understand this involvement the kinds of imaginary social relationships that people develop with sport figures must be examined.

In our culture, virtually everyone with any perceived interest in a sport figure is simply classified as a "fan." With associations of "fantasy" and "fanaticism" the term is suggestive. But as a classifier it is inadequate. The term does not begin to do justice to the variety of different sport attachments that exist in American society nor to the subjective experience of these attachments.

Interviewed in depth about their interest in a given figure, many "fans" attempted to explain their attachment by specifying an actual social relationship whose emotional quality is similar to that which they feel to the star. Thus one informant viewed basketball player Wes Unseld as the ideal "big brother." Many fans have attachments to unmet sport figures that are directly analogous to actual social relationships with real "brothers," "fathers," "lovers," and "friends." In the most significant type the sport figure is viewed as hero, alter ego, and friend. But before examining that relationship I will briefly consider two other examples.

Several of my informants described attachments to opposite sex sport figures (e.g., Bjorn Borg, Scott Hamilton, Chris Evert, Cal Ripkin, Jr., and Doug Flutie) in which the basis of the imaginary relationship is clearly romantic: The individual casts the sport figure in the role of imaginary lover. When the individual enters the realm of sport spectatorship her (or his) involvement is structured by this relationship. The individual admires the figure's physical beauty ("he's cute and I love his muscular legs") and relates to the performance with sympathetic concern. While activities such as the collecting of magazine photographs, posters, and newspaper clippings may be significant, the "heart" of such relationships involves imaginary social interactions. In the midst of nondemanding situations, the individual mentally slips away and plays out imagined social encounters with an image of the sport figure.

One young woman, studying to be a lawyer, described her "love" relationship with O.J. Simpson. Like other informants she fantasized about dating and marrying her star. One often repeated fantasy involved vivid imaginings of "the meeting," a social situation in which O.J. first interacts with the fan.

> We sometimes meet because he needs help. On these occasions, I am the best lawyer in town . . . a willing soul ready to do battle (for him).
>   This time O.J. Simpson is still active in the NFL. As he runs a "fly pattern" and makes the game-winning touchdown, he crashes into me and my cameras in the end zone. As he helps me up, he notices the "twinkle" in my eyes and I notice his "twinkle." We fall in love and live happily ever after.

The glamour of such sport figures includes their grace and physical beauty, but they are also paragons of success. Recognized, admired, and worshiped by millions of others, the sport figure has a powerful appeal lacking in the boy (or girl) next door. Landing such a person, in fantasy, raises you up to the level of the American gods.

A second sport figure relationship is based on antagonism. Most informants can readily list sport figures they dislike or despise. Examples include controversial figures like Howard Cosell, George Steinbrenner, John Elway, Jimmy the Greek, Phyllis George, Joe Theisman, and Martina Navratilova (many of whom were strongly admired by other people in my sample). Given that the individual has never met these people, the level of hostility is surprisingly high. One woman spoke forcefully of her antagonism to Mark Gastineau whom she viewed as ''the epitome of the dumb violent football player.'' In some cases these negative feelings lead the individual into the formulation of an elaborate social relationship that is the inverse of the stereotypic fan relationship; the basis of the relationship is hatred, anger, envy, or disgust.

As with the love relationships, media consumption is often intense. Several informants taunted or talked back to sport announcers they disliked. Others took satisfaction in watching a player fail: ''I thoroughly enjoy and certainly get thrilled when I see Danny White get sacked.'' Such relationships have a fantasy dimension as well. Serious participants conjure up fantasy meetings with the objects of their displeasure. Here they beat these figures at their own game or carry out an imaginary debate with them. In one woman's daydream, ''I just tell him (an announcer) how rotten he is and that Howard Cosell is Superman compared to him and walk away.'' Imaginary criticizing, taunting, or outdoing of the disliked figure seems to allow the person to deny a potentially feared self-image and to experience feelings of superiority to a disliked but ''successful'' rival.

Admiration Relationships

The most common and significant group of pseudosocial relationships are those in which the sport figure becomes the object of intense admiration. Such relationships approximate the stereotypic conceptualization of the ''fan,'' but much more is involved than aesthetic appreciation of sport performance. Characteristically, the admired figure comes to represent some combination of idol, hero, alter ego, mentor, and role model. The diverse sport figures around whom informants have built such relationships include: Larry Bird, Chris Evert, Rocky Balboa (from the movie *Rocky*), JoJo Starbuck, Joe Montana, Cal Ripkin, Julius Erving, Eric Liddell (from the movie *Chariots of Fire*), Don Meredith, Olga Korbut, and Mary Lou Retton. Women are much more likely than men to mention admiration relationships with opposite sex sport figures, and they also tend to draw their admired figures from somewhat different sports (see Tables 1 and 2).[3] As with other involvements, people frequently compare the attachment to a real social relationship; their hero is like a friend, older sister, father figure, guide, mentor, and so forth. As with the love relationships, the appeal is clear. These sport figures seem better than mere mortals, and the absence of actual social contact leaves admiration unchecked by the direct experience of faults and limitations.

From hundreds of glamorous alternatives, why does the fan seize on one particular figure rather than another? The appeal that the chosen figure holds is complex, but several different factors seem to be involved. Sometimes people mention a seemingly superficial parallel in backgrounds—the player's name is similar to one's own, she came from a similar part of the country, and so forth. Sometimes someone significant in the individual's actual social world "introduced" the person to their idol. Thus a young golfer's attraction to Arnold Palmer originated in part because he came from a neighboring town and because his father deeply admired Palmer. Most significantly, however, the admired figure dramatically expresses culturally approved personality attributes, values, and competent styles of behavior that the individual longs to realize in himself. The figure represents an *ideal self-image*.

Once the identification has been made, patterned forms of behavior develop. The individual may collect posters, news clippings, stadium programs, totem-like autographed sport equipment, and the like. Spectatorship—live or via the media—is likely to be intense:

> I feel everything these athletes are feeling—I'm actually in it with them—everything from precompetition nervousness, to the excitement of the routine, to the waiting for the final score—and finally to cheering in their victories.

Another woman adds, "I tape all his big competitions on TV so I can watch these dramatic performances over and over." Personal identification is strong and emotional. "Sometimes I get so involved in his (Scott Hamilton's) routine that I lean when he goes around corners and I rise up a little in my seat when he does a jump."

> The greatest euphoric feeling I receive is when a tribute is being given to him. (Commentators) talk about him being a great human being as well as a gifted ball player. When I hear this—and they show highlights, a chill goes through my body and tears of joy come to my eyes.

Fantasy Interactions

Admiration relationships also have an important fantasy dimension. As with love relationships, fantasies connect the individual with the sport hero. Although they often seem to fade from one into another, several distinct types of fantasies are apparent. In the first the individual daydreams *about* the idol. In the second he or she *meets* the idol, in the third the individual *resembles* the idol, and in the fourth he or she *becomes* the idol. In daydreaming about the admired figure (real or fictional), the

Table 1   Admiration of Male Sport Figures

Sport	Male fans		Female fans	
	Number	Percent	Number	Percent
Football	49	(30)	41	(27)
Basketball	40	(24)	12	(8)
Baseball	19	(12)	20	(13)
Boxing	17	(10)	19	(13)
Golf	12	(7)	4	(3)
Car racing	8	(5)	1	(1)
Hockey	5	(3)	1	(1)
Tennis	4	(2)	7	(5)
Wrestling	3	(2)	0	(0)
Skating	2	(1)	10	(7)
Track	2	(1)	13	(9)
Skiing	2	(1)	7	(5)
Weight lifting	1	(1)	3	(2)
Gymnastics	1	(1)	12	(8)
	165	(100)	150	(100)

individual imagines the hero in various life situations, often playing well in sport. One informant described a repeated scenario in which he pictures his favorite quarterback throwing brilliantly after returning to the field from a serious injury. In such a fantasy the individual remains somewhat apart from the hero, but through identification he not only "sees" but also "feels" the quarterback's success. Sometimes these fleeting daydreams gradually develop into very detailed mental structures.[4]

In the second type of fantasy, the individual imagines himself interacting with the idol. Such fantasy encounters are not mere meetings; an intimate social relationship develops. A standard variant involves establishing a professional sport relationship with the admired figure. One fan admires Philadelphia Phillies' pitcher Steve Carlton.

> Steve Carlton is a 6-ft, 5-in., 220-lb pitcher for the Philadelphia Phillies. Since I myself am a frustrated athlete I admire Carlton. He was given a great body specimen and he has made the best possible use of it. Carlton possesses all the physical attributes I wish I had. . . . Carlton is also an expert in martial arts and is intellectual, having studied psychology and Eastern philosophy. I admire the man because he is the type to accomplish tasks and achieve goals.

This fan has several different fantasies about establishing a social relationship with his idol.

Table 2   Admiration of Female Sport Figures

Sport	Male fans		Female fans	
	Number	Percent	Number	Percent
Gymnastics	4	(67)	57	(56)
Tennis	2	(33)	18	(18)
Skating	0	(0)	17	(17)
Track	0	(0)	3	(3)
Bodybuilding	0	(0)	3	(3)
Swimming	0	(0)	1	(1)
Golf	0	(0)	1	(1)
Jockey	0	(0)	1	(1)
	6	(100)	101	(100)

One has me in the Big Leagues pitching for the Phils and Carlton becomes my friend, takes me under his wing, and I become his protégé. I have also imagined that one day I will become Carlton's manager and that we have a great relationship. He admires me for my managing and coaching ability.

The dynamics of such fantasy interactions are complex, but a crucial dimension is the elevation of the self-involved. Acceptance by the admired figure is the vehicle for indirect self-acceptance. (I admire them—I am like them—they accept me—I am a good person.)

In a third type of fantasy the individual becomes someone similar to the admired figure. Often a curious new self emerges here that represents an imaginative combination of the skills, body, and personality of the fan and the admired figure. In this new identity the fan lives out experiences similar to those of the idol. Often this includes playing the idol's sport with professional prowess, perhaps by going "head to head" with the hero's rival. One fan began his account of a golf fantasy as follows: "Before I hit my tee shot, Jack (Nicklaus) and I shook hands and both wished each other luck."

An important part of the appeal here involves attaining success similar to that of the idol. This includes the confirmation of self-worth, which comes through the imagined admiration and recognition of others. In the following account the individual imagines himself as a successful baseball manager and "hears" himself being described by Howard Cosell. Note the language here—the "showing" of others.

Hello again, everybody, this is Howard Cosell and "Speaking of Sports." The Red Sox did it again last night; they won their seventh straight game, downing the Orioles 2–1. . . . Every critic who laughed when Jones was hired has already swallowed his words. Last night was no exception. With the score tied 1–1 in the ninth, Jones had Carlton Fisk squeeze in Rick Burleson with a bunt to win it. . . . Those who thought Jones to be a joke are no longer laughing. In fact, they are choking on their own words. This is Howard Cosell.

Indirectly this acclaim can often be interpreted as an implicit winning of respect from those in the individual's actual social world. Sometimes this is explicit; the star's family and friends are pictured cheering in the stands. Often present also are those who have offered rejection in the past: parents, former teachers, ex-spouses, and critics of any kind. One not only gets the pleasure of their acclaim; in addition, past social failures are magically transcended and avenged.

One step further, in the fourth type of fantasy, the fan abandons his or her self and becomes the admired figure. This is a common desire ("I would change places with him in a moment"). In fantasy the desire is realized. The person achieves and experiences the ideal self by transmuting into the hero and reliving the figure's past successes or experiencing those of the future. Imaginary interviews are common.

I'd heard earlier in the day that Eric Dickerson had broken O.J. Simpson's rushing record and I was wondering how he would react—this appeared as a vague mental question, "how will he handle it?", which shifted, without any deliberate intention, into hearing him speaking—"I have mixed feelings . . ," and then into my saying his words, I became O.J. giving a "classy" performance in the interview. "Sure, I'm sorry to see the record go. We got it through a lot of work. . . . But records are made to be broken— just like we broke the old one in '73. Eric is a great runner. . . ."

These four kinds of fantasies represent a neglected but pervasive dimension of American sport experience. Americans not only "play" sport through participation and spectatorship, they also experience sport through the medium of these internal mind games. These imaginary self-transformations are also significant because of their effects on actual social behavior. One minor but elaborate example involves board games such as "dice baseball." Here participants come together in an actual social situation in order to play out imaginary baseball games in which the roll of the dice determines the course of play. The "American Professional Baseball Association" (APBA) includes cards with information based on the professional players' previous performance. The game puts participants into the role of manager and allows them to make player trades as well as managerial decisions during the game. One informant described a college league in which he and several other young men played out an entire season rotating from one dorm room to another for games. They appointed a league commissioner to settle disputes and developed a variety of associated traditions; managers wrote out "professional" reports to the commissioner on a weekly basis, and most chewed tobacco during the games. Despite a variety of deliberately humorous touches, the games were taken very seriously by the participants and disputes were often heated.

Dice baseball evokes powerful feelings from the participants, who often become deeply engaged in the imaginary action. A lawyer says the game is "more real" to him than real baseball. "I don't get as excited about anything else as I do about APBA. I'm looking forward to retiring, so I can play all day, every day" (Lidz, 1980:17). Participants explain the appeal of the game as a "diversion." As one suggests, "APBA is the greatest escape mechanism I've ever found" (Lidz, 1980:17). Like various other role-playing games, its appeal has to do with fantasized identity transformations and imaginary social relationships.[5] In the game world, the participant acts out the big-league manager identity and may even gain some public recognition for success in this role. Furthermore, the participant attains special social relationships with big-league players. An excerpt from an informant's "report to the commissioner" illustrates both aspects.

> Since the word has been out that Joe Smith will be manager of the Phillies this season, title hopes have risen in Philadelphia. In five seasons of minor league managing . . . Smith won 5 world championships. I think the first thing I should do is orient myself with the players and work from there . . . not only are personal relationships important, but they are vital to a team's continuity. . . . Robin Roberts is looking forward to playing for Smith. "He (Smith) called me on the phone and sounded terrific. I can't wait to pitch."

Another way in which fantasy relations with sport figures affect actual social behavior is through imitation and role modeling. While some researchers are skeptical of the importance of imitative media effects, this perspective may be related to behavioristic research methods that overlook the power of imaginary processes (Caughey, 1984:61). Certainly it is easy to observe that many fans, especially young people, seek to imitate the appearance of a favorite sport figure by wearing a jersey with the star's uniform number or by adopting some other characteristic of dress or hair style. This superficial imitation is often a surface manifestation of the kind of deeper identification described above. Such identification may lead to behavioral imitation as well. This is conspicuous in children's sport play. As one informant reported, "At bat I imitated his (Jim Gentile's) typical mannerisms, spitting in the dirt, measuring the plate with my bat, kicking dirt in the batter's box, and assuming an extremely wide stance. . . ." It is common, in fact, for children to announce publicly the assumption of a professional player's identity prior to starting a real game. "It was typical for the friends I was playing with to adopt the character of their favorite players too. Occasionally, someone else would want to be Jim Gentile and a heated argument would ensue."

As athletes become older the public announcement of a fantasy identity falls away but, often, identification and imitation do not. Clearly, many, and quite possibly most, American athletes are affected by media exemplars. Even the most successful professional athletes regularly report such role modeling. O.J. Simpson, for example, deliberately patterned himself after Jim Brown. Many of my own informants reported the same process. The successful young golfer whose hero was Arnold Palmer not only read all the Arnold Palmer how-to books, studied his game on television, and practiced his style of shots, he also pretended to be Arnold Palmer while actually playing golf. Unlike some older athletes, he was not embarrassed by public recognition of the derivative nature of his style of play. "It made me proud to think others saw an 'Arnie Palmer' in me."

An all-American college basketball player described her close relationship to a favorite professional player.

> Among the most significant persons who have contributed to my life thus far is Bill Walton. Since Bill's college years, I've followed him closely, read about him in magazines, watched him on television, and seen him on talk shows. . . . Many times I sit and stare at a basketball court and imagine Bill down there warming up with a series of left- and right-handed hook shots. . . . And still there are other times when after seeing him play on TV I imagine myself repeating all his moves. . . . On the court I pattern many of my offensive moves from Bill Walton.[6]

As is typical, the imitation of sport behavior is part of a wider influence. "Since the beginning of this relationship in my junior year of high school, similarities have shown up in the lifestyles of both Bill and myself." In this case the young woman not only wears a bandana headband, like her hero, she has also become a vegetarian and an avid fan of the Grateful Dead. A young tennis star shows vividly how his pattern of play is but one manifestation of a larger imitation of values and lifestyle.

> I'm extremely aggressive on the court, I guess. I really like Jimmy Connors' game. I model myself after him. I read somewhere that he said he wants to play every point like it's match point at Wimbledon. . . . I like the individualism of tennis. It's not a team sport; it's an ego trip. You get all the glory yourself. That's what I thrive on—ego. . . . I want to become like Vitas Gerulaitis, with the cars, the shopping in Paris, and the girls.[7]

Thus the sport figure often becomes a mentor and role model for behavior in the paramount reality of everyday life. One woman admires Martina Navratilova for her "competitive" and "unfeminine, tough" style of play.

> One of the effects that Martina has had on my outlook on life is that I play tough. . . . I am tough when it comes to my ambi-

tions. I am very confident in myself and do not feel less of a woman because I want to do a "man's" job.

Here we can see how the hero provides an ideal self-image, not only for sport fantasy but for the social world of work as well. Many other informants spoke of having learned particular values and styles of action through identified admiration relationships: "He's living proof that one can succeed against the odds," "I hope I can retain the dignity she has," "I realized the importance of self-confidence—in this respect he affected much more than my baseball playing." In some cases the fan may attempt to induce a self-transformation in the midst of social life: "Sometimes I find myself saying, 'You are Carlton. Believe you are and so will everyone else.'"

Conclusion

Many studies of American sport assume that involvement consists only of actual participation and spectatorship. This approach neglects a sometimes significant psychological dimension—imaginary sport involvement. To take but one example, Roberts and Chick (1984) have recently provided an important examination of game involvement in which three basic stages are specified: (a) the "recruitment period" (when players are introduced to the game); (b) the "involvement period" (when players show a high degree of actual participation); and (c) the "disengagement period" (when a player drops a game). This discussion overlooks the fact that people may be vicariously involved with sports outside these stages. Loy (1981:270) has observed that various psychological processes, including those of Roberts and Sutton-Smith's "conflict-enculturation model," may apply to spectatorship as well as actual sport participation. The same is true of imaginary sport experience. People may be imaginatively engaged in a game well prior to actual involvement, and they may continue to "play" it long after actual disengagement. One informant reported various forms of imaginary participation, including the reexperiencing of plays he had formerly made as well as fantasy plays, more than 20 years after actual disengagement from organized football. Thus the various psychological functions ascribed to game involvement may still be operating despite actual disengagement.

Imaginary sport experience cannot be observed directly. One must rely instead on introspective self-reports. Such data may not be as reliable as direct observation, but it certainly parallels self-report interview data commonly relied on in ethnographic studies (cf Caughey, 1982:117–125, 1984:23–27). As I have shown here, self-reports can provide some detailed, interesting, and revealing information on imaginary sport involvement. Apparently, from the material collected and reviewed here, a basic feature of American sport involvement includes imaginary social relationships with unmet sport figures. These include romantic and antagonistic relationships, but the most significant seem to be those in which the fan relates to the sport figure as idol, alter-ego, and mentor. These imaginary relationships involve a variety of patterned activities including collecting and identified media consumption, but they center around fantasy interactions.

Asked about such sport relationships, many informants explain them as escape. Their involvement provides an "outlet," "recreation," a "vacation," "an escape from the dull routines of everyday life." Critics of compensatory interpretations of sport involvement (e.g., Gelber, 1983:4) tend to assume that such informant explanations are mistaken. While I agree that much more goes on in sport than "escape," fantasy material helps us to see that, at a certain level, escape is involved. Fantasy also helps us to see how escape works at the level of personal identity. Through imaginary relationships, the fan sloughs off his own problematic actual identity and enters a better world by assuming an improved, more successful self. Through identified media consumption and through fantasies, such as those of becoming someone like the idol, the fan experiences a gratifying sense of release and heightened self-worth.

But an examination of the contents of imaginary social relationships also shows us how they reflect or recreate culture. In escaping self and society in order to play out interactions with sport figures, the individual is not escaping the values of society at all. In fact, the individual is taking a bath in the American dream. He or she is psychologically soaking up some of the most significant assumptions and values of American culture: the notion that personal worth is defined by individual competitive achievement and success, that happiness is attained by the ego glow of "winning," and that self-worth is attained by the recognition, envy, and applause of others. As we have seen, many fans also indicate that they have internalized particular cultural values and identity attributes through their imaginary association with admired sport figures. In this sense as well, these relationships seem to represent not escape but vicarious enculturation.[8] Thus people may return from their pseudosocial experiences with sport well primed to conform to the values of the society they just felt that they had escaped.

Notes

1. An earlier version of this paper was presented to the 1985 Annual Meeting of the Association for the Anthropological Study of Play, Washington, DC, March 16, 1985. Some of the material included here was previously published in a different form in chapter 2 of Caughey (1984). This material is used with the permission of the University of Nebraska Press.

2. For a review of spectatorship with attention to identity dynamics, see Loy (1981). For a compensatory study of spectatorship, see Rader (1983).

3. Fifty-six informants (members of an undergraduate class that was not about sport) were asked to list 20 sport figures who were "significant" to them and to indicate "how the figure was important." Ten people (3 men and 7 women) said that *no* sport figures were significant to them and one woman disliked several sport figures but admired none. Tables 1 and 2, then, list the figures toward which the remaining 32 women and 13 men indicated that they felt some admiration. Vander Velden (1986) noted a similar pattern of male versus female admiration in his large scale questionnaire study. He also found variation in the attributes valued in sport heroes by black and white fans.

4. For an example, see Singer (1966:18–20).

5. On social aspects of fantasy games, see Fine (1983) and Caughey (1984:190–196). For a fictional portrait of psychological involvement in dice baseball, see Coover (1968). In the related world of "video sport," players competitively manipulate miniature sport figures on a screen. Again it seems that they project their own identity into the image.

6. This player's use of images of her hero's style of play points to another aspect of imaginary sport, deliberate preplay "visualizations" intended to improve performance. For a review of the literature, see Feltz and Landers (1983).

7. This case is discussed by Rogers (1978).

8. For a general review of the socializing aspects of sport with attention to self-development, see Loy and Ingham (1981:189–216). Once again, fantasy involvement is overlooked.

References

Berger, P. (1970). The problem of multiple realities: Alfred Schutz and Robert Musil. In T. Luckmann (Ed.), *Phenomenology and sociology* (pp. 343–367). New York: Penguin.

Berger, P., & Luckmann, T. (1966). *The social construction of reality*. Garden City, NY: Anchor.

Caughey, J.L. (1984). *Imaginary social worlds: A cultural approach*. Lincoln: University of Nebraska Press.

Coover, R. (1968). *The Universal Baseball Association*. New York: New American Library.

Feltz, D., & Landers, D. (1983). The effects of mental practice on motor skill learning and performance: A meta-analysis. *Journal of Sport Psychology, 5,* 25–57.

Fine, G.A. (1983). *Shared fantasy: Role playing games as social worlds.* Chicago: University of Chicago.

Gelber, S.M. (1983). Working at playing: The culture of the workplace and the rise of baseball. *Journal of Social History, 16,* 3–21.

Lidz, F. (1980, December 8). APBA is the name, baseball is the game, and obsession is the result. *Sports Illustrated,* pp. 17–18.

Loy, J.W. (1981). An emerging theory of sport spectatorship: Implications for the Olympic Games. In J. Segrave & D. Chu (Eds.), *Olympism* (pp. 262–294). Champaign, IL: Human Kinetics.

Loy, J.W., & Ingham, A.G. (1981). Play, games and sport in the psychosociological development of children and youth. In J.W. Loy, G. Kenyon, & B. McPherson (Eds.), *Sport, culture and society* (pp. 189–216). Philadelphia: Lea and Febiger.

Rader, B. (1983). Compensatory sports heroes: Ruth, Grange and Dempsey. *Journal of Popular Culture, 16,* 11–22.

Roberts, J.M., & Chick, G.E. (1984). Quitting the game: Covert disengagement from Butler County eight ball. *American Anthropologist, 86,* 549–567.

Rogers, T. (1978, April 26). Groetsch isn't hazy about tennis goals. *Philadelphia Evening Bulletin,* p. C3.

Schutz, A. (1962). On multiple realities. In M. Natanson (Ed.), *Collected papers of Alfred Schutz* (pp. 207–259). The Hague: Martinus Nijoff.

Singer, J. (1966). *Day dreaming: An introduction to the experimental study of inner experience.* New York: Random House.

Vander Velden, L. (1986). Heroes and bad winners in North America. In L. Vander Velden & J. Humphry (Eds.), *Psychology and the sociology of sport: Current selected research: Vol. 1.* New York: AMS Press.

How They Play in Peoria: Models of Adult Leisure

John R. Kelly

The place of leisure in the lives of older people has been subjected to more careful attention in the last decade. Interest was stirred by the careful study in Kansas City by Havighurst (1957), Neugarten (1968), and their associates in which various forms of leisure were found to be significant elements in the lives of older adults. More recently, Atchley (1976) has studied the functions of leisure in retirement. Gordon, Gaitz, and Scott (1976) discovered that expressive activity remained important through the later life course. Perhaps most compelling has been Palmore's (1979) longitudinal analysis documenting that later life adaptation is strongly related to activity and social contexts outside the home.

On the other hand, just how leisure makes its contribution remains somewhat obscure. One possibility is simply that it fills time in pre-retirement and retirement periods in which formerly central roles are losing salience. This paper, however, is a refutation of that simplistic position. A second, related suggestion is that leisure provides opportunities for effectual action in the years when work and family commitments have lessened. The third possibility is that leisure activities provide a context in which important social relationships are developed and expressed.

The latter two possibilities were examined in a research program with a sample of adults age 40 and over in Peoria, Illinois. A sample of 400 were interviewed using a telephone protocol. Then a subsample of 120 participated in "collaborative interviews" in their homes.

The aims of the study are reflected in a chapter by the principal investigator titled "Leisure in Later Life: Roles and Identities" (Osgood, 1982). A number of propositions were offered that were based primarily on research in adult leisure completed in several communities between 1972 and 1982 (Kelly, 1983).

In this report, a model of leisure in adult life will be presented. The sharp decline in some forms of leisure participation in later life will be examined for patterns related to activity forms and life-course factors. Styles of life and leisure will be analyzed using both the survey and intensive interview data. The results of the two approaches will be compared for consistency and complementarity.

Later Life Roles and Identities

The main thrust of the argument is that when studied in a life-course perspective, leisure is a multidimensional set of activities, relationships, contexts, and commitments (Rapoport & Rapoport, 1976). The interests and choices of leisure are related to both role sequences and developmental preoccupations. They are not fixed at some point to remain static until old age closes off opportunities and reduces resources. Rather, leisure has a place in the existential life-developing thrust of life as well as in coping with changes mandated by external events. It is more than filling time. Leisure is a full domain of life along with work, family, and community.

Definitions of leisure are less important than what people actually do and what they mean by their actions. In general, leisure may be defined as "activity chosen primarily for its own sake" (Kelly, 1982:23), with the dimensions of choice or relative freedom and intrinsic meaning seen as defining. However, this approach does not mean that leisure is some sort of esoteric activity segregated from the ongoing and more central contexts of life.

From one perspective, leisure is activity. The activity model emphasizes that an essential element of intentioned action exists in its actualization. However, the activity model has too often been reduced in research to a counting and summing of the number and/or frequency of engagements. A more accurate interpretation incorporates the dimension of intensity (Kelly, 1983:148–150). Some activity is more or less residual and of low intensity and salience. Almost without exception, we are told by adults of almost any age and either sex that the leisure they value most either involves interaction with significant others or is expressive activity in which they have invested considerable effort in gaining competence. They may spend more time watching television, but they define themselves by and invest themselves in more intense engagement.

A more useful model is that of the "core and balance" (Kelly, 1983:87–88). Rather than stereotyping leisure styles as monothematic, adults are found to have a core of leisure that persists through the life course. This core consists of accessible activities, usually in or near the residence, that form an integral part of the ongoing round of daily life. Informal interaction with household companions, media use, reading, walking, and interstitial conversation and play are the expressive stuff that forms the other side of task-orientation. However, a balanced set of engagements also exists that is more likely to shift through the life course as roles, self-definitions, aims, and opportunities change. For midlife adults this balance may include some quiet as well as physical activity, being alone as well as being with others, and high-demand engagement as well as relaxation. For later life persons, often a reduction of physical exertion and a constriction of the range of the social world occur that bring more of the balance close to home. Such a balance is best interpreted within a dialetic perspective that includes both individual self-definitions and intentions and social aims and opportunities.

Adding to the "core and balance" model is another approach that locates significant meanings in how persons define themselves in their roles (personal identities) and how they perceive themselves to be defined by others (social identities). Life is seen as a dialectic in which lines of action and self-presentations are initiated, responses interpreted, and revisions made (Kelly, 1983). In the social process, we come to learn who we are in the perceived and interpreted responses of significant others. This lifelong process of becoming takes place in all life domains including leisure. In fact, for some individuals in some life periods, leisure identities may be most central to who we are and who we are trying to become.

Leisure, then, is a life domain with its role expectations and opportunity structures, personal agendas and outcomes, and social contexts and purposes. It is a social space in which relative freedom exists to orient action toward the immediate experience, self-developing activity, and the expression of various levels of social bonding. It is opportunity for expression, development, and community. And one major dimension of adult leisure is that it is frequently a context for social integration and for activity that brings us together in common activity that fosters communication and intimacy.

The question, then, for later life leisure is the extent to which it provides a social space for significant expression and community. If not for all, does leisure become for some a central set of role identities in which individuals develop and actualize self-definitions central to their personal identities? Are the meanings of later life leisure both personal and social in significant rather than trivial ways?

Leisure in Life's Second Half

The research program conducted in Peoria consisted of three parts: a telephone survey, intensive interviews, and a mail follow-up. The first part has yielded evidence that leisure is, indeed, an important element in life satisfaction and social integration.

"Sociology"—The Telephone Survey

The initial part of the research program employed traditional sociological methods of inquiry and quantitative analysis. In the spring of 1983, 400 telephone interviews were conducted with adults age 40 and above in Peoria, Illinois. In age, gender, income levels, occupational distribution, and education level, Peoria is within 2 to 4% of national distributions. The sample of 400 was obtained by applying a table of random digits to the telephone directory. Callbacks were continued until it was determined that no one within the sample frame resided in the household or participation was refused. A summary of the findings relating age category to leisure participation follows.

Eight types of leisure activity were factored out of the list of 28 about which subjects were asked. Participation levels varied by age and type. Sport, exercise, and outdoor activity had lower rates for each older age category. Travel, cultural, and home-based activity were lower only for those aged 75 and older. Family activities were slightly lower only for older widows. Social activity participation was slightly higher for men over 75 and lower only for women over 75. Social, home-based, and family activity, which generally represent the "core" of adult leisure, were the most common for all the over-40 sample with participation in community organizations least frequent.[1]

Life satisfaction as measured by a summary Havighurst scale (LSI) was found to be strongly associated with level of leisure activity when measures of income, age, sex, marital status, and occupation level as well as health, income, and housing problems were subjected to prior control. Further, the measure of social integration—frequency of interaction with family and friends—was also strongly related to leisure participation levels (Steinkamp & Kelly, in press). In multiple regression analysis, no other factor contributed as much to life satisfaction and social integration as leisure participation. When age, gender, education level, family status, health, and occupation level were entered first, general activity level still accounted for an additional 6.2% of the variance in life satisfaction. When entered stepwise in order of contribution, leisure activity level accounted for 13.3% of the variance, far and away the most powerful variable.

The types of leisure that differentiated the four age categories in life satisfaction were:

Age 40–64: Travel and cultural activities
Age 65–74: Social and travel activities
Age 75+ : Family and home-based activities

These findings are consistent with the shift for those over 65 to social integration as the most important factor in life satisfaction and the availability of family for those 75 and above.

Although the familiar overall decline in leisure activity levels associated with age is supported, significant differences exist when the main types of activity are examined separately. Previous research may have been somewhat biased by focusing on activities with a public recreation provision base. Further, a covert assumption may have been that those "poor old folks" would be burdened with all kinds of time to fill and that the main leisure problem would be boredom. Shifts in leisure locales evidently do not create a time void unfilled by other engagements.

Later life leisure demonstrates considerable continuity with the earlier adult period. Even limited cross-sectional research that cannot measure cohort differences over time suggests certain patterns of continuity as well as change. The overall decline in leisure participation rates is differentiated by both age category and context. Participation in sport and exercise and resource-based outdoor recreation are considerably lower for each age category. However, along with community organizations, these were always the three types of activity with the fewest regular participants. On the other hand, family, social, and home-based activity have relatively low rates of decline for the over-65 age categories. Cultural activity, which includes some home engagement, remains at a high level for about 60% of the sample, and travel is sharply lower only for the 75+ age category.

Continuity is demonstrated in the "core" of accessible and relatively informal leisure that makes up the ongoing day-to-day center of non-required engagement (Kelly, Steinkamp, & Kelly, 1986). Further, extra-residential activity that does not call for a high level of physical output is also maintained, especially if social interaction with significant others is the central meaning of the activity. The balance shifts somewhat toward social engagement and away from strenuous physical activity for the older segments of the sample. The overall decline found in various studies is in reality a shift away from organized and resource-based activity requiring considerable physical exertion and effort.

The lowered rates of participation for older adults are uneven. Sport and exercise and outdoor recreation are found to have a steep slope down-ward for the 55 to 64 age category. While there is a cohort confounding the possibility that younger adults will have somewhat different experiences and values when they are retirement age, the finding is consistent with national surveys completed over a 20-year period. Travel, on the other hand, not only continues at a relatively high level for the pre- and post-retirement segments, but is found to be salient for satisfaction. Only for those aged 75 years and over—the segment most likely to have health deficits, financial limitations, and the loss of companions to death or severe illness—do the significant locales of leisure become constricted inward around the residence.

Certain patterns of change can be identified amid the continuity. First, health and physical ability rather than age itself seem to be related to a reduction in certain kinds of activity. A confounding factor, however, may be that older cohorts do not expect to continue such activity in later years. Second, a marked disjunction exists between those in the first post-retirement period and the 75+ "old old." The oldest segment demonstrated considerable constriction in leisure, both in social contexts and geographical range. Their activity scope becomes much more home-based. Their social range is concentrated more on family, close friends, and friendly neighbors. Travel loses its previous predictive association with life satisfaction. Third, interaction and support from family members become *the* major factors in coping in the final life period. Because all members of the Peoria sample were still functioning at some viable level in a residential environment, health traumas and social loss may have been severe but were not totally debilitating. Continuity is found in primary relationships and accessible activity along with the constriction.

Leisure for second-half adults is neither specialized devotion to a single activity nor to time-filling activity but is a context for what is central to later life—stimulating interaction with family and friends as well as opportunities to be and become selves of ability and worth. In the telephone interviews, a base was laid for the later collaborative interviews with the subsample. Considerable evidence showed that leisure was important to later life adults achieving personal satisfaction with life (a) as a context for expressing and maintaining primary relationships and (b) as an opportunity to express and develop self-definitions of ability. In summary, both the core and balance elements of leisure styles were maintained. However, for the "old old" aged 75 and above, the contexts seemed to be constricted inward around the residence and in smaller social circles of intimates. All of this is consistent with previous work in social gerontology and provides a plausible basis for more intensive investigation with the sample. In this sociological approach, the telephone interviews laid the groundwork for the more anthropological collaborative interviews.

Collaborative Interviews and Convergence

A stratified subsample was selected from the first 400 interviewed for in-home interviews in which the subjects were asked to share in the interpretation process. The interviews stressed interchange and empathy as life-course traumas, and transitions were examined and styles of coping identified. Those being interviewed were asked to "tell their stories" as well as provide "data." Further, the taped interviews were subjected to multiple analysis by the research team in producing summaries and seeking consistent styles of coping and social investment. This interpretive approach was the central part of the overall research design.

In the collaborative interview part of the Peoria research, salient transitions and traumas of later life were identified and modes of coping examined with open-ended questions. The place of leisure in responding to changed roles, resources, and life conditions was probed directly and indirectly. Quite distinct styles were identified in a multistep program of analysis.

First, three types of life course were defined.

- *Straight arrow* (40%): SAs had a life course that proceeded "normally" with the predictable transitions of launching children, employment shifts, and retirement but without major disruption. The transitions could be anticipated and handled with the support of others in the same cohort dealing with the same on-time changes.
- *Turning point* (23%): A single event redirected life and had major impacts for the remainder of the life course requiring major personal and social adaptation. Such events included early death or incapacitating illness of a spouse, incapacitating mental or physical illness for self, alcoholism, divorce for a family-centered person, and catastrophic economic loss.
- *Zigzag* (37%): Two or more events required significant change. Such a life course might have several stops and restarts, especially when a low level of economic resources compounded impacts of health or other trauma.

Patterns of coping were found to be cumulative and consistent by the time adults reached preretirement and retirement periods. Although the interview formats examined work, family, health, and other disrupting events separately, the subjects were found to have characteristic response patterns that they employed to cope with a variety of impacts. However, no significant relationship between the life-course pattern and the styles of coping was shown.

Only 3% were classified as "leisure-invested" in the typology developed. Leisure was seldom the central or dominant life domain through the later life course. Nor did the "work-centered" (3%) or "faithful members" (4%) in voluntary organizations prove to be major response patterns. However, leisure was found to be one life domain along with work and/or family in the lives of "balanced investors" (40%) that fit no one-dimensional typology. Balanced investors both invest in and receive support from at least two of the major domains of life-work, primary relationships, and leisure. Leisure has a place, usually a rather important one, in the overall scheme or balance of life.

For those who are more "family-focused" (19%), the family is the primary context for life and social resources. Leisure tends to be defined primarily in terms of providing environments for familial interaction and the expression of relationships. Balanced investors were more likely to devote time and other resources to at least one leisure engagement that provided a significant personal identity through life-course transitions. For both types, however, leisure is at least in part a social context for expressing and building intimacy, relationships with family and "real friends." Leisure, then, tends to be more integrated into a set of life orientations and commitments than to be a separate and "special" realm of activity.

Further, the "balanced investors" were clearly those with the highest levels of life satisfaction. They were followed by the "family-focused" and the tiny group of "faithful members" who found a primary community and purpose in their churches. The contribution of leisure is more than activity that occupies time and fills emptiness left by lost opportunities and relationships. Rather, leisure is most important when it is integrated into an overall lifestyle that incorporates engagement with intimate others as well as with activity that is personally expressive and developmental.

Discussion of Results

In summary, a "convergence" exists between the findings of the two approaches. Both the telephone survey with its quantitative analysis and the collaborative interviews with their interpretive framework lead to the same conclusions. Leisure can contribute to both social integration and personal identities. Such a contribution is made when leisure is a context for the expressive and bonding dimensions in life. Whether we use the vocabularies that refer to "leisure," "adult play," or "expressive behavior" may be of little significance. Recognizing the integral functions and meanings of behaviors that are oriented toward meaning within the experience rather than extrinsic ends is important. Such meanings are not confined to the episode or event, but become part of investment in lines of action that have outcomes related to both personal identities and significant relationships.

Thus most second-half leisure is not "recreation" in the sense of organized activity. Certainly most leisure is not in the special environments of public recreation venues or programs. In fact, when asked whether leisure had been a help in coping with change, almost 80% of our Peoria sample said "Yes." The kind of help varied. The most common response (32%) was that leisure had been a context of maintaining or developing important relationships. Filling time or escape from problems was seen as the primary contribution by 23%. Personal expression and development was reported by 12% with another 12% reporting both personal expression and social integration. Yet, these same persons were almost universally at a loss when asked to identify any public program in which these contributions had been found.

Sources of Leisure Styles

How do people develop their leisure styles? Within the core-plus-balance metaphor, styles are seen as related to both role sequences and developmental aims through the life course (Kelly, 1983). However, all do not display the same styles in either activity choice or orientations.

From the perspective of meaning, leisure styles are based in the life orientations of individuals as they move through the life course. In their sequential or interrupted roles, they respond to the immediate contexts of their lives as well as to age-related role expectations. Leisure is, for the most part, integrated into overall life patterns that differ only in detail from those common to other persons in the same social strata and life period.

From the perspective of activity, leisure styles are more a response to resources. Community, occupation, education, marital and family situation, geography, and culture along with personal conditions such as health tend to determine what is available. Leisure socialization, then, is a cumulative learning response to available resources. We develop styles in the context of accessible and appropriate resources.

Leisure socialization is a process in which orientations and resources have an interplay of reciprocal effects. Changes in resources can lead to different activity choices that, in turn, influence orientations. Those altered attitudes help shape what we perceive as appropriate and beneficial as well as what we choose.

Leisure, within the framework of this analysis, is a part of a more comprehensive lifestyle. On the one hand, the environments, forms, and meanings of leisure change through the life course as we move through anticipated transitions and cope with unexpected traumas. On the other hand, considerable consistency exists in both the core of engagements and the central meanings of leisure through the life course. For later life adults, the multivalenced meanings of leisure have a dual orientation that persists from launching parents to preretirement to active retirement and even into final fragility and constriction. One pole is that of personal expression, a desire to invest in activity that expresses and enhances the self. The other pole is tied to primary relationships, the significant others who are enjoyed and who share the realities of life's journey with us.

How do the second-half adults play in Peoria? They seem to be much like those in other communities. For most, leisure is neither the peripheral and residual life domain nor the life-transforming elixir that some assume. Leisure is a part of life that journeys through changes in ways that are both critically limited and marvelously resilient.

Acknowledgments

This is a revision of a paper presented at The Association for the Anthropological Study of Play, Washington, DC, March, 1985. This research has been supported by the National Institute on Aging research grant 1R01 AG02933-01 and -02, "Aging Adaptation, Role Changes, and Leisure Resources," J.R. Kelly, principal investigator. The author is especially grateful to Dr. Marjorie W. Steinkamp for her coordinating work.

Note

1. The 28 activities were categorized as follows: Travel—car trips, other travel; Cultural—reading for pleasure, music, drama, dance and arts programs, going to concerts, plays, or exhibits; Exercise and Sports—going for walks, swimming, golf, tennis, other sports; Outdoor—fishing, boating, hunting, camping; Family—getting together with family, family outings, talking with others at home; Social—socializing with friends and family, entertaining at home, going to bars and clubs, eating out, talking on the phone; Community organization—church participation, clubs and organizations; Home-based—gardening or raising plants, watching TV, hobbies at home, fixing or building things at home. "Doing nothing" was not categorized. "Anything else you do for enjoyment?" responses were individually categorized by form.

References

Atchley, R. (1976). *The sociology of retirement*. Cambridge: Schenkman.

Gordon, C., Gaitz, C., & Scott, J. (1976). Personal expressivity across the life cycle. In R. Binstock & E. Shanas (Eds.), *Handbook of aging and the social sciences*. New York: Van Nostrand Reinhold.

Havighurst, R. (1957). The leisure activities of the middle aged. *American Journal of Sociology*, **63**, 152–162.

Kelly, J.R. (1982). *Leisure*. Englewood Cliffs, NJ: Prentice-Hall.

Kelly, J.R. (1983). *Leisure identities and interactions*. London: Allen and Unwin.

Kelly, J.R., Steinkamp, M.W., & Kelly, J.R. (1986). Later life leisure: How they play in Peoria. *The Gerontologist, 26*, 531–537.

Neugarten, B. (Ed.). (1968). *Middle age and aging*. Chicago: University of Chicago Press.

Osgood, N. (Ed.). (1982). *Life after work*. New York: Praeger.

Palmore, E. (1979). Predictors of successful aging. *The Gerontologist, 16*, 441–446.

Rapoport, R., & Rapoport, R.N. (1976). *Leisure and the family life cycle*. London: Routledge and Kegan Paul.

Steinkamp, M., & Kelly, J.R. (in press). Leisure activity level, role involvement, and subjective well-being of older adults. *The International Journal of Aging Human Development*.

The Manliness Paradox in Ernest Thompson Seton's Ideology of Play and Games

Jay Mechling

In 1937, in the 77th year of his life, Ernest Thompson Seton, aided by his wife, Julia Buttree, set down in one final volume his accumulated wisdom about American Indian cultures. Seton, the Englishman raised in Canada, was coming to the end of a lifetime appreciation of American Indian ways, an appreciation that began with boys' work in the 1890s and reached its apotheosis in 1932 when he and Julia founded the College of Indian Wisdom on their property near Santa Fe, New Mexico. He intended *The Gospel of the Redman* to be to Americans in 1937 what the original Gospels were meant to be—"good news." The good news was that a philosophy, an ethic, and a way of life existed that could save the white man from ruinous civilization, from modernity. Seton's "Epilogue" is his jeremiad and his promise of revitalization. "The Civilization of the White man is a failure," he begins, "it is visibly crumbling around us. It has failed at every crucial test." Seton poses a series of questions, a test to measure one's civilization, such as: "Is your Civilization characterized by justice in the courts and gentleness in the streets?" or "Does your Civilization grant to every individual the force and rights of humanhood?" or "Does your system guarantee to each man the product of his industry?" or "Does your system discourage large material possessions in one man?" (Seton, 1937:106–107).

On each of these tests Seton finds white civilization a failure. Then comes his stern challenge.

> Men of the White Race! We speak now as representative of the most heroic race the world has ever seen, the most physically perfect race the world has ever seen, the most spiritual Civilization the world has ever seen.
>
> We offer you the Message of the Redman, the Creed of Manhood. We advocate his culture as an improvement on our own, if perchance by belated repentance, remorse, restitution, and justification, we may save ourselves from Divine vengeance and total destruction, as did the Ninevites in their final stance; so that

we may have a chance to begin again with a better, higher thought. (Seton, 1937:107–08)

This is strong stuff for an audience not yet out of the Depression and sensing already the pathology of European political events. Nonetheless, Seton's view is quite in keeping with a respectable tradition of European and American intellectuals' using Native American cultures to criticize bourgeoise society. This tradition is as old as the *philosophes*, Robert Berkhofer (1978) reminds us, and the Seton compound at Santa Fe was at the geographic heart of this American tradition of the 1920s and 1930s, not far from Taos and its community of disaffected intellectuals.

But an important difference existed between Seton and the group that gathered around D.H. Lawrence. Whereas the Mary Austins and the Willa Cathers and the Oliver LaFarges created a "literature of reverence" around Native American cultures of the Southwest, and the John Colliers molded institutional forms to better the lives of Native Americans, Ernest Thompson Seton translated this same ideology into a plan that would have whites actually adopt Indian ways. Neither the *philosophes* nor the Taos crowd wanted whites actually to become the Noble Savage. Seton did want that, and he left his mark on youth groups that have touched the lives of more than 60 million American children.

But *The Gospel of the Redman*, published in 1937, comes near the end of Seton's story, so we must go back to the 1890s and his first "tribe" of boy Indians to understand this complex man and the precise ways in which he would design games for social change. My thesis is that Seton had in mind an institutional order that we might call *androgynous*; that is, one that displays the most valued human traits of both the masculine and feminine in a society. This application of gender research to a retrospective interpretation of Seton's use of Native American materials could be seen as a "presentist" fallacy. But I believe that sufficient textual evidence is present in Seton's writing and in the details of his biography to warrant the notion that Seton's ideology and program were a good deal more revolutionary than they seem at first glance and that they strike at the heart of the American patriarchal, bureaucratic, and capitalistic social order. At the same time, Seton was very much a man of the 19th century, never comfortable in the 20th.

My argument will proceed as follows. First, I shall describe briefly (from feminist theory and gender research) what the characteristics are of institutional androgyny. Second, I shall describe Seton's model of the American Indian as cultural ideal and of American Indian customs as the template for white youth activities. An aspect of this second section is an inquiry into the characteristics of Seton's games. What would constitute, say, an androgynous game structure, and do Seton's games fit that definition? Third and finally, I shall address the obvious paradox in my thesis. Given the heavy focus of this period in American history upon "manliness" and worry about the "feminization" of American culture, how is it that I can insist that a central figure in this call for manliness was, in fact, advocating an androgynous institutional order?

Institutional Androgyny

One of the bonuses of the women's movement since the 1960s has been the broad social science research program around questions of masculinity and femininity. Among those studying the psychology of masculinity and femininity, the tendency is to move away from the bipolar approach—that is, one that poses masculinity and femininity as extreme ends of a single dimension—toward a dualistic approach that sees masculinity and femininity as quite separate qualities of self-concept, qualities that can vary independently and appear in every individual. The dualistic approach entertains the possibility of psychological androgyny in persons whose self-concept includes both masculine and feminine desirable traits. Bem (1974), for example, developed the Bem Sex-Role Inventory (BSRI) in order to measure psychological androgyny. The BSRI, a self-report inventory, contains items that describe desirable masculine traits (e.g., "Acts as a leader," "Assertive," "Independent," "Self-reliant," "Willing to take risks"), desirable feminine traits (e.g., "Affectionate," "Cheerful," "Compassionate," "Gentle," "Sensitive to the needs of others," "Tender," "Yielding"), and a number of "neutral items" judged to be no more desirable for one sex than for the other (Bem, 1974:156–157). Spence and Helmreich (1978), also taking the dualistic approach, developed their Personal Attributes Questionnaire (PAQ) that asks respondents to rate themselves on a series of scales for separate traits (e.g., "Not at all independent" to "Very independent," "Not at all helpful to others" to "Very helpful to others," "Not at all competitive" to "Very competitive").

Although technical differences exist in the construction and application of the BSRI and PAQ, they operate from similar assumptions. Their most important shared assumption is that all human beings need two distinct and sometimes antithetical clusters of traits in their own personalities and in their social organization. Parsons (1955) labeled these clusters "instrumental" and "expressive," whereas Spence and Helmreich borrow Bakan's (1966) terms, *agency* and *communion*. Agency and communion, argues Bakan, must be balanced in both the individual and society. An imbalance in either direction would be detrimental. "Since men tend to be dominated by a sense of agency and women by a sense of communion," write Spence and Helmreich, "the developmental task of each is different: Men must learn to 'mitigate agency with communion,' women the reverse" (Spence & Helmreich, 1978:18).

Obviously people have different levels of success meeting these developmental challenges. Thus in Spence and Helmreich's results four "types" emerge (Spence & Helmreich, 1978:35):

- The "androgynous" individual whose self-concept is above the median for both masculine and feminine traits
- The "masculine" individual whose self-concept is above the median on masculinity but below the median on femininity
- The "feminine" individual whose self-concept is above the median on femininity but below the median on masculinity

- "Undifferentiated" individuals whose self-concept falls below the median on both qualities

On Bem's inventory, as well, the androgynous individual is one whose total sex-role includes significant amounts of both masculine and feminine desirable characteristics (Bem, 1974:158).

As one might expect, this whole research tradition is fraught with definitional and conceptual disputes, not helped the least by the disputants' lack of an interdisciplinary perspective. Critics doubt that androgyny has any usefulness as a psychological concept (Henley, 1985:104–106), arguing that we ought not use the terms *masculine/feminine* or *masculinity/femininity* because these "tend to reify qualities which may be situationally, culturally, or socially determined, and have little intrinsic relationship to male or female status" (Harrison, 1978:325). The disfavor of androgyny as a concept lies in the larger movement within psychology to abandon personality as a construct (or, worse, to turn increasingly to biological processes to explain personality). Bem (1983) herself, for example, has moved away from androgyny as a gender-related self-concept and has begun writing about the "gender aschematic" individual within a society that generally processes information according to "gender schema." Similarly, Pleck (1975) prefers to speak of "sex role transcendence." As psychology discovers the social construction of reality (Berger & Luckmann, 1966; Gergen, 1982), the term *androgyny* seems more and more an embarrassing reminder that psychologists once committed the error of thinking of masculinity and femininity as "real" qualities of human beings.

But the concept of androgyny and the psychological and feminist research on androgyny are useful here precisely because they identify what Americans take to be masculine and feminine traits. These are native categories, even if they are abandoned by the scientists. If we are to undertake historical culture studies we must pay attention to the native categories. Seton did not have available to him the term *androgyny* in its full social-psychological meaning, so he was forced instead to hold up the Native American as an extended example of the concept for which he had no name. For these reasons I have decided to brave the controversy and continue using *androgyny* in analyzing Seton's ideology. Moreover, I use the term *feminist* to describe not the narrow political movement but the broader critical perspective that weds gender research with value judgment in a critique of patriarchy. In this sense we might call "feminist" an ideology of play that seeks to restructure game form and content away from culturally masculine (even patriarchal) patterns toward a balance between what the society values as masculine and feminine. We are prepared to ask, now, to what extent a socializing institution avows these traits and is organized to create them in its members. To be specific, what is the masculinity/femininity profile of the institutions Seton helped design?

Seton's Androgynous Model

Born in England in 1860 and raised in Canada, Seton established himself as an artist, naturalist, and author of animal stories before he embarked on his boys' work near the end of the century (Keller, 1984; Seton, 1940). In the 1890s Seton began to formulate his "Woodcraft Idea," a theory for youth work based upon the instinct psychology of G. Stanley Hall. The model woodcrafter, thought Seton, was the American Indian, and in 1898 Seton (at the urging of Rudyard Kipling) began casting his wood-craft idea into the form of a novel. Over the next few years Seton worked simultaneously on the novel, *Two Little Savages: Being the Adventures of Two Boys Who Lived as Indians and What They Learned* (1903), and on a hand-book for the organization he envisioned. In 1902 the *Ladies Home Journal* agreed to establish a new "Department of American Woodcraft for Boys," helping Seton launch his organization by publishing a Seton article each month. The magazine published excerpts from *Two Little Savages* in 1903, and the entire book appeared later that year. The publication of the organi-zation's handbook, *The Birch Bark Roll of Woodcraft*, that same year com-bined with the articles and novel to provide a complete ideology and program for Seton's Woodcraft Indians.

Seton's visibility as a genius of boys' work grew in the next few years, so it is not surprising that he chaired the committee that met in 1910 to found the Boy Scouts of America (Murray, 1937). Seton was made Chief Scout of the organization and he wrote the bulk of the first *Handbook for Boys* (1911), a manual that closely resembled the *Birch Bark Roll* and out-lined a program based upon the Woodcraft Idea. The founders of the Boy Scouts were a mixed group, including on the one side such pioneers in boys' work as Dan Beard and John L. Alexander and on the other side Progressive Era bankers, lawyers, and businessmen. Seton increasingly felt alienated from the rest of the Boy Scout leadership, accusing them of abandoning the Woodcraft Idea. In 1915 the conflict came to a head over the fact that Seton never took out American citizenship. The position of Chief Scout was abolished amid very bitter public exchanges, and Seton left the Boy Scouts to redevote himself to his Woodcraft Indians.

In 1916 Seton incorporated his Woodcraft League and sought to give his movement a greater sense of national organization. The Woodcraft League never really rivaled the Boy Scouts, and throughout the 1920s Seton held out hope that the Boy Scouts would return to the Woodcraft Idea (he even drafted a proposal to that effect). Seton deplored the militarism he saw in the Boy Scout organization and in the revised *Handbook for Boys*, complaining to friends that "the philistines" were in command of the Boy Scouts and that people like chief executive James E. West were "totally lacking any knowledge of things spiritual" (Seton, 1927). The Boy Scouts never did return to Seton's model, and he lived out the rest of his 86 years writing on Native American arts, crafts, and lore from the Wood-craft leader training camp, the College of Indian Wisdom, that he and his wife established near Santa Fe in the 1930s (Seton, 1967).

Within Seton's woodcraft idea lay an ideology of androgyny and a program for youth work designed to empower both boys and girls for androgynous adult roles. Seton never called himself a "feminist," though he admired historical feminists and counted among his friends several feminist women.

His model for youth work was markedly feminist within the context of a male institution, as I believe I can show with a few examples. Consider the ideal American Indian he takes as the model for his movement. Seton's writing over 4 decades, stretching from *Two Little Savages* in 1903 to *The Gospel of the Redman* in 1937, constructed a meticulously documented argument that the prereservation American Indian was the noblest human in history. Seton consulted written documents and live informants to distill "The Indian's Creed." Whereas the redman believed in many gods, he accepted "one Supreme Spirit." The redman revered his body and his parents, and he respected "the sacredness of property" such that theft was unknown. The redman believed in cleanliness of body and purity of morals, always speaking truly and never breaking a trust. He "believed in beautifying all things in his life" and kept his life simple. The redman "believed in peace and the sacred obligations of hospitality." For the redman, "the noblest of virtues was courage," and he never feared death (Seton, 1921:11–12).

The materialism of the white civilization was ruinous, said Seton, and he insisted that the redman's religion is simply the latest in a tradition of revitalization movements that include those of Moses, Buddha, and Christ (Seton, 1932:35–36). To prove his thesis that the redman's religion could revitalize 20th-century white society, Seton described in detail the redman's traits: He was reverent, clean, chaste, brave, thrifty, cheerful, obedient, kind, hospitable, truthful, honorable, and temperate, the model of physical excellence (Seton, 1921:19–59).

What is so striking about Seton's portrait of the ideal American Indian is how androgynous a figure it is in the context of early 20th-century American culture. The great Shawnee chief Tecumseh, whom Seton held as the finest example of the ideal, was known for his compassion, gentleness, and kindness—three decidedly feminine traits (Seton, 1921:18). Also feminine are the ideal Indian's spirituality and desire to beautify all things. The attraction of the ideal American Indian as a role model for American youth, therefore, was that the model was androgynous as Bem defines it. The model demonstrates qualities of personality and behavior that are "*both* masculine and feminine, *both* assertive and yielding, *both* instrumental and expressive" (Bem, 1974:155).

Also important to Seton's case for the American Indian ideal was the relatively high status of women in Native American societies. Seton devotes several pages of *The Book of Woodcraft and Indian Lore* to excerpts describing the contribution of Native American women to the commonweal. Indian women must do hard and dreary work, admitted Seton.

> But the Indian woman had several advantages over her white sister. She owned the house and the children. She had absolute control over her body. There could be no war without her consent; she could and often did become the Head Chief of the Nation. (Seton, 1921:40)

Seton clearly admired strength in women, as is evidenced both by his choice of women friends and by his support for girls' lodges in the Woodcraft

Indians and for the Campfire Girls. In describing the Woodcraft Woman, Seton offered as a model for American girls "one of the first great women of America, Wetamoo, the woman Sachem of Pocassett (1662)," and listed as her heirs such women as Susan B. Anthony and Elizabeth Cady Stanton (Seton, 1920:3–4).

Such was the texture of the ideology of androgyny composed by Seton the artist/naturalist. But the portrait of Seton's model for the Boy Scouts is not finished, for what distinguished Seton from other ideologists of this period is the fact that he designed an institutional structure to realize his ideal model. Seton took his Woodcraft Idea and his American Indian ideal as the basis for what we would have to call a feminist model of social organization. Let me explain this rather extravagant claim.

One of the important dilemmas of human social organization is the balance between cooperation and competition. The word "balance" may be inappropriate in that one version of the argument would insist that cooperation and competition are not bipolar opposites but are independent characteristics of social organization. In any event, several theorists concur that the instrumental, agency tendencies of males incline them toward competition, whereas the expressive, communion tendencies of females incline them toward cooperation in social arrangements. Bem (1974:156), for instance, lists "Competitive" as a masculine trait, and Spence and Helmreich (1978:232–233) consider "Very competitive" a high-masculine response and "Very warm in relations with others" a high-feminine response. Gouldner (1965) describes the effects of a male "contest society" upon Greek culture and Tiger (1969) makes a sociobiological argument to explain the role of competition in the social organization of males.

In contrast, Jean Baker Miller insists that one of the devalued strengths of women's psychology "is their greater recognition of the essential co-operative nature of human existence." Miller defines *cooperative* as "behavior that aids and enhances the development of other human beings while advancing one's own" (Miller, 1976:41). For men, says Miller, cooperation means losing something or giving it away. "To women, who do not have the same experience, cooperativeness does not have the same quality of loss." Miller is one of those who sees women as naturally competitive, but in a different proportion and within a different interpretive context (Miller, 1976:42–43).

If we take some of these distinctions and return to Seton's model for youth work, Seton clearly advocated this feminine principle for both his youth organization and for American society. Much of Seton's appreciation of American Indian societies is rooted in his Populism. A long-time friend and correspondent with Hamlin Garland, Seton consistently criticized white American civilization for its materialism and its economic system that allowed great wealth to accumulate in the hands of a few. American Indians were the world's "successful socialists," claimed Seton. Like the early Christians, the American Indians shared their resources. "Only personal property was owned by the individual," wrote Seton, "and even that, it was considered a shame to greatly increase. For they held that greed grew into crime, and much property made men forget the poor" (Seton, 1921:55). Moreover, Seton valued the small, face-to-face group. His Woodcraft Indians took as their model the tribal form of organization, and Seton always preferred the local autonomy of Woodcraft "tribes" to the building of a national, bureaucratic organization.

Most revealing of his feminine approach to socialization, however, was Seton's principle of "Honors by Standards." It is worth quoting Seton in full on this matter.

> The competitive principle is responsible for much that is evil. We see it rampant in our colleges to-day, where every effort is made to discover and develop a champion, while the great body of students is neglected. . . . A great deal of this would be avoided if we strove to bring all individuals up to a certain standard. In our non-competitive tests the enemies are not *"the other fellows,"* but *time* and *space*, the forces of Nature. We try *not to down the others, but to raise ourselves.* (Seton, 1921:7, emphasis his)

The almost revolutionary importance of this principle should not be underestimated (Lasch, 1979). First, this principle means that many contests in the Woodcraft Indians and, later, in the Scouts of America, *are not zero sum games*. In other words, unlike the Greek contest system described by Gouldner (1965:49–50), a person's "winning" does not depend upon another person's "losing." Honors by standards does not undermine the social order, as did the Greek contest system (Gouldner, 1965:54). The *Handbook for Scoutmasters* makes clear to the adult leaders the difference between this principle and the usual understanding of competition. The opening paragraphs of the chapter on Scout contests, for example, emphasize this distinction in darker type, a sign that the authors assume most adults coming into the organization would expect contests to be zero sum games.

> Scout contests and competition differ from ordinary physical contests in that emphasis is placed not only on group competition, but an opportunity is provided whereby the boy can compete against his own record or against a record which is set up. As well as this form of competition, each patrol or group is concerned in bringing up its weaker members and indeed does so.
>
> Scout contests do not represent the development of one champion in each event—but rather that every Scout develops his "best" in every event, thus giving each Scout breadth of experience. (Boy Scouts of America, 1924:319)

The second significant point about the honors-by-standards principle is the value it places upon the learning of a large repertoire of skills, rather than upon specializing in a single skill and trying to excel in that skill alone. In a sense, *quantity* and not quality, "Scout breadth" (as the *Handbook for Scoutmasters* calls it), is the goal of the program. Competition exists, to be sure, and in this competition there are winners and losers. But the contests come only after each boy has learned the skill required for the contest, and the contests are almost always between small groups, usually no larger than a patrol of eight boys. Thus first aid races, Morse-signaling races, and knot-tying races are speed events that are possible only after each boy has learned his bandages, his Morse code, and his knot tying. The goal is to learn the skills, a mastery that cannot be taken from the boy. The contests are for fun and to build speed and proficiency in the skills. Furthermore, because every boy is expected to learn every skill (working up to First Class Scout means the boy has just about every skill he needs for the contests), the individual boy might find that he does excel in one or another of the skills.

The same principle is applied to games. Here, again, winners and losers occur, but the point of the games is still didactic. "While [play's] competitive spirit gives morale," advises the *Handbook for Scoutmasters*, "it further provides opportunity for teaching the Scout how to win or lose in the right spirit. Selfishness is absorbed in team play and cooperation, and loyalty lays foundations for democracy" (Boy Scouts of America, 1924:333). A secret agenda always exists to the play and games in Seton's Woodcraft Indians and, later, in the Boy Scouts. Seton is careful to specify the benefits of each of the games he puts into his publications, and he linked many of the games to his list of instincts. The *Handbook for Scoutmasters* suggests games under the following categories: "Games for Instruction," "Games Demanding Attention," "Games Demanding Cooperation," "Games of Vigorous Action," and "Games for Fun."

Seton and some Boy Scout authors were attempting to make an important distinction between the play experiences they were providing boys and those provided by the two more well-known contest societies—sport and the military. Team sport provided Americans with the perfect model for the sort of "muscular Christianity" that linked muscles and morals at the turn of the century (Cavallo, 1981), and Seton knew that he was making his case against that background. But organized sport was subordinating means to ends, in Seton's view, so that sport came to stand for the bureaucratic, conformist, competitive American society that Seton felt was doomed. The military was unsuitable as a model for youth work for much the same reason; although Seton admired much in the initial program of Lord Baden-Powell's Boy Scouts in England, Seton was never comfortable with the military origins of that movement. Despite the apparent cooperativeness and male bonding in team sport and military organizations, Seton saw both settings as symptoms of a sick civilization, not as models for its revitalization.

Sutton-Smith (1971:80) asks us to see games as models of power. If we bring this view to the games played by Seton's two little savages, by the Woodcraft Indians, and by the Boy Scouts, we discover a model of power (I believe) far more androgynous than the usual models of power in boys' play. Seton's philosophy and the games he chooses for his handbooks reinforce cooperation, are nonhierarchical, favor nonspecialized roles, and feature a special style of competition, "honor by standards." These are characteristics of the play of female children (Goodwin, 1985; Lever, 1978;

Sutton-Smith, 1979), wed by Seton with some traditional forms of male play to form a wholly new, androgynous style of game and play for American boys (Mechling, 1986). Seton takes away from affiliation and cooperation any sense of loss or danger and makes service to others one of the highest ideals of his youth movements. Thus in his ideology, in his philosophy of play, in the institutional organization he creates for the socialization of American youth, and in the actual games and contests he designs for the organization, Seton holds an androgynous ideal that combines masculine and feminine traits, agency and communion, into an integrated human ideal.

What is remarkable, finally, is that Seton's program of activities and skills, awards, and badges actually *empowered* both boys and girls to enter adulthood with a broader repertoire of sex-role possibilities. The Wood-craft Indians and, later, the Boy Scout program empowered boys to cook, clean, and otherwise care for themselves, while encouraging in them a devotion to servicing others, helpfulness, kindness, and an appreciation of beauty that were not characteristic male qualities in the first half of this century.

What's more, Seton also aimed at empowering the girls. The Wood-craft Indians very early included girls and made no gender distinctions in requirements and activities. Seton was also an active ally in Luther Gulick's founding of the Camp Fire Girls (Buckler, Fiedler, & Allen, 1961). In these settings, Seton was eager to help girls acquire such positive mas-culine traits as assertiveness, independence, and self-reliance and to be able to develop their athletic and leadership abilities. The success of individual boys and girls in achieving the androgynous ideal, of course, must have varied greatly, and no doubt Seton's programs were training these boys and girls for an ideal society that did not really exist for adult Americans for most of this century (not even today). But such was Seton's aim, which is why I want to insist that Seton introduced into youth work in this century—and into the Boy Scout *Handbook* and program in particular—an androgynous model for human beings.

The Manliness Paradox

If I am correct in my claims that Seton's use of American Indian customs for youth work was in the interest of creating androgynous human beings, then a stunning paradox exists in Seton's work because the early part of this century was a period when American adults were creating male youth organizations precisely to encourage *manliness* in boys in the face of what these adults worried was the "feminization" of American culture (Hantover, 1978; Macleod, 1983). How shall we explain this seeming paradox?

One way to explain the strong feminist/feminine streak in some of the male leaders of youth work at the end of the 19th century is to resort to psycho-biographies of those men. Dorothy Ross's fine biography of G. Stanley Hall, for instance, views Hall's work after 1890 as a strategy aimed at reconciling his own masculine and feminine natures.

Hall had never been able to escape the feminine ideal he carried within him, and this was especially true after 1890 when the collapse of his more masculine efforts threw him back on himself. Although Hall wished for a magical and complete union, the most he was able to achieve was a kind of feminization of his own identity and sublimation of his desires into intellectual creation. (Ross, 1972:258)

Hall's eventual choice of adolescence as the focus of his work was no accident, in Ross's view, for Hall experienced "a long and troubled adolescence" not unlike that of his sometimes friend and sometimes competitor, William James (Feinstein, 1984). "Hall," writes Ross,

used his concept of adolescence to escape the narrow limits of his sex role. The idea contained and expressed his enlarged concern with the "feminine" realm of the feelings, religious experience, and youth. It was really a means by which he could restore these aspects of human nature to masculinity. In adolescence, the normal male could indulge in the feelings Hall's own constraints and narrow view of masculinity had denied him. (Ross, 1972:338)

Similarly, Wadland, who follows Seton's life up to 1915, pays delicate attention to Seton's Calvinist upbringing and his subsequent relationships with the three most important women in his life—Charlotte Schreiber, art teacher, mentor, and confidante to Seton while he was an 18-year-old art student at the Ontario School of Art (Wadland, 1978:58–59); Grace Gallatin, an independent American feminist and author whom he married in 1896; and Edith Lees, who, with her husband Havelock Ellis, was a frequent visitor to the Setons' estate in Connecticut and whom Seton considered "a prophetess from the wilderness, neither wholly woman nor wholly man" (quoted in Wadland, 1978:314). Wadland calls Seton's ideas "ecological" and "misunderstood and attacked" because they came 60 years before their time. But the cognitive style Wadland is calling "ecological," that is, appreciative of a whole systems approach, trying to balance the objective and subjective, emphasizing cooperation and communion, is better termed androgynous, I think, or even feminist. Certainly feminist theory regarding masculinist, exploitive attitudes toward nature (Griffen, 1976; Kolodny, 1975) would applaud Seton's ideology as being precursor to their own. It is clear to me, then, that Wadland's two points, Seton's relations with women and his ecological consciousness, are really one.

Another Seton biographer uses Seton's autobiography to push a case like Ross's for Hall. Writing about Seton's teenage years, Redekop makes a major point of something Wadland relegates to a footnote (Wadland, 1978:71). Referring to Seton's childhood hernia and the heavy truss he had to wear, Redekop writes

His painful and embarassing medical condition combined with the late onset of puberty and a dose of Victorian prudery to make life miserable for him. He fought against what seemed to him a constant and monstrous state of sexual excitement. He studied the life of St. Anthony and, having heard that the eating of meat fed sexual appetite, became a vegetarian. He bathed in icy water, went on fasts, and avoided pictures of naked women in the National Gallery.

It was a power struggle between natural instinct and will; his will won the battle. His reward came in the form of voices which spoke to him in the early mornings, just after waking. In the early hours of a summer day in 1881, a compelling voice came to him, urging him to leave London and go to the plains of western Canada. (Redekop, 1979:20–21)

The biographers of both Hall and Seton (and of William James, for that matter) all tend (some more explicitly than others) to attribute these men's theories about adolescence to the figures' own unresolved adolescent conflicts. Through their intellectual work, in short, these men were able to regain their feminine natures and seek a new, *culturally uncharacteristic* integration that would be a later-life solution to the conflicts.

Although I am quite in agreement with these interpretations, I believe that one need not resort only to an ego-psychology explanation in order to account for the paradoxical interest of men like Hall and Seton in recovering the feminine traits of human nature for males while at the same time writing about "manliness." A good many historical forces at the end of the 19th century were making the gender arrangements that had characterized the Victorian era and that had made the advanced stages of the industrial revolution possible in the United States problematic (Lasch, 1977; Sennett, 1970; Zaretsky, 1976). Anxiety about gender roles and about appropriate behavior was prevalent in the social class of these men. The anxieties are in the journalism of the period, and they are a central element of the formula fiction adults wrote for young people. In the Boy Scout novels that appeared after 1910, for example, but also in the Woodcraft Boys and Woodcraft Girl novels written by Lillian Elizabeth Roy during these same years (1918–1928), the most common formula is of the transformation of a character who begins the novel with "a lack" but, through the Boy Scouts or through Woodcraft, is reborn into a redeemed state of happy, healthy, socially constructive adolescence. What most boys lack in these plots is manliness; what most girls lack is self-reliance.

The important point to realize is that Seton certainly (and Hall probably) was using the term *manliness* to describe the entire range of desirable human traits, some thought to be characteristically masculine, others feminine. Seton's calling the American Indian "manly" and his description of the androgynous American Indian ideal makes Seton's meaning clear for us. Similarly, Hall's and Seton's attacks upon "feminization" is not misogynous. Quite the contrary, the attack is against weakness, dependence, lack of self-reliance, lack of trustworthiness, and lack of honor, all of which are as likely to be found in males as in females. Labeling these traits "feminization" certainly sounds misogynous and was in hindsight a rhetorical error. One is reminded here of Freud's reluctance to gender-ize what he considered to be the basic opposition in human traits, namely, active versus passive. Seton argues against the weak, passive traits, and I believe Seton was addressing both young men and young women when he urged upon them the independence, self-reliance, trustworthiness, and honor that he called "manliness."

So no paradox really exists behind Seton's creation of more feminist institutional structures and activities for youth work and the androgynous character of the young people he expected would emerge from those institutions. Seton's games would provide experiences structured by feminist principles, teaching the young people of both sexes that a workable and satisfying alternative existed to the masculinist institutional structures that the young people encountered elsewhere in their everyday lives in America. Seton's games were a sort of planned "conflict enculturation" (Sutton-Smith, 1971) aimed at mediating the youths' anxieties over rapidly changing gender arrangements by putting the youths into game worlds that solved the cultural oppositions by favoring the best of gender possibilities into the androgynous ideal. Cultural contradictions are not resolved so easily, we know, but Seton's effort is remarkable both in its critique of patriarchal civilization and in its longevity in the official ideologies of American youth movements.

Acknowledgments

This is an expanded version of a paper delivered at the Seventh Annual Meeting of The Association for the Anthropological Study of Play in Fort Worth, Texas, April 1–4, 1981. The author wishes to thank Dee Seton Barber, her family, and the staff of the Seton Memorial Library and Museum for their generous assistance on the research for this essay. The Research Committee of the Academic Senate of the University of California, Davis, supported this research.

References

Bakan, D. (1966). *The duality of human existence*. Chicago: Rand McNally.

Bem, S.L. (1974). The measurement of psychological androgyny. *Journal of Consulting and Clinical Psychology, 42*, 155–162.

Bem, S.L. (1983). Gender schema theory and its implications for child development: Raising gender-aschematic children in a gender-schematic society. *Signs, 8*, 598–616.

Berger, P.L., & Luckmann, T. (1966). *The social construction of reality: A treatise in the sociology of knowledge*. Garden City, NY: Anchor/Doubleday.

Berkhofer, R.F., Jr. (1978). *The white man's Indian: Images of the American Indian from Columbus to the present*. New York: Knopf.

Boy Scouts of America. (1911). *The official handbook for boys*. New York: Author.

Boy Scouts of America. (1924). *Handbook for scoutmasters* (2nd ed.). New York: Author.

Buckler, H., Fiedler, M.F., & Allen, M.F. (1961). *We-He-Lo: The story of the Camp Fire Girls, 1910–1960*. New York: Holt, Rinehart and Winston.

Cavallo, D. (1981). *Muscles and morals: Organized playgrounds and urban reform, 1880–1920*. Philadelphia: University of Pennsylvania Press.

Feinstein, H.M. (1984). *Becoming William James*. Ithaca, NY: Cornell University Press.

Gergen, K.J. (1982). *Toward transformation in social knowledge*. New York: Springer-Verlag.

Goodwin, M.H. (1985). The serious side of jump rope: Conversational practices and social organization in the frame of play. *Journal of American Folklore*, **98**, 315–330.

Gouldner, A. (1965). *Enter Plato*. New York: Basic Books.

Griffen, S. (1976). *Women and nature*. New York: Harper and Row.

Hantover, J.P. (1978). The Boy Scouts and the validation of masculinity. *Journal of Social Issues*, **34**, 184–195.

Harrison, J.B. (1978). Men's roles and men's lives. *Signs*, **4**, 324–336.

Henley, N.M. (1985). Psychology and gender. *Signs*, **11**, 101–119.

Keller, B. (1984). *Black Wolf: The life of Ernest Thompson Seton*. Vancouver, Canada: Douglas and McIntyre.

Kolodny, A. (1975). *The lay of the land: Metaphor as experience and history in American life and letters*. Chapel Hill: University of North Carolina Press.

Lasch, C. (1977). *Haven in a heartless world: The family besieged*. New York: Basic Books.

Lasch, C. (1979). *The culture of narcissism: American life in an age of diminishing expectations*. New York: Norton.

Lever, J. (1978). Sex differences in the complexity of children's play and games. *American Sociological Review*, **43**, 471–483.

Macleod, D.I. (1983). *Building character in the American boy: The Boy Scouts, YMCA, and their forerunners, 1870–1920*. Madison: University of Wisconsin Press.

Mechling, J. (1986). Male border wars as metaphor in capture the flag. In K. Blanchard (Ed.), *The many faces of play* (pp. 218–231). Champaign, IL: Human Kinetics.

Miller, J.B. (1976). *Toward a new psychology of women*. Boston: Beacon.

Murray, W.D. (1937). *The history of the Boy Scouts of America*. New York: Author.

Parsons, T. (1955). Family structure and socialization in the child. In T. Parsons & R.F. Bales (Eds.), *Family, socialization and interaction process* (pp. 35–131). Glencoe, IL: Free Press.

Pleck, J.H. (1975). Masculinity-femininity: Current and alternative paradigms. *Sex Roles, 1*, 161–178.

Redekop, M. (1979). *Ernest Thompson Seton*. Ontario, Canada: Fitzhenry and Whiteside Limited.

Ross, D. (1972). *G. Stanley Hall: The psychologist as prophet*. Chicago: University of Chicago Press.

Sennett, R. (1970). *Families against the city: Middle class homes of industrial Chicago, 1872–1890*. Cambridge, MA: Harvard University Press.

Seton, E.T. (1903). *Two little savages: Being the adventures of two boys who lived as Indians and what they learned*. New York: Doubleday, Page.

Seton, E.T. (1920). *The Woodcraft manual for girls: The eighteenth birch bark roll*. Garden City, NY: Doubleday, Page.

Seton, E.T. (1921). *The book of woodcraft and Indian Lore*. Garden City, NY: Doubleday, Page.

Seton, E.T. (1927). *A history of the Boy Scouts by: Ernest M.T. Seton, Chief Scout, 1910–15*. Unpublished manuscript, Seton Papers, Seton Village, Santa Fe, NM.

Seton, E.T. (1932). The message of the redman; or The gospel of manhood. *Totem Board, 11*, 6–36.

Seton, E.T. (1937). *The gospel of the redman*. New York: Doubleday.

Seton, E.T. (1940). *Trail of an artist naturalist, autobiography*. New York: Scribner's.

Seton, J.M. (1967). *By a thousand fires*. New York: Doubleday and Company.

Spence, J.T., & Helmreich, R.L. (1978). *Masculinity and femininity: Their psychological dimensions, correlates, and antecedents*. Austin: University of Texas Press.

Sutton-Smith, B. (1971). Play, games, and controls. In J.P. Scott & S.F. Scott (Eds.), *Social control and social change* (pp. 73–102). Chicago: University of Chicago Press.

Sutton-Smith, B. (1979). The play of girls. In C.B. Knopp & M. Kirkpatrick (Eds.), *Becoming female: Perspectives on development* (pp. 229–257). New York: Plenum Press.

Tiger, L. (1969). *Men in groups*. New York: Vintage/Random House.

Wadland, J.H. (1978). *Ernest Thompson Seton: Man in nature and the Progressive Era, 1880–1915*. New York: Arno Press.

Zaretsky, E. (1976). *Capitalism, the family, and personal life*. New York: Harper and Row.

Making Work Play

John R. Bowman

This was no time for play
This was no time for fun
This was no time for games
There was work to be done.
                    —Dr. Seuss

In contrast to our culture's traditional way of viewing play and work as separate activities that are polar opposites and sociological investigations of work that are based on the arbitrary dualism of formal/informal organization, this study seeks to identify the many ways both work and play are interwoven during the work process.

Employing a qualitative methodology, the topic of spontaneous forms of playing was approached and described by a variety of field research strategies. In addition to personal observations and informal interviews, information about making work play was collected from 70 accounts written by individuals (primarily college students) who participated in such play forms. These accounts provide us with firsthand descriptions of what went on in these situations by supplying details such as the context (setting) of the interaction, who is involved, and how these playful interactions are routinely accomplished. Furthermore, these accounts are written from the perspective of the participants and provide us with a unique subjective orientation to the experiences they describe. As will be demonstrated, not only what people do but also how they perceive, interpret, and feel about what they are doing leads them to conclude that play is occurring in the situation.

Because not all work takes place in the context of paid employment, consideration will also be given to playful variations of activities that participants themselves regard as "work." In addition, data will be provided from recent ethnographic accounts done by anthropologists in various work settings throughout American society.

As will be shown, many occasions occur in which individuals spontaneously play on their jobs. In fact, workers as players may engage in a variety of joking activities, horseplay, and practical jokes throughout the working day. Moreover, many of these play forms are repeated, and may even become routine features of some work settings.

The Work Society

Kando (1980) has described American society as the "work society," noting that historically this was the result of a number of cultural, natural, and economic conditions. Foremost among these conditions that contributed to the development of a work-oriented society was the cultural context of Puritan Protestantism. The Protestant ethic exalted work, while it detested idleness and prohibited all forms of amusement. Work became a duty, and as Weber (1958:53) noted, the spirit of capitalistic societies involves "the acquisition of more and more money, combined with the strict avoidance of all spontaneous enjoyment."

Play is often defined in terms of what it is not. From the perspective of the Protestant ethic, perhaps one of the most important things that play is not is work. Moreover, not only is play not work, but the two terms are seen as being polar opposites. Traditionally, contrasting play with work has produced a number of consequences for how we ordinarily perceive play. The following oppositions can be cited as prime examples:

- If work is serious and important, then play is trivial and insignificant.
- If work is productive, then play is unproductive and inconsequential.
- If work is for adults, then play is for children.
- If work is disciplined and compulsory, then play is free and spontaneous.
- If work is encouraged, then play is to be avoided.

In this way, play and work can be seen to define one another by a process of dialectical contrast.

A number of noteworthy exceptions exist to the prevailing tendency of viewing play and work as opposites. Marx's conception of work and alienation represents one such exception. According to Marx's humanistic conception of work, work, too, can be intrinsically satisfying and not be imposed by external circumstances alone (cf. Giddens, 1971:12). In fact, Marx's notion of unalienated labor transcends the play/work antithesis by suggesting that such labor may ideally be "something that gives play to one's bodily and mental powers" (Marx, 1964:89).

Along these same lines, anthropologists (Bohannan, 1963; Norbeck, 1971; Salter, 1978) have argued that perceptions of play and work are very much related to culture. The previously discussed complex of values and beliefs referred to as the Protestant ethic formed the basis of American culture's dualistic conception of play and work. However, this separation of play and work has been found to be frequently absent in nonindustrialized cultures. Unfortunately, this taken-for-granted separation of play and work has made it almost impossible for members of Western industrialized societies to recognize the possibility that what is regarded as work can in fact be play, and that on some occasions that which is normally perceived as play can be experienced as work. As Csikszentmihalyi (1975:202) notes, "One way to reconcile this split (between play and work) is to realize that work is not necessarily more important than play and that play is not necessarily more enjoyable than work."

Instead of viewing play and work as mutually exclusive activities, the data that are to be presented here raise serious questions concerning the traditional play/work dichotomy. All of the following examples of adult play occurred in social settings where individuals were working.

Playing on the Job

Sociologists who study the work world have traditionally directed their attention toward the following six themes:

- The changing nature of work, including the increasing division of labor and occupational specialization (Caplow, 1964; Durkheim, 1964; Miller, 1981)
- The social nature of work and related phenomena such as increasing leisure time (De Grazia, 1964; Faunce, 1968)
- The study of individual occupations (e.g., Spradley & Mann, 1975)
- The relationship between occupations and systems of social stratification (Noscow & Form, 1962:3)
- The management of labor, with particular emphasis on work conditions and worker productivity (Gardner & Moore, 1950)
- The experience of working, including the experience of alienation (Blauner, 1964; Terkel, 1974)

Despite the fact that these and other topics have been examined extensively by sociologists, these studies provide little or no details on how workers routinely construct organized events in work environments. As Speier (1973:160) notes, the sociological literature on work and occupations provides "almost no data at all that present how work routines of the most mundane sort are accomplished as interactional phenomena." Following Speier's recommendations, this chapter concerns how individuals manage to accomplish a sense of play while working.

Sociological investigations of work have also focused attention on the formal organizational levels of such activities. Actions that failed to conform to these formal models of organizational structure are regarded as informal, and this informal organization is said to develop in response to various failures in formal systems of communication (cf. Bittner, 1965). According to Handelman (1976:434), this formal/informal dualism resulted in according "primacy to formal organization in the social life of 'serious' settings, instead of analyzing their coherence and unity as an integrated whole fashioned by members of the setting in question." Moreover, a second consequence of this arbitrary dualism "was to prevent researchers from perceiving how expressive behavior . . . could come to signify the integration of a work setting to much the same degree as could formal directives" (Handelman, 1976:434).

The present examination seeks to overcome this dualistic relationship between play and work by stressing the importance of pursuing integrated, as opposed to segregated, studies of play and work. In short, a sociology of work necessarily entails a sociology of play.

Very little research has attempted such integrated descriptions of the work environment. One noteworthy exception was a study done by Roy (1959–1960); however, this study has been largely ignored. Roy observed workers' behaviors in a relatively small industrial setting, noting that in such repetitive work environments many times occurred when workers played on their jobs. Roy concluded that these various forms of rule breaking (e.g., horseplay, pranks, and joking) on the job actually functioned to alleviate boredom and other manifestations of worker alienation.

Although Roy was not specifically concerned with how these play forms were socially organized and accomplished, he nevertheless did note that certain groups of workers engaged in such actions throughout the working day, that these actions were frequently repeated, and that the workers obviously enjoyed these times of fooling around on the job.

A number of the observations made in the present investigation of adult play were made in work environments similar to the Roy study. For example, the following account described a series of spontaneous pranks played in a factory that produced automobile tires.

> I work in this tire room where they have about a hundred machines all controlled by one builder to each machine. One night I was steadily working when this piece of rubber comes flying by my head. I looked around and saw the guy beside me with a big grin on his face. A few seconds later I picked up a piece of rubber and threw it at him. Then another one came back at me. Well, this went on until break time and we both left our machines. I came back a little earlier than he did so I decided to adjust his machine a little. I moved his ply light over just a little bit where he couldn't run his ply on right. As soon as he figured out what happened he came over and cut my turret off. Next I set the speed on his machine up a little. All of a sudden his machine starts going faster and faster until he couldn't control it. He looked over at me and I was just dying laughing. He then took another piece of rubber and threw it at me. I was afraid the supervisor would catch us so I let him get away with that and proceeded to build more tires.

Sometimes such horseplay and pranks are even institutionalized in some work settings.

> This play observation was one which I observed while working in the factory. One day when the workers learned that one of the men in the department was going to get married, they decided to give him a shower to celebrate the occasion. This particular morning the line stopped temporarily. Immediately, all the employees in the department proceeded to carry their victim to the shower. Before they were finished a water fight had developed and almost everyone was completely soaked. I later learned this was a very

common sight in this department. It seemed like someone was getting a shower for some odd reason almost everyday.

Playing on the job is not limited to factory workers. It turned out that quite a few of the participants and observers involved in this study of spontaneous forms of adult play were nurses or nursing students. Despite the rather "serious" context and constraints of most medical environments, nurses too are able to find occasions where they can engage in playful interactions.

> The setting of this interaction was the Fairhaven Home for the Aged, where I work as a nurse's aide. Two nurses' aides were taking a linen cart down the hall, one in front of it pulling it, and the other in the back pushing. As they were going down the hall the one in the back jumped onto the cart and rode it down the hall. I knew it was play because both the participants were laughing, and trying to show off for the other aides who were watching. I thought the interaction was funny because it was humorous to see adults in their forties and fifties riding down a hall in a linen cart.

Numerous other episodes of playing on the job were documented, including two coworkers throwing a Styrofoam airplane around a drugstore and a make-believe game of baseball at a Pizza Hut, where a rolling pin was used as a bat and pizza dough was used as a ball.

One of the most frequently observed examples of playing on the job involved various joking relationships among certain groups of workers. Name-calling, cursing, and mock insults were very characteristic of such relationships. For example, a nurse described an instance of two nurses trying to out-insult the other.

> The first time I worked this floor two of the nurses were really cutting each other down. I didn't know what to do. I just sat there and stared at them. They were really nasty. For example, they called one another "fat slob," "witch," and "super dud." Nobody else paid any attention to them. All at once it was over and they started laughing. They all thought it was funny because I took them seriously. I had no way of knowing they were best friends.

Although such mock insults are often mistaken for expressions of hostility and aggression by outsiders, these behaviors actually connote friendship and personal affection.[1]

Pilcher's (1972) observations of the joking behaviors of dock workers are most relevant to this discussion. Pilcher describes various examples of name-calling, particularly the use of nicknames, which are nearly always derogatory (e.g., Bignose, Cesspool, Jowls, and Snake). Pilcher stresses that these names are seldom given to persons who are not well liked, and that these names are used only in the work context. This type of play is generally only recognized by the workers themselves.

> After the men begin work, the behavior begun in the pre-work period changes in tone. Although the shift is slight among those men who perform their tasks on the dock, there is a very clear change aboard the ships. All forms of profanity become more frequent and more serious in tone. The insults are more often directed toward individuals, are more serious in nature, and the mock assaults although less frequent are more realistic than ever. While the tone of the banter becomes lighter on the docks, and is often clearly playful even to outsiders, it becomes more serious on the ships. Again, outsiders often mistake the insults and horseplay on the ships for real hostility and aggression. (Pilcher, 1972:107)

In spite of the many ways that work settings inhibit play, many workers manage to fool around on their jobs. Spontaneous play and games are a characteristic part of some work experiences, and workers routinely manage to blend both work and play. For example, a worker behind the counter at a sandwich shop participated in such playful happenings as the following:

> We sometimes pretended to misunderstand orders or repeated something back totally different. At clean-up, we'd sometimes create little races and see who could do this or that first. The loser would owe the other a beer, or would have to stay and clean longer. Sometimes we'd actually say "Ok, ready go!" then start pushing mops around real fast and throwing chairs up on tables.

Playing at work is not always antithetical to getting the job done. As was seen in the last example, making a game out of cleaning up still accomplished this particular work task. Many of the accounts of workers who participated in play episodes stressed just this: Although they were playing, they were still working. This point is made in the following account of a laboratory technician.

> In the medical laboratory field there are difficult jobs and easy jobs. While working at a hospital there was a game we played to resolve who would get the arduous job of cross-matching blood for patients scheduled to have surgery. (We were all licensed and competent personnel so we weren't playing games with people's health.) Bloodbanking was not the favorite job of any of us, so we would choose a number from 1 to 24 and turn on one of the lab centrifuges. Whoever came the closest to the number on which the centrifuge stopped was quickly resigned to his job for the evening. We went through this ritual each Sunday night.

Although most of these playful episodes were interspersed throughout the working day, many of these spontaneous forms of play occurred at certain junctures in the working day. Most notably, playful exchanges were likely to take place right before work started, or near the end of the working period. One of the most common times for playing on the job was when work was slow or monotonous. As one worker/player stated,

> I was having fun during this play episode. I had never acted this way at work before, and the play probably wouldn't have even taken place if a customer had been present. It was play because it was so out of place, but we still had to keep our ''professional image'' by keeping an eye out for customers.

Almost always these various play forms took place when supervisors and other ''bosses'' were absent and ended when those in charge arrived on the scene.

Making Work Play

Not only were workers found to engage in various forms of pranks and horseplay, but sometimes the work task itself was accomplished playfully. As previously noted, playing on the job does not always mean that work goes undone. Workers performing instrumental tasks sometimes attempt to do these tasks in a way that provides an alternative to the more formal conception of the daily work routine.

One example of playing on the job that deviated from the normal ''professional'' model is the following description.

> The setting of this playful event occurred in the pharmacy where I am employed. Picture in your mind hundreds of pills—how about thousands. The major goal is counting out a required amount of pills for prescriptions. This goes on continuously for about three or four hours. After a few hours of this one seeks to find some type of variation in counting, which we did this afternoon.
>
> The object was to add some variety to the counting and still fill the prescription correctly. One of the pharmacists played a guessing game. He took a bottle of 1,000 pills and tried to pour out as close to the prescribed number of pills as possible. The other pharmacists joined in and they even attempted to pour the pills out with their eyes closed. They got braver and were even pouring behind their backs. This became quite a playful event and was accomplished with amazing speed and accuracy. The play got a lot of laughs and broke the boredom of being a professional pharmacist.

Many other instances of playing on the job that occurred during repetitive and "boring" work experiences were observed. As one player remarked, "Sometimes it was real necessary to play these little games just to break up the monotony." Most of these activities were described as just something to do while the workers were bored.

Being bored on the job was found to be related to the monotony of the work task, the workers' experience of time as moving too slowly, or the simple fact that the workers had no work left to do. Thus many instances of playing on the job occurred during these periods of boredom, with workers attempting to make the job more bearable or simply to make work time pass more quickly.

Not only do workers play to reduce boredom and monotony, but another important reason for playing while working is to make the job experience more enjoyable. Just as players experience pleasure while playing, players may also experience pleasure and enjoyment while working. In this sense, making a job enjoyable may sometimes involve transforming work into a play- or game-like situation. Indeed, many examples of playing on the job made such transformations. Thus a woman described how a routine job of bricklaying may be played with and actually experienced as fun.

> My father is a brickmason and I help him very often. Well, we went to stock out a house Saturday morning, and the bricks were at each end of the house. So we each took a set of tongs and opened a stack of bricks. Daddy said, "Let's have this house stocked by 11:00." So we began and the point was to see who could stock out their end of the house first. I stocked out my end first because Dad had to stop to put up corner posts. I told him I won, but he said he had more to do than I did. I helped him finish. It was fun because we played and got the work done.

Similarly, two farmers acted as if their shovels were guitars and played along to the music on a radio; this playful action was said to bring enjoyment to the arduous job of shoveling soybeans into a truck. A mother described how she transformed the unpleasant job of washing her baby's ears into a more pleasant job.

> I started pretending to see various vegetables in her ears, like potatoes, beets, carrots and onions. She loved it and laughed. In this way we were having fun doing a not so pleasant job. Now ear washing is the highlight of her bath.

Finally, a college woman described how a sorority changed the dreadful task of writing invitations to their alumnae into a playful occasion.

> We sat down and began the dreaded job and everyone was very seriously busy at work. Two of our sisters just started laughing and racing to see who could write the fastest and therefore write

the most invitations. The craze spread and before long everyone was racing. In the midst of all this fun we didn't realize we were all working and doing the dreaded job. I couldn't believe how much fun invitation writing could be.

As can be seen, a variety of work activities can be transformed into play and game-like experiences. Like play, such work activities are experienced as fun and enjoyable.

Conclusions and Theoretical Implications

All of the above examples illustrate various ways in which both paid employment and other work-related tasks may be transformed into playful activities. Although some of these episodes of playing on the job interrupted the ongoing work process, other examples were provided where workers successfully turned work into play and managed to accomplish work objectives while playing.

The fact that work activities can be accomplished playfully suggests the theoretical possibility that play activities can correspondingly be accomplished and experienced as work-like. Huizinga (1950:199), for example, recognized that games can be played too seriously, as is sometimes the case in sport where "we have an activity known as play but raised to such a pitch of technical organization and scientific thoroughness that the real play-spirit is threatened with extinction." Thus the data that was presented here on how work is made into play suggests a parallel area of research on the topic of how playful activities can be transformed and experienced as work.

The previously discussed research findings of Handelman (1976) and Pilcher (1972), as well as the works of Coser (1960), Sykes (1966), Brown, Brannen, Counsins, and Samphier (1973), and Handelman (1974), have emphasized the integrative functions of playing on the job. According to these functional approaches to the study of play, playing on the job provides a means for releasing tension, relieving pent-up emotions, and controlling and preventing aggression. Most importantly, play relationships serve as a symbol of group membership and perform the integrative function of helping to create and maintain group solidarity.

All of the above functions of playing while working may indeed be true, and to a certain extent the data presented in this study could be used to replicate and support the above research findings. However, that was not the objective of this research and according to the accounts of those engaged in play activities while working, such functional explanations were not really a significant part of their motives for playing.

Rather than stressing the integrative functions of playing on the job, this research has focused its attention instead on the participants' subjective experiences of playing while working. As viewed by the participants, a distinction is often employed to distinguish between certain work environments or between the way that certain jobs are actually accomplished. From the players' perspective, work was transformed into play to make jobs more interesting and bearable and, in some cases, to make jobs actually fun and enjoyable.

In conclusion, the data presented in this chapter suggest that our culture's traditional ways of viewing play and work as separate activities that are polar opposites are far too simple and must be severely criticized. Moreover, sociological investigations of work that are based on the arbitrary dualism of formal/informal organizations fail to identify the many ways that both play and work are interwoven in certain work settings. Handelman (1976:434) makes a similar recommendation when he states that both work and play "should be considered cognate modes of expression whose contrastive realities complement one another to compose a unity of experience." More efforts are needed to overcome these traditional dichotomies by examining everyday work and play experiences in such a unified manner. When it is realized that both play and work are interactional events, attention then must be directed to the many ways these activities are related and socially achieved. As demonstrated here, sometimes work activities are accomplished quite playfully.

Note

1. An important rule of these mock insults is that they are accomplished in a most serious manner. In this sense, the accomplishment of such insults is very similar in form to pranks and practical jokes. A more detailed discussion of the social organization of harmless pranks and practical jokes can be found in Bowman (1982).

References

Bittner, E. (1965). The concept of organization. *Social Research, 32,* 230–255.

Blauner, R. (1964). *Alienation and freedom.* Chicago: University of Chicago Press.

Bohannan, P. (1963). *Social anthropology.* New York: Holt, Rinehart, and Winston.

Bowman, J.R. (1982). On getting even: Notes on the organization of practical jokes. In J. Loy (Ed.), *The paradoxes of play* (pp. 65–75). West Point, NY: Leisure Press.

Brown, R., Brannen, P., Counsins, J., & Samphier, M. (1973). Leisure in work: The "occupational culture" of shipbuilding. In C.A. Smith (Ed.), *Leisure and society in Britain* (pp. 97–110). London: Allen Lane.

Caplow, T. (1964). *The sociology of work.* New York: McGraw-Hill.

Coser, R.L. (1960). Laughter among colleagues. *Psychiatry, 23,* 81–95.

Csikszentmihalyi, M. (1975). *Beyond boredom and anxiety*. San Francisco: Jossey-Bass.

De Grazia, S. (1964). *Of time, work, and leisure*. Garden City, NY: Anchor Books.

Durkheim, E. (1964). *The division of labor in society*. New York: Free Press.

Faunce, W. (1968). *Problems of industrial society*. New York: McGraw-Hill.

Gardner, B.B., & Moore, D.G. (1950). *Human relations in industry*. Chicago: Irwin.

Giddens, A. (1971). *Capitalism and modern social theory*. New York: Cambridge University Press.

Handelman, D. (1974). A note on play. *American Anthropologist*, **76**, 66–68.

Handelman, D. (1976). Rethinking "banana time": Symbolic integration in a work setting. *Urban Life*, **4**, 433–448.

Huizinga, J. (1950). *Homo ludens*. Boston: Beacon Press.

Kando, T.M. (1980). *Leisure and popular culture in transition*. St. Louis, MO: C.V. Mosby.

Marx, K. (1964). *Selected writings in sociology and social philosophy*. New York: McGraw-Hill.

Miller, G. (1981). *It's a living: Work in modern society*. New York: St. Martin's Press.

Norbeck, E. (1971, December). Man at play. *Natural History Magazine: Play* (Suppl.), pp. 48–53.

Noscow, S., & Form, W.H. (1962). *Man, work, and society*. New York: Basic Books.

Pilcher, W.W. (1972). *The Portland longshoremen: A dispersed urban community*. New York: Holt, Rinehart and Winston.

Roy, D.F. (1959–1960). Banana time: Job satisfaction and informal interaction. *Human Organization*, **18**, 158–168.

Salter, M.A. (1978). *Play: Anthropological perspectives*. Champaign, IL: Leisure Press.

Speier, M. (1973). *How to observe face-to-face communication*. Pacific Palisades: Goodyear.

Spradley, J.E., & Mann, B.J. (1975). *The cocktail waitress: Women's work in a man's world*. New York: John Wiley.

Sykes, A.J.M. (1966). Joking relationships in an industrial setting. *American Anthropologist*, **68**, 188–193.

Terkel, S. (1974). *Working*. New York: Pantheon Books.

Weber, M. (1958). *The Protestant ethic and the spirit of capitalism*. New York: Charles Scribner's Sons.

PART III

Children's Play
Under Constraint

Playing Around: Children's Play Under Constraint

Caroline Zinsser

Children's play is usually studied in places designated by adults as spaces suitable for play—researchers' observation rooms, nursery school classrooms, public school playgrounds, parks, yards, and neighborhood play areas. What has largely been omitted from research on play is the study of how children play in places that are not meant to be used for that purpose and how they adapt their play to circumstances constrained by adults. Although the unauthorized play of children in school classrooms has been widely recognized in pedagogical writings, it has been described from the viewpoint of teachers whose task it is to eliminate these activities in the cause of discipline. King (1982) and Zinsser (1984), taking the children's point of view as well as the teachers', have described how children interact with teachers and use such classroom play as a form of resistance to the demands of adult authority.

Unauthorized classroom play, however, is only one manifestation of a much larger phenomenon. Children are put in situations daily where their activities are constrained by the demands of public demeanor—in stores, on public transportation, on sidewalks, in church, and in many other social situations in their families and communities. Such social settings generally call for behavior of seriousness rather than "funfulness" (Sutton-Smith, 1971), and the role of play becomes problematical. What I would like to suggest is that not only do children continue to play under such circumstances, but they adapt their play to boundaries of behavior that they negotiate with adult arbiters.

The setting used for observations for this study was Alexander's department store in Manhattan, a large store known for its moderate prices and located at a subway stop that draws shoppers from the greater metropolitan area. I observed during 6 days over 2 winter months, usually in the children's department, during the mornings and again during after-school hours and on two Saturdays when many families shopped together. My method of observing was to walk around with my coat on (so as to blend in with shoppers) and to make notes on a clipboard. Evidently the clipboard gave my notetaking an official aspect, for no shoppers appeared to take particular note of my presence.

Play Under Constraining Circumstances

An example of the behavior that I term play under constraining circumstances is a sequence I observed in the adult shoe department of the store. Two boys, about 5 and 7 years old (I have estimated all the children's ages) had been told to wait in chairs while their mother tried on shoes. The boys first engaged in a tug-of-war with a wool hat. The older boy wrested the hat out of the younger one's grasp and threw it over his shoulder where it landed in the aisle. They both raced after the hat, laughing. The older boy reached the hat first, snatched it, and used it to pummel the younger boy as they returned to their seats. The younger boy began to cry audibly.

Their mother, hearing the crying, came over to the chairs and whacked both boys with a boot she had been trying on. She separated the children by moving one boy over two seats and then returned to the shoe counter. The boys sprawled in their chairs and rocked back and forth swinging their legs. One fingered his crotch as he stared into the middle distance. The other sang. The older boy suddenly turned around in his chair, put his back flat on the seat, and waved his legs in the air while looking for the other's reaction. The younger boy picked up on the action and they eyed each other while waving their legs, evidently pretending to be non-human creatures.

The older boy next converted the chair into a climbing apparatus, first standing up on the seat, with the younger child following suit, and then balancing himself on the chair arms. At this point, a shoe salesman approached and ordered, "Sit down!" Both boys sat. Their mother returned saying loudly, "I want you to be quiet for awhile. Shut your mouth. Stop playing around." She sat down between the boys and began to gather her belongings. The boys purposefully pulled their clothes into order, and all three departed.

The boys' behavior illustrated several aspects of play under constraint. They had been assigned a space where they would supposedly be kept safe from harm and out of trouble by the surveillance of their mother, other shoppers, and the salesman. The children converted this space into a place for play, first using an object at hand, a wool cap, as a plaything and then converting the chairs into play apparatus. They managed to continue to play together even when separated physically. They also, at one point, retreated into private worlds of their own. At no point was the play noisy. Only when they climbed on top of the chair arms did a salesman decide to enforce rules of appropriate store behavior. At that point, their mother also made an overt display of rule enforcement and moved the children away from the scene.

A department store is a semipublic place and calls for a way of behaving, a public demeanor, as Goffman (1963) points out, that is characteristic of people in public places. Shopping, the selection of goods for purchase, also calls for an expected set of behaviors. When children are taken along on shopping expeditions, they are under considerable pressure to behave in ways different from those at home. Children who do not behave "properly" are considered to display an unfavorable reflection of their parents' standards of behavior and training abilities.

Some idea of the amount of control shopping calls for can perhaps be better understood by my observations of very young children who had not yet learned the rules. A 2-year-old reached above her head to the counter and pulled down whatever protruded over the edge and threw it to the floor. She removed items from a display rack and carried them with her. She tipped over a wastebasket and pulled out some wrapping paper. Another small boy grabbed a package of underwear bearing a picture of a robot and refused to let it go.

When children are taken along with shopping adults, children can do very little to join in the activity of shopping—the business of estimating size, inspecting workmanship, judging styles, looking for fabric content and washing instructions, and making decisions about value and price. Children are allowed to touch the goods but not to contaminate them or to remove their tags or to take them from their designated places. They must not use the merchandise for play. Even toys on display are off limits. They, therefore, have the problem of maintaining their "public front" but at the same time finding activities of their own that are not only satisfying but allowable within the setting.

Establishing Space to Play

Adults (almost all shoppers-in-charge were mothers) had a double concern. They were shopping, an activity that took concentration and the use of both hands, but they were also taking care of their children, keeping them under surveillance. In moving from place to place, mothers usually put infants and toddlers in strollers and sometimes held the hand of an older child. Hand holding was also used as a way of leading a child to a new setting, as when leaving an escalator to enter the children's department or when moving toward the cashier. Variations were an older sister grabbing the cloth of a boy's jacket, a father steering his son by the back of the neck, and an older woman holding a 5-year-old boy by the arm.

But in the children's department, where low counters held goods on display for customers to inspect, the most prevalent arrangement for staying together was for the adult to lead and the child to follow at distances ranging from close by to nearly 40 feet away. So intent were mothers on shopping that they seldom looked back at following children. The space between them was used as a territory in which parent and child could separate and reattach (with children coming close and then falling behind, and with mothers moving ahead and then pausing), rather like a moving flight distance zone used for safety (Anderson, 1972; Carpenter, 1958; Nice, 1941).

Within this zone or territory, children managed to play while they were following. Almost all children ran their hands along the edge of the counter, often as though their hand were a detached object making a journey of its own, either vehicular or otherwise. A boy searched the floor for fallen pins. Another picked up a plastic tag, aimed it as though playing basketball, and threw it into a nearby wastebasket. Another systematically touched every shirt on display. Another tried to balance a package on his head. Two boys played peek-a-boo, sticking their heads forward and then back behind a pillar. A girl and her brother played hide-and-seek, chasing each other around counters until the boy was caught and taken to "jail" as his sister questioned,

> You going to jail?
> Yes.
> Behind bars?
> Yes.
> In a tiny room you can't read in?
> Yes.

Space could be delineated by using a marker, as when a stroller piled with coats marked the center of a space in which a father circled with a toddler while an older child stood close by and a mother moved at greater distances looking at goods. Coats could also be piled on the floor along with a shopping bag to mark the space within which parents and children moved. In these cases children "privatized" the space (Lofland, 1973) and used it for play. A boy pushed his brother's stroller back and forth saying "Vroom, vroom!" A girl and her brother used a wall mirror to take turns making faces.

When adults lined up at the cashier to pay for their purchases (and their activity changed to waiting), children used the space around the counter informally, abandoning their "public front" (Goffman, 1971). Instead of controlling their posture, they leaned, sprawled, sagged, and dropped to the ground, giving way to gravity. Some sat with their back to the counter or even crawled along on their stomachs. Because a floor-length mirror was nearby, children played games of autoinvolvement, making faces and motions, touching the surface freely with their hands and even, in full defiance of contamination rules, licking the mirror.

More complicated forms of dramatic play took place in what might be called niches or out-of-play areas (in this case out of the public behavior game). The two boys in the shoe department described earlier played in such an area. But the shoe department was the only place where chairs were provided. In other departments children sat on the low platforms that supported the mannequins used for clothing displays.

These islands within the flow of shoppers provided places where children considered themselves free from the constraints of shopping behavior. Because children were "parked" in these areas while their mothers shopped, they sometimes stayed as long as 30 minutes within the confines of the platform. Because they were left in pairs (never alone, presumably for safety's sake), they were able to devise imaginative games with each other.

Adapting Play to Limitations

Two boys of about 7 and 10 used two plastic tags, which they had found on the floor, as motorboats. The carpeting became the sea, the metal brace holding the mannequin a weapon that went "Pow." The dialogue was dramatic.

> This is a motor boat. It can go fast.
> Let's have a monster right here. You saw this thing pulling you in the hold.
> It pulled me, and then I crashed.
> You saw it getting bigger and bigger.

On another platform one girl sat in a relaxed posture while the other stretched out full length on her side. They wound rubber bands around their fingers and shot them at each other with gunplay motions. On another platform two girls played a game of trying to slap each other's wrists.

In adapting their play to this semipublic place, children did not usually play with strange children, although they eyed them with interest. Children were already learning how to scan, screen, and code other people as sources of possible danger in public places (Lofland, 1973). The only exception observed was the two boys, strangers to each other, who played peek-a-boo, a game that was started with the challenge, "You can't scare me!" but thereafter required no words.

When children were companions, however, they turned to each other in organizing play—games such as hide-and-seek, keep away, and wrist slapping that required few preliminaries, no equipment, and were adaptable to varying circumstances of time and space. When children were of different ages, they managed to find games in which both could participate with enjoyment such as when the older brother pushed his toddler sibling's stroller in imitation of a powerful vehicle.

In a department store whose general rules were that no store items could be used for play, children nevertheless were able to find objects to which the rules didn't apply and to use them as playthings—plastic tags, rubber bands, pins, mannequin stands, and mirrors. Lacking these, children used what was at hand of their own possessions—a hat, bubble gum, a family stroller, and a purchased package.

Children also withdrew from the scene at hand by going into individual reveries or entering games of dramatic play. When children apparently entered imaginary worlds of their own, their behavior appeared to lose focus. The child gazed into the middle distance, slid along the counter, trailed his hand over the merchandise—his actions lacked clear definition in terms of purpose. Other behavior indicated boredom, such as when children leaned against a wall, propping a bent leg by placing one foot on top of the other or when children engaged in what we might call "body doodling," manipulating their cheeks and mouths or swinging a package back and forth. Dramatic play was more elaborate, and when two children played together, involved the assignment of roles and the establishment of an imaginary scene that could be enacted within a confined space with few props.

Negotiating Boundaries of Play

Using Goffman's terms, we could say that the children used play as a way of moving "away" from participation in the "situational proprieties" demanded by the social situation of shopping (1963:69). This process required a good deal of judgment on the children's part because they should not have engaged in activities so deviant as to go beyond what was tolerable by adults. Inevitably, such play sometimes brought children in conflict with adults such as when the boys in the shoe department were chastised by the salesman and their mother. But more often, children and their parents successfully negotiated boundaries of acceptable behavior.

When a 4-year-old waited by the cashier's line, he sat on the floor with his back to the counter, legs outstretched. Next he crawled across the carpet to a mirror where he ran his hands back and forth across its surface, looking at his reflection and singing to himself. His mother came up and mildly remonstrated, "Don't do that," but the child disregarded her and stretched out full length on the floor. The mother then hissed from her place in line for him to stand up. The child hesitated a few moments, as though assessing the situation, resting his head on his arm and waving his legs in the air, and then he reluctantly stood up and joined his mother in line.

Children develop a fine sense of what their parents or other adults in charge will allow in social situations. These constrictions vary, of course, according to children's ages but are consistent enough so that children can adjust their play so that it does not disrupt the overall social organization of public behavior. On the contrary, such play is so adaptable as to almost disappear from adult awareness. Children do not appear to want to disrupt the rules for social settings so much as to create an alternate realm of their own, a world of play that provides refuge from the adult world but does not challenge its basic social structure.

Offsetting the Demands of Public Demeanor

Children, through their play, manage to balance out their own concerns against the pressing ones set by adult standards. What children appear to be struggling with are the demands of public demeanor. Goffman (1963) has described and thus made explicit the amount of discipline, tension, and control over the body that is required in American society in the regulation of ordinary, day-to-day interaction. These are the rules for bodily comportment, which when they are followed go unnoticed, but if not performed, mark one as a deviate or a child.

Children use unauthorized play not so much to counteract the harshness of adults but to counteract the role adults play as arbiters of the socialization process. Even the most permissive parent or teacher must necessarily, as an adult representative of the culture, enforce the standards for socially acceptable behavior in children. As adults who take these complicated standards for granted, we may forget the amount of effort required to learn and conform to the rules, an effort from which children seek the periodic relief provided by play.

Play allows the players a sphere of autonomy where they can arbitrarily make and break their own rules and so offset the demands of adult-like behavior. Although adults may recognize children's need to play in public places, they themselves do not join in the play. Instead, children must carve out their play activities within the interstices of adult demands of public demeanor. When they find themselves in social situations where play is, in adult terms, not appropriate, they must not only accommodate their play to limiting circumstances but also negotiate its terms with adults. For although the play that takes place in a department store might be labeled unauthorized, it is nevertheless tolerated under terms that are negotiable and require mutually understood communication between the players and those in authority. A situation of play must be mutually recognized (Bateson, 1955/1972; Goffman, 1974; Sutton-Smith, 1971), and this depends upon the child's abilities to convey the message, using Bateson's terminology, of "This is play."

Messages of Play

Children must indicate by their behavior that they are playing, but because the constraints of the department store as a social context deprive them of the usual accoutrements of child play—playthings, play equipment, and play spaces—they must demonstrate their intentions by behaving in a way such that adults (as well as potential child fellow players) will understand that even without the trappings play is taking place. Children accomplish this by playing as though the usual supports of child play do, in fact, exist. Thus a child ran his hand along a countertop as though he were playing with a toy car. His motions were so precise that an observing adult "read" the message. By acting out the behavior of a young child playing with a toy, the boy aided the adult in identifying the framework of play by including a representation of a recognizable plaything in his actions.

Similarly, another boy used a plastic tag as though it were a basketball and threw the tag into a wastebasket as though he were shooting at a basketball hoop. The child's actions conveyed a message of play, in this case, of a specific sport. Lacking both basketball equipment and play-designated space, the boy was nevertheless able to communicate that he was engaged in an activity that fell within the framework of sport.

These messages of play systematically serve to transform a social situation so that the child tosses the plastic tag in the expectation that his actions will not be judged by the context of adult store behavior—where plastic tags are used as security measures against pilfering—but instead will be viewed, within a context of play, as using a piece of sporting equipment. Similarly, a younger child stretched out full length on the floor indicates by his playful movements that he is not to be judged by the same expectations of public demeanor as are brought to bear on an adult in a department store. Play, by shifting sets of expectations within a social context, effectively allows children to purposefully escape or remove themselves from the constraints of adult rules and take refuge in play.

How much play will be tolerated by adults or how much play can be accommodated within a social situation without undue disruption varies with individual situations and necessitates establishing limits. Adults must enforce rules of social behavior, but rules, even such explicit ones as not destroying store property and not endangering oneself, allow interpretation. Children's play under constraint sometimes escalates as children test to find the hidden limits of a play situation. The boys in the shoe department first moved from sitting to lying on their chair seats. Then they stood on the seats, and finally, they stood on the chair arms. At this point the shoe salesman told them to sit down. A limitation of how much play was allowed had been reached.

When the 4-year-old played as his mother waited in the cashier's line, he started by sitting near her with his back to the counter. Then he crawled toward a nearby mirror where he played for a while before stretching full length on the floor. His actions, from sitting to crawling to lying, grew progressively more deviant from expected adult postures, and the child appeared to be testing the limits of the play situation both in terms of his mother's tolerance of his different actions and of the length of time he would be allowed to continue to play.

Conclusion

Children at play define themselves simultaneously as players and as actual persons in a social context (Schwartzman, 1976). Children in school may seek play as a relief from the demands of their roles as students so that they become players as well as students. But children in a social situation that does not allow for their participation, such as a department store, face a different problem. They are in the common predicament of children who have been dragged into an adult situation that cannot be shared. A child has no role as a shopper, only as a person who is being taken along. In these circumstances, it is commonly expected, although not explicitly stated, that children will play. Play provides children with a framework for self-directed action. Those who can "amuse themselves" within tolerable limits of play can win adult approval, for they have by this means provided themselves at least temporarily with an autonomous activity of their own that relieves the adult-in-charge of some caregiving responsibilities.

Children, however, were not the only nonparticipants in the department store shopping activity. Occasional adult and adolescent males also appeared to have been dragged along. They, too, engaged in activities distinctly different from shopping behavior. A man, for example, followed his wife while running his hand along the counter. He scratched his knee, hooked his thumbs in his jeans, counted the money in his wallet, stared into the middle distance, and finally removed himself from the scene to make a telephone call. To an onlooker, he appeared to be behaving so as to distance himself from the immediate situation. His actions were not those of a shopper but of someone who sought other activities to keep himself occupied.

King (1985) and Willis (1977/1981) have documented the ways in which adults, socialized as children in schoolrooms into patterns of illicit play, carry these play activities into the workplace as a form of resistance to authority. In these circumstances the patterns of students as players persist into those of workers as players. But the observations in the department store illustrate a different pattern of child play carried into adult life. Adults as well as children often find themselves in situations of social constraint, in places not of their own choosing, in groups where they have no involvement of their own. Adults in such circumstances may draw on the patterns of play set in childhood in seeking imaginative escape from uncomfortable settings.

Children, through their play, manage to balance their own concerns against the pressing ones set by adult standards. Perhaps traces of such play activities can be seen in adults who doodle, fiddle with eyeglasses, paper clips, and jewelry and mentally abstract themselves from social situations where they, like children, seek relief from the demands of propriety.

References

Anderson, J.W. (1972). Attachment behavior out of doors. In N. Blurton-Jones (Ed.), *Ethnological studies of child behavior* (pp. 199–215). Cambridge, England: Cambridge University Press.

Bateson, G. (1972). A theory of play and fantasy. In *Steps to an ecology of mind* (pp. 177–193). New York: Ballantine Books. (Reprinted from *American Psychiatric Association Psychiatric Research Reports: Vol. 2*, 1955)

Carpenter, C.R. (1958). *Territoriality: A review of concepts and problems*. In A. Roe & G. Simpson (Eds.), *Behavior and evolution* (pp. 224–250). New Haven, CT: Yale University Press.

Goffman, E. (1963). *Behavior in public places*. New York: Free Press.

Goffman, E. (1971). *Relations in public*. New York: Harper and Row.

Goffman, E. (1974). *Frame analysis*. New York: Harper and Row.

King, N.R. (1982). Children's play as a form of resistance in the classroom. *Boston University Journal of Education*, **164**(4), 311–329.

King, N.R. (1985, March). *The paradox of resistance as play*. Paper presented at the American Anthropological Association Annual Meeting, Washington, DC.

Lofland, L. (1973). *A world of strangers: Order and action in urban public space*. New York: Basic Books.

Nice, M.M. (1941). The role of territory in bird life. *American Midland Naturalist, 26,* 441–487.

Schwartzman, H.B. (1976). Children's play: A sideways glance at make-believe. In D.F. Lancy & B.A. Tindall (Eds.), *The anthropological study of play: Problems and prospects* (pp. 200–215). Champaign, IL: Leisure Press.

Sutton-Smith, B. (1971). Boundaries. In R.E. Herron & B. Sutton-Smith (Eds.), *Children's play* (pp. 99–111). New York: John Wiley.

Willis, P. (1981). *Learning to labor.* New York: Columbia University Press. (Reprinted from *Learning to Labour,* 1977, Farnborough, England: Saxon House)

Zinsser, C. (1984). *My Bible says I should obey: Child resistance to adult control in a fundamentalist Sunday school.* Paper presented at the Ethnography in Education Research Forum, University of Pennsylvania, Philadelphia.

Researching Play in Schools

Nancy R. King

School play is not, as some might assume, a contradiction in terms. Although the environment is organized to emphasize the importance of work, teachers and others who observe classroom activity see numerous examples of play in school. The classroom setting fails to inhibit the children's playful tendencies for several reasons. Perhaps the most important reason is that most adults believe that children's play is essential for healthy growth and development. Further, teachers often find that play activities encourage attention to academic lessons and serve as a valued reward for participation in assigned tasks. Consequently, adults tolerate a considerable amount of spontaneous play in school, and at times, teachers organize and promote classroom play activities.

The issue of play in the elementary school is approached from two perspectives. First, the children's definitions of play and the changes in their definitions as they move through the elementary grades will be presented. The categories of play that emerge will also be discussed. Second, the children's definitions will be used to organize the research relevant to each category of play. Finally, implications for future research will be explored.[1]

Children's Definitions of Play in School

Adult recollections about childhood play do not help researchers understand play in school settings from the children's perspective. Only children can define classroom play from the children's point of view. Consequently, three related studies designed to explore children's definitions of work and play in schools relied on data collected by observing classroom interaction and interviewing participants. The 94 children involved in these studies represented predominantly white class populations (King, 1979, 1983).

The Studies

Fifteen different classroom settings, kindergarten through the fifth grade, in three different elementary schools, were observed for two consecutive school days, and the children's official and unofficial activities were recorded. The children were observed participating in math lessons, reading assigned stories, doing seat work, running relay races in physical education, painting puppets in art, and taking spelling tests. The children were also observed passing notes, laughing together, playing tag during recess, gazing out the window, and talking informally with the teacher.

With the teachers' help, three boys and three girls from each of the 15 classrooms were selected so that each group of six children included a range of academic achievement and conformity to norms of classroom behavior. Each child was interviewed individually in a quiet area in the school building. After a number of open-ended questions that asked the children for examples of work and play in school, each child was asked to categorize activities in which he or she had been observed to participate during the preceding 2 days as either work or play. In some cases, children were also asked why they had placed an activity in the category they chose.

Results

The elementary school children who participated in these studies defined work and play as opposites; from their point of view, the categories are entirely separate, and the differences between the categories preclude the possibility that any activity could belong to both. The children see the differences as obvious, and they have no difficulty placing their school activities in one category or the other.

While work and play maintain their stability as distinct categories in the minds of the children, the categories themselves change significantly as the children move through the elementary grades, and the reasons for the categorization of particular activities change. Kindergarten children use the social context of their activities to differentiate work from play. Those activities that the teacher requires are examples of work, and although kindergartners may enjoy participating, they never place assigned activities in the category of play. Play includes only those activities that the children perceive to be voluntary and free of direct supervision by the teacher.

Because kindergartners focus on the social context of classroom interaction, their categorizations of the same activity are identical. The categorizations of older elementary school children, on the other hand, differ from child to child because older children introduce the psychological criterion of personal pleasure when labeling activities.

Although pleasure is important to younger children, they do not use it as a criterion that differentiates between work and play. Definitions based on pleasure first appear in the primary grades; enjoyment gradually assumes importance until it eventually becomes the dominant factor dividing work experiences from play experiences in schools. By the fifth grade, children rely almost exclusively on psychological criteria as they draw fine distinctions in categorizing their activities. For example, an activity will be labeled play if the child "feels like it" or work if the child "isn't in the mood." Further, the categorizations of particular activities are not stable because an activity that is enjoyable one day may be considered tedious on another day.

Although work continues to be identified with required academic lessons, all required activities are no longer labeled work. Required activities that older children enjoy or that they find unusually easy or entertaining are labeled play. The category of work is thus narrowed to include only those activities that are required and tedious or difficult. The category of play, on the other hand, includes all activities the children enjoy. Consequently, play in elementary school becomes a broad category that includes a range of dissimilar activities and apparently contradictory elements.

Categories of Play in Elementary School

A closer examination of the children's responses reveals that within the broad category of play three distinct types of classroom play are evident in elementary school. These subcategories can be labeled instrumental play, real play, and illicit play.

Instrumental Play

Instrumental play activities are those that are assigned and required by the teacher but that older elementary school children label play because they enjoy participating. Examples of instrumental play named by the children in these studies include listening to records, playing math games, writing poems, doing a science experiment, listening to the teacher read a story, and making pictures for a Thanksgiving mural. Children enjoy instrumental play for many reasons. These activities may permit energetic physical activity, or they may be undemanding and require little effort. They may allow or require social contact among children, encourage individual expression or include interesting content.

Although upper elementary school children label these activities as play, numerous differences exist between instrumental play activities and the spontaneous play activities usually associated with children. Most importantly, instrumental play activities are not voluntary or self-directed, and they serve goals beyond the purposes of the participants. Teachers organize these activities so that playful elements are included, but the teacher controls the situation, and the playful elements of the experience are not permitted to obscure the academic messages.

During instrumental play, entertainment becomes part of the curriculum as teachers provide instructional games and other playful curricular events. Simultaneously, achievement as measured by external standards becomes part of play.

Real Play

Real play includes activities that are voluntary and self-directed as well as enjoyable.[2] These activities meet both the social criteria and the psychological criteria of play, and the elementary school children interviewed in these studies labeled such experiences "play." Activities during recess are examples of this type of play in school.

All the children said they like recess, and many called it the best part of the school day. Children value recess because it provides them with opportunities to participate in active, often boisterous, physical activities, to interact with the children they choose, and to control the flow of events without direct adult intervention. Their comments emphasize the freedom and autonomy they have during recess to shape activities to suit themselves. In this way, play during recess resembles the spontaneous play of young children.

Recess differs from spontaneous play in two important respects, however. First, recess is used by many teachers as a reward for adequate participation in classroom events. Children who fail to complete assigned tasks or to exhibit adequate diligence during periods of work may be denied the opportunity to participate in recess. Second, teachers include recess in their daily schedules for additional reasons other than those of the participants. Recess is expected to fulfill the children's need to exercise and to relax so that they will return to the classroom refreshed and ready to work again.

Furthermore, children are carefully supervised during recess, and participation is not, strictly speaking, voluntary. However, because adults rarely intrude directly upon children's activities, children ordinarily proceed to organize their interaction without reference to the adults present. From the children's point of view, then, recess is a period of virtually unrestricted play during the school day.

Illicit Play

The third category of play includes all unsanctioned interaction among children during classroom events. Whispering, passing notes, and clowning around are examples of illicit play. Such play is intrinsically motivated and occurs in spite of the rules and regulations of the classroom. Teachers usually see illicit play as a disruptive nuisance, and they move quickly to prevent and control it. The children know their illicit play activities are unwelcome in the classroom, and they are ordinarily careful to hide these activities from the teacher.

Illicit play activities were evident in every classroom included in these studies. At various times, teachers ignored the children involved, reminded them to get back to work, or instructed them to move to a separate area of the room for the remainder of the lesson. In every observed instance, the teacher's actions or remarks convinced the children to discontinue their play.

In summary, all the examples of play activities identified by the children fall into one of these three categories of school play. Taken together, they encompass the meaning of play in the elementary school from the children's point of view. It is easy to use the children's definitions to organize recent research about elementary school play and to explore what researchers have learned about each category.

Research About Elementary School Play

The belief that play is a natural mode of learning for young children and the use of instructional strategies based on play activities have a long history in the field of education. At the turn of the century, for example, the playschool movement captured the attention of many educators and produced numerous experiments and curricular innovations (Hetherton, 1914; Pratt, 1948; Winsor, 1973). Currently, the theories of developmental psychologists and the observations of early childhood educators support those who believe that children learn important cognitive and social skills during play. Play, then, continues to be an important element in the instructional repertoire of most elementary school teachers.

Instrumental Play

Play activities designed to teach academic lessons are examples of instrumental play in school. Instrumental play is the category most widely researched and discussed by educators. Unfortunately, few educational researchers acknowledge the difference between play and games, and in most research studies instrumental play is usually equated with classroom games.

Play and games are actually distinct concepts; they may or may not include common characteristics (Makedon, 1984). Games, for example, are not playful if the children do not enjoy participating. In such cases, children would categorize the games as examples of work in spite of the teacher's intent to organize the lessons as play. At best, classroom games include a substantial element of pleasure and playfulness, without sacrificing the academic messages. When the organization and goals of the game coincide with the organization and goals of the academic content, the game is likely to be both a learning and a playful activity.

Every academic subject can, and, according to many educators, should include classroom lessons that are organized as instrumental play. Physically active games, puzzles, and brain teasers are typical examples of the games that are suggested and recommended for use in the classroom (Hollis & Felder, 1982; Hounshell & Trollinger, 1977; Kraus, 1982). For example, logical reasoning skills can be taught both on the playground and inside the classroom using a variety of games and play experiences (Van de Walle & Thompson, 1981). Other social studies concepts can also be taught in the form of games (Shears & Bower, 1974); simulations, for example, can provide children with the opportunity to experience work on an assembly line and are not difficult to organize in a classroom setting. Such activities can be used to introduce children to economic concepts, social relations skills, and the work reality of many adults (Palermo, 1979).

Riddles and activities involving sociodramatic play are often recommended for the teaching of reading (Gentile & Hoot, 1983; Tyson & Mountain, 1982). Singing games that take advantage of the children's natural interest in games and play are said to facilitate learning and engender positive attitudes in math and science. Finally, interest is growing in the ways that computers lend themselves to instrumental play (Malone, 1980). Computers can be used to offer children a wide variety of experiences with simulations and games in many curricular areas; in addition, lessons in programming can also be designed as games (Goodman, 1984; Kraus, 1981).

Although numerous books and articles have been published extolling the virtues of instrumental play and exhorting teachers to provide such play in their classrooms, the research literature includes surprisingly little evidence that instrumental play actually increases learning, and the evidence that does exist is inconclusive and fragmentary. Still, a number of studies compare the merits of lessons organized as games to the outcomes of lessons using traditional instructional strategies. Zammarelli and Bolton (1977), for example, studied 24 children aged 10 to 12 and concluded that those who had used a toy designed to teach a mathematical concept achieved greater insight into the nature of the concept and exhibited greater short-term memory of the concept than did children who had not used the toy.

Bright, Harvey, and Wheeler (1979) studied the effects of games on the cognitive achievement of upper elementary children in mathematics. The children played games that required them to practice using multiplication and division facts. The authors found an overall improvement in the post-test scores of the children, and concluded that instructional games are an effective way to review and retrain math skills. Because the research design did not include a control group, however, the authors could not conclude that instructional games are preferable to other instructional strategies.

Other studies indicate that a play environment is not conducive to learning cognitive skills. For example, a study of 10 primary grade classrooms found that the play-based curricular programs used by some of the teachers were less successful in teaching reading and math skills than the formal traditional programs used by other teachers (Evans, 1979). Baker, Herman, and Yeh (1981) also found that the use of play materials in academic lessons was negatively correlated with academic achievement. They concluded that play activities distract children and hinder academic growth.

In spite of the lack of conclusive supporting evidence, most educational researchers and theorists continue to urge teachers to use instructional games and other forms of instrumental play in the classroom (Hollis & Felder, 1982; Schoedler, 1981). Play advocates are careful to emphasize, however, that games should not replace traditional instructional strategies; rather, teachers are encouraged to use play activities to enhance and enliven academic lessons (Cruickshank & Telfer, 1980). The most frequent reasons given by authors for including instrumental play in the classroom have more to do with the children's attitudes than with their achievement (Avedon & Sutton-Smith, 1971; Block, 1984). It is usually argued that games are particularly effective motivators, and that children who are given the opportunity to play participate willingly and energetically in classroom events. The wholeheartedness of their participation seems, to many educators, to be an overriding positive consequence of play in the classroom.

Real Play

Educators study real play far less often than they study instrumental play; most studies of real play are written by anthropologists, linguists, or folklorists. These researchers ordinarily focus on playground activity and neighborhood play groups, though there are also a small number of studies of classroom interaction.

Sylvia Polgar (1976) is one of the few researchers to compare classroom play in a teacher-directed situation to school play that is initiated and controlled by children. Polgar studied the experiences of sixth-grade boys during physical education class and during recess. The activities in which the boys participated were similar in the two settings, but the experiences the boys had were quite different.

The games the teacher organized during physical education classes included many teacher-imposed rules and regulations, and they focused on goals beyond the playing of the games themselves. In contrast, peer groups on the playground developed games with fewer rules that were played simply because the children enjoyed them. The differences Polgar found convinced her the experiences children have during play depends on the context in which they participate. Furthermore, she found that only experiences during recess included elements of spontaneous play.

Polgar's research points to the important differences between real play and instrumental play. Her study also indicates some of the reasons why researchers studying real play ordinarily choose to observe playground activity. In most school settings, recess is the only time of the day when children are not subject to the direct supervision and control of teachers. Consequently, it is the time of the school day when real play activities are most likely to occur.

Most research studies of real play explore one of three major categories of playground activity. First, studies have been made of children's word play; these studies focus on storytelling as well as on childhood rhymes, jingles, puns, and riddles (Opie & Opie, 1959). Word play is often the framework children use to devise tricks, choose teams, and create games (Knapp & Knapp, 1976). Singing games and word plays create a sense of community among children of different ages and abilities; they are an important element in the culture of the play group.

McDowell's (1979) study of the speech play of 50 Chicano children demonstrates the ways in which children's word play helps to create and maintain their peer culture. In addition, his research emphasizes the importance of understanding the children's peer culture in the context of the larger ethnic culture in which it is embedded. In the case of word play, for example, it is necessary to understand how various social groups play with language before their speech play can be properly understood (Kirschenblatt-Gimblett, 1979). This is particularly true when children use their ethnic heritage as an immediate source and foundation of such play (Bauman, 1982; Leventhal, 1980).

Although most studies of word play focus on playground interaction, Reifel (1984) found examples of spontaneous word play among children eating in an elementary school cafeteria. Because the children were confined to their seats and expected to attend to their food, they could not participate in physically active games. In spite of the constraints of the setting, the children contrived numerous opportunities for real play based on games such as riddles, teasing, dramatic play, and clever repartee.

The primary cafeteria activity, eating, shaped the children's play, and the themes and focus of their word games had to do with food. The children who initiated and directed play events emerged as group leaders and other children admired their ability to entertain themselves and others. The adults in the cafeteria seemed unaware of the children's play. If the children were reasonably quiet and seemed to be eating reasonably quickly, the adults paid little attention to other aspects of their cafeteria behavior.

The study of active games is the second major category explored by researchers. These studies focus on playground activities and investigate both the games themselves and the nature of the peer groups that emerge during game activity.

Recess is ordinarily the only time during the school day when children are permitted to create and maintain self-initiated peer groups. Because recess is also the only time when most school children are permitted to play spontaneously, play activities are, not surprisingly, ordinarily the basis for the formation of peer friendships. Peer groups are, for the most part, based upon and maintained by the children's interest in common play activities.

The content of children's playground games is an important aspect of real play in the elementary school. Researchers who observe children at play relate that the experience of participating in a game is not to be confused with a description of the game rules. Children shape game rules to suit themselves, and, throughout the game, the activity remains under the children's control (Opie & Opie, 1969).

Although the games children choose are clearly influenced by adult society (Sutton-Smith, 1972), adults are rarely involved in organizing and directing children's activities during recess. Playground games are not, however, leaderless, chaotic, or confused. Even very young children organize games with clear rules concerning participants' behavior.

During real play activities the children negotiate the rules of their games to suit the skills and desires of the players involved. Sometimes initiating a playground activity requires little discussion; at other times, establishing the rules for a game activity requires lengthy debate (Borman, 1979; Hawes, 1974; Hughes, 1983). Some games such as tether ball and jacks ordinarily include variations, and negotiating these variations is required by the rules themselves. However, even during games such as soccer and baseball, which have rules established by adults, participants discover or create the opportunities they need to introduce changes.

While some playground games require complex social or cognitive skills, many games require considerable physical strength or agility. Rough-and-tumble play and play fighting are examples of the active physical play of some children during recess. Most episodes of play fighting last only a few seconds and follow an observable pattern that makes it clear that participation in this seemingly haphazard play also involves the recognition and acceptance of established rules of conduct (Aldis, 1975).

Play fights and other organized playground games reveal aspects of the exercise of leadership and the nature of status on the playground. These are important elements of the children's peer culture that flourishes during recess (Sluckin, 1981). The study of the children's culture is the third major category of playground activity that attracts the attention of researchers exploring real play in school.

During real play the children's desire and ability to create their own cultural context can be realized (Glassner, 1976). The study of playground interaction indicates that elementary school aged children are capable of creating their own subculture complete with values, loyalties, traditions, rules, and rituals. Children's games also teach the astute observer about the larger cultural context in which the children live.

Though fewer studies of real play have been made than of instrumental play, the research about real play is more richly detailed, more descriptive, and more informative. We may learn more about children and their play experiences because they are freer to express themselves during real play than they are during instrumental play. It may also be that the research methodologies preferred by most researchers of real play permit a close look at the play phenomenon itself without the need to evaluate or prescribe.

Illicit Play

Illicit play is the category about which we have the least information. Few research studies are available, and those we have often begin by assuming that illicit play behaviors are aberrant and dysfunctional. Consequently, the focus of the researcher is on controlling or eliminating rather than on exploring and understanding the children's illicit play.

The fact that researchers rarely study illicit play does not reduce the importance of this play phenomenon. Though it involves some risk to the participants, illicit play is important to the children because it provides a sphere of autonomy within the structure of the classroom. Children use illicit play activities to avoid assigned tasks or make contact with peers during periods of classroom work. Despite the danger, or, perhaps in part because of it, children appear to delight in episodes of undetected voluntary illicit play.

Children's illicit play appears in individual acts such as doodling, playing with a small toy behind an open textbook, and sneaking food during a lesson. Pairs of children or small groups may pass notes, whisper, comb each other's hair, make faces, or giggle together. Illicit play may also take the form of speech play when children sing new words to familiar tunes in order to challenge authority, ridicule adults, and satirize established norms of behavior (Jorgensen, 1983). Such parodies are particularly popular in elementary schools; they enable children to express their resentment and disdain for schooling in general and for selected teachers in particular. Composing these satirical songs, writing notes, and trading ritual insults often require linguistic fluency and social skills ordinarily admired by school officials. In the context of illicit play, however, these competencies become offensive (Gilmore, 1983).

The teacher's organization of the curriculum influences the nature of the illicit play activities in the classroom. The organization of classroom work and the teacher's leadership style are particularly important factors that shape the children's illicit play (Bossert, 1979). For example, in classrooms where children were grouped by ability for academic lessons, Schwartz (1981) observed that the ability groups developed distinctive forms of illicit play. The most academically able students interacted covertly and quietly during teacher-directed lessons. They developed a variety of subtle devices for passing notes and maintaining peer contacts, although the teacher openly discouraged such interaction. During those times when the teacher did permit peer interaction, their covert network dissolved, and the children substituted a system of informal peer contact.

Children who were in the least academically able groups, on the other hand, participated in overt, disruptive, illicit play during academic work periods. Their illicit play distracted the teacher and undermined the academic efforts of other children. Illicit play thus became a substitute for rather than an accompaniment to academic lessons. These children were viewed as disruptive and uncooperative by the teacher, and, from the teacher's point of view, the appropriateness of their placement in a low-ability group was confirmed by their behavior during teacher-directed lessons.

Spencer-Hall (1981) also found that among intermediate-grade children, potentially disruptive behavior is often quietly and carefully concealed. Children who are sufficiently accomplished at avoiding detection are seen as compliant and cooperative by teachers, though their illicit play activities are as numerous and as varied as those of other pupils who are less clever about concealing their play. The children teachers think of as disruptive are those who are more often caught playing, not those who play more frequently.

Occasionally, illicit play can be a group effort. For example, Williams (1981) observed a group of students stage a mock fight. Though the other children in the classroom realized that the fight was not serious, they reacted with fear, horror, cheers, and jeers. The teacher did not recognize the fight as play and devoted considerable time and effort to stop the "fight," settle the "dispute," quiet the children, and reestablish order in the classroom. The children met later to laugh at the teacher's gullibility.

Such examples of group illicit play are not common, and the disorders caused by illicit play are not usually a serious challenge to the authority of the teacher. Still, the opportunity to be disorderly may be one of the principle attractions of illicit play. Illicit play permits children to deny the relevance of the school's agenda and create a peer community that excludes the teacher. Children thus assert their control over both their loyalties and their activities during illicit play.

Although most teachers find illicit play activities to be disruptive, annoying, and exhausting, such play has value for them as well. The children's social life, ordinarily hidden from teachers, becomes visible during periods of illicit play. Furthermore, episodes of illicit play are conducted in an area easily observed by teachers and researchers alike. If taken seriously, the study of illicit play provides the opportunity to explore both the children's peer culture and the nature of play itself.

Conclusion

In each category of play, researchers have gathered and shared evidence concerning the experience and the meaning of play activities to the children and/or to the educational enterprise. The majority of the work by educators has been in the area of instrumental play. They view classroom play as one possibility in a range of instructional alternatives; it is, or is intended to be, controlled by adults in the interest of adult goals. Largely because of the instrumental attitude educators have toward school activities in general and toward school play in particular, the category of instrumental play is of overriding interest to educational researchers.

Although their focus on instrumental play is not surprising, it is surprising that despite the large number of studies about instrumental play, educational researchers have actually learned little from these studies. Findings tend to be suggestive rather than definitive and most conclusions are, in fact, inconclusive. Furthermore, because studies are designed to establish a causal relationship between classroom play activities and academic achievement, the quality of the participants' experiences is rarely examined in detail. This does not, however, prevent educators from extolling the contribution of play and urging teachers to include play in academic lessons. Hortative rather than reasoned, much of this body of literature is seriously flawed as a source of understanding about play in the elementary school. Unfortunately, the literature also appears to be limited as a source of understanding about its primary focus, the relationship between the academic goals of schooling and play.

With their research focus shaped so decisively so early in the research process, many educational researchers have an extremely narrow view of play, its manifestations in the classroom, and its meaning to participants. Their focus on instrumental goals blinds researchers to the importance of real play and illicit play as aspects of children's experiences in school. The children continue to play, of course, but their play is invisible to researchers; it conceals rather than reveals.

Researchers who choose to study real play rarely affiliate themselves with the educational establishment, and their findings rarely reach the educational community. They naturally seek out situations where children are relatively free from adult supervision and institutional constraints because it is in these circumstances that children's play becomes visible and children's culture becomes accessible. Consequently, they rarely focus on classroom play or play during teacher-controlled experiences.

A thorough study of school play, however, requires a noninstrumental, richly descriptive account of play experiences in classrooms as well as on playgrounds. Research that neither narrows nor purifies the categories of play studied is necessary if we are to understand the nature of play in settings established for and dedicated to work.

Notes

1. Portions of this chapter appear in somewhat different form in "When Educators Study Play in Schools," *Journal of Curriculum and Supervision*, 1(3), 233–246 (Spring, 1986). The discussion here emphasizes those aspects of play in school that traditionally have been of interest to anthropologists and ethnographers.
2. This label was provided by the children themselves in their interview responses. After categorizing a number of instrumental play experiences as play, the children differentiated between these classroom experiences and their activities during recess by saying, for example, "The math game was play, but when we go out after lunch, that's *real* play."

References

Aldis, O. (1975). *Play fighting*. New York: Academic Press.

Avedon, E.M., & Sutton-Smith, B. (Eds.). (1971). *The study of games*. New York: John Wiley and Sons.

Baker, E., Herman, J., & Yeh, J. (1981). Fun and games: Their contribution to basic skills instruction in elementary school. *American Educational Research Journal*, **18**, 83–92.

Bauman, R. (1982). Ethnography of children's folklore. In P. Gilmore & A.O. Glatthorn (Eds.), *Children in and out of school* (pp. 172–186). Washington, DC: Center for Applied Linguistics.

Block, J.H. (1984). Making school learning activities more play-like: Flow and mastery learning. *Elementary School Journal*, **85**, 65–75.

Borman, K. (1979). Children's interactions on playgrounds. *Theory Into Practice*, **18**, 251–257.

Bossert, S. (1979). *Tasks and social relationships in classrooms*. New York: Cambridge University Press.

Bright, G.W., Harvey, J.G., & Wheeler, M.M. (1979). Using games to retain skills with basic multiplication facts. *Journal for Research in Mathematics Education*, **10**, 103–110.

Cruickshank, D.R., & Telfer, R. (1980). Classroom games and simulations. *Theory Into Practice*, **19**, 75–80.

Evans, M.A. (1979). A comparative study of young children's classroom activities and learning outcomes. *British Journal of Educational Psychology*, **49**, 15–26.

Gentile, L.M., & Hoot, J.L. (1983). Kindergarten play: The foundation of reading. *The Reading Teacher*, **36**, 436–439.

Gilmore, P. (1983). Spelling 'Mississippi': Recontextualizing a literacy-related speech event. *Anthropology & Education Quarterly*, **14**, 235–256.

Glassner, B. (1976). Kid society. *Urban Education*, **11**, 5–21.

Goodman, F.L. (1984). The computer as plaything. *Simulation and Games*, **15**, 65–73.

Hawes, B.L. (1974). Law and order on the playground. In L.M. Shears & E.M. Bowers (Eds.), *Games in education and development* (pp. 12–22). Springfield, IL: Charles C. Thomas.

Hetherton, C.W. (1914). *The demonstration play school of 1913*. Berkeley, CA: University of California Publications.

Hollis, L.Y., & Felder, B.D. (1982). Recreational mathematics for young children. *School Science and Mathematics*, **82**, 71–75.

Hounshell, P.B., & Trollinger, I. (1977). Games for teaching science. *Science and Children*, **15**, 11–14.

Hughes, L.A. (1983). Beyond the rules of the game: Why are rooie rules nice? In F.E. Manning (Ed.), *The world of play* (pp. 188–199). Champaign, IL: Leisure Press.

Jorgensen, M. (1983). Anti-school parodies as speech play and social protest. In F.E. Manning (Ed.), *The world of play* (pp. 91–102). Champaign, IL: Leisure Press.

King, N.R. (1979). Play: The kindergartner's perspective. *Elementary School Journal*, **80**, 81–87.

King, N.R. (1983). Play in the workplace. In M. Apple & L. Weis (Eds.), *Ideology and practice in schooling* (pp. 262–280). Philadelphia: Temple University Press.

Kirschenblatt-Gimblett, B. (1979). Speech play and verbal art. In B. Sutton-Smith (Ed.), *Play and learning* (pp. 219–238). New York: Gardner Press.

Knapp, M., & Knapp, H. (1976). *One potato, two potato. . . .* New York: W.W. Norton and Company.

Kraus, W.H. (1981). Using a computer game to reinforce skills in addition basic facts in second grade. *Journal for Research in Mathematics Education*, **12**, 152–155.

Kraus, W.H. (1982). Math learning games: Simple vs. complex. *School Science and Mathematics*, **82**, 397–398.

Leventhal, C. (1980). Afro-American speech play in integrated schools: Some preliminary comments. In A.T. Cheska (Ed.), *Play as context* (pp. 259–266). Champaign, IL: Leisure Press.

Makedon, A. (1984). Playful gaming. *Simulation and Games,* **15,** 25–64.

Malone, T.W. (1980). *What makes things fun to learn? A study of intrinsically motivating computer games.* Palo Alto, CA: Xerox.

McDowell, J.H. (1979). *Children's riddling.* Bloomington: Indiana University Press.

Opie, I., & Opie, P. (1959). *The lore and language of schoolchildren.* Oxford: The Clarendon Press.

Opie, I., & Opie, P. (1969). *Children's games in street and playground.* Oxford: The Clarendon Press.

Palermo, J. (1979). Education as a simulation game: A critical hermeneutic. *Journal of Thought,* **14,** 220–227.

Polgar, S.K. (1976). The social context of games: Or when is play not play? *Sociology of Education,* **49,** 265–271.

Pratt, C. (1948). *I learn from children.* New York: Simon and Schuster.

Reifel, S. (1984, April). *Play in the elementary school cafeteria.* Paper presented at the annual meeting of The Association for the Anthropological Study of Play, Clemson, SC.

Schoedler, J. (1981). A comparison of the use of active game learning with a conventional teaching approach in the development of concepts in geometry and measurement at the second grade level. *School Science and Mathematics,* **81,** 365–370.

Schwartz, F. (1981). Supporting or subverting learning: Peer group patterns in four tracked schools. *Anthropology and Education Quarterly,* **12,** 99–120.

Shears, L.M., & Bower, E.M. (Eds.). (1974). *Games in education and development.* Springfield, IL: Charles C. Thomas.

Sluckin, A. (1981). *Growing up in the playground.* Boston: Routledge and Kegan Paul.

Spencer-Hall, D.A. (1981). Looking behind the teacher's back. *The Elementary School Journal,* **81,** 281–289.

Sutton-Smith, B. (1972). *The folkgames of children.* Austin: University of Texas Press.

Tyson, E.S., & Mountain, L. (1982). A riddle or pun makes learning words fun. *The Reading Teacher,* **35,** 170–173.

Van de Walle, J.A., & Thompson, C.S. (1981). Fitting problem solving into every classroom. *School Science and Mathematics,* **81,** 290–297.

Williams, M.D. (1981). Observations in Pittsburgh ghetto schools. *Anthropology and Education Quarterly,* **12,** 211–220.

Winsor, C. (1973). *Experimental schools revisited*. New York: Agathon Press.

Zammarelli, J., & Bolton, N. (1977). The effects of play on mathematical concept formation. *British Journal of Educational Psychology, 47*, 155–161.

The Effects of Traditional Playground Equipment on Preschool Children's Dyadic Play Interaction

Chris J. Boyatzis

The playground is perhaps the most traditional sanctuary for children's play. The thought of children playing evokes images of youngsters digging in the sandbox, whooshing down the slide, climbing on the jungle gym, and sailing away on the swings. All of these activities are associated with the playground setting.

Interest in playgrounds in this country flourished in the early part of this century. Prior to 1900 only 10 American cities had playground areas under the supervision of "play leaders," but by 1916 at least 480 cities featured more than 3,000 playgrounds (Park, 1982). During these early decades the playground movement gained considerable force, and the leaders of the movement argued that children's play should be regulated and ordered to insure "health, morality, and the social good" (Park, 1982:100).

This view may have led to playgrounds that typified what one architect (Allen, 1968) has called the "prison" and "ironmongery" periods in the evolution of playgrounds. The "prison" period featured play areas of a barren tract of asphalt or concrete enclosed by a high fence. This was, in Allen's words, "an administrator's heaven and a child's hell" (1968:18). Playground developers later added large metal structures such as swings, jungle gyms, slides, and seesaws. These play areas characterized the "iron-mongery" period in playground construction, and became the standard playground in America; they have thus been called traditional playgrounds. Virtually no change has occurred in these traditional playgrounds over the past 50 years, primarily due to their indestructibility and low need for maintenance.

In one of the earliest studies of how play behavior is influenced by play equipment and play areas, Johnson (1935) observed children playing in two play settings: a traditional playground with the large stationary metal equipment and an "enriched" traditional playground that had, in addition to the large equipment, many small manipulable toys. Johnson found that in the enriched setting children preferred to play with the small manipulable items rather than the traditional playground equipment, but in the enriched setting fewer social contacts occurred than on the traditional playground without small toys. Apparently the distraction of attractive, small toys reduced social interaction.

Children's play on playgrounds has been investigated in several recent field studies. Sluckin (1981) observed the growth of social-cognitive skills on the playgrounds of England, and Sutton-Smith (1981) provides a fascinating account of the relationship between children's play on New Zealand playgrounds and changing social conditions in that country. Due to its rapid population growth and industrialization, turn-of-the-century New Zealand, holding a view similar to that of the United States, promoted the organization of children's play. Another study (Farrer, 1977) examined how the Mescalero Apache Indian children of New Mexico play their version of the game of "tag," which was never observed anywhere but on the jungle gym. Groups of three to eight children would race around the structure in a clockwise direction, bodies often touching, but with a "tag" occurring only when the "it" child touched another child's body with a deliberate motion.

In addition to this ethnographic information, a small body of recent systematic research exists on how ecological factors such as playground equipment affects children's play interaction. One study (Frost & Campbell, 1977) discovered that on traditional playgrounds most second graders' play was physical exercise with very little pretend or fantasy play, whereas social forms of play were much more common on creative playgrounds (those with movable and adaptable parts and equipment). Another study (Weilbacher, 1981) compared the behaviors of kindergarten girls in two types of indoor settings: a static play environment (one with stationary equipment) and a dynamic play environment (one with movable equipment). Weilbacher found that significantly more cooperative and pretend play occurred in the dynamic environment than in the static environment, suggesting that movable equipment fostered cooperative and advanced levels of play interaction for young girls.

Some information, then, does exist about the effects of equipment, but less is known about the ways that specific pieces of traditional playground equipment influence children's play interaction. How is children's play with peers affected by the swings, sandbox, slide, and so on? These are important questions in light of the venerable status given to the traditional playground as a forum for children's play. These questions are also important in that the answers to them could have significant applications to playground design.

Method

Subjects

The subjects were 91 preschoolers (52 boys, 39 girls) between the ages of 3 and 6 years old. While race and social class were not specifically controlled for, the subjects were predominantly white and middle-class.

Setting

The requirement for a playground to be included in this study was that it have at least three of the following pieces of equipment designated as traditional: swings, slide, seesaw, sandbox, and jungle gym, and a somewhat less traditional item, enclosures (i.e., any structure that children could climb under or into, such as play tubes, tunnels, or fort-like structures). The settings consisted of three private, three school, and five public playgrounds for a total of 11 playgrounds. Each was visited once, and the average stay for observation was approximately 45 minutes at each playground. The school playgrounds were visited primarily on weekends or during after-school hours, and all of the playgrounds were visited during the fall season. The swings, sandbox, and slide were found on nearly all of the playgrounds, and enclosures and jungle gyms on about half, but only two seesaws were seen and therefore dropped from further analysis.

Procedure and Scoring System

Data were collected by observing dyads of children playing on traditional pieces of playground equipment. The purpose of the observations was to assess children's play interaction, and therefore children playing alone were not observed. All possible combinations of dyads (boy-boy, girl-boy, and girl-girl) were used in this study.

Observations were made with a time-sampling method in which children were observed at 30-second intervals at play on the equipment and had their highest level of play interaction during the interval recorded. The scoring system is an ordinal scale consisting of four levels that are based on the quality of socially interactive play between the children. The system reflects an increasing degree of "socialness" from one level to the next. The first level is *solitary play*, in which the children are together on a piece of equipment but play alone (e.g., sitting next to each other in the sandbox but with no regard for one another). The second level, *parallel play*, occurs when there is limited involvement between children on the equipment (e.g., playing beside rather than with and occasionally looking at or talking with each other). The third level, *social interaction play*, occurs when the children exchange social behaviors (e.g., smiling, talking, and offering/receiving objects) while on the equipment together. The fourth level, *social fantasy play*, occurs when the children are socially interacting but play with a pretend or fantasy theme such as superheroes or monsters, sociodramatic play (e.g., "house"), or other forms of make-believe. (This level requires interaction between the children; thus a pair of children independently building houses in the sandbox would score at the first level, solitary play.)

The author and two trained observers watched dyads of children at play on the equipment and the interrater agreement for the level of play interaction ranged from 83 to 91%, with a mean agreement of 87%.

Results

Table 1 contains the actual frequencies and percentages for level of play interaction on each piece of equipment. The column totals show that the sandbox and swings were the most commonly used pieces of equipment, and the enclosures were the least used. These findings are primarily due to the sandbox and swings being the most common pieces on the playgrounds visited, and the enclosures being the least common. The row totals show that solitary play and social interaction play were observed most frequently, followed by parallel play. Social fantasy play was very rarely observed, making up only 5% of the total observations.

A chi-square analysis comparing the observed versus expected frequencies at each level of play interaction by each piece of equipment yielded a highly significant effect, $\chi^2 (12) = 186.70$, $p < .001$, indicating that a piece of equipment does influence the level of play interaction occurring on it. As seen in Table 1, the swings were strong elicitors of solitary play, with little facilitation of parallel and social interaction and none for social fantasy play.

Table 1   Frequency and Percentage of Preschooler's Level of Play Interaction by Equipment

Level of play	Piece of equipment					
	Swings	Jungle gym	Slide	Sandbox	Enclosures	Totals
Solitary						
Frequency	132	24	18	64	4	242
Percentage	66	22	19	29	7	36
Parallel						
Frequency	34	32	32	52	8	158
Percentage	17	29	34	24	14	23
Social interaction						
Frequency	34	48	40	94	30	246
Percentage	17	44	42	43	53	36
Social fantasy						
Frequency	0	6	4	8	15	33
Percentage	0	5	4	4	26	5
Totals						
Frequency	200	110	94	218	57	679
Percentage	29.4	16.3	14	32	8.3	100

$\chi^2 (12) = 186.70$, $p < .001$.

On the jungle gym, the modal level of play was social interaction, closely followed by parallel and solitary play. The jungle gym was also poor at promoting social fantasy play. Both the slide and sandbox produced levels of play interaction extremely similar to the jungle gym. On all three pieces of equipment, social fantasy play was quite infrequent. The results indicate that the enclosures influenced play interaction in markedly different ways. The enclosures promoted more social play than the other pieces, with more than half of the obervations on them scored as social interaction and more than a quarter as social fantasy play.

Because the scoring system reflects an increase in the degree of social interaction from one level to the next, the four levels can thus be categorized as either "nonsocial" (consisting of solitary and parallel play) or "social" (consisting of social interaction and social fantasy play). The nonsocial category is so-called because of the relative lack of social participation within the first two levels, and the social category is named because of the highly social quality of interaction in the last two levels. When the observations are combined into these two broader categories, 59% of the children's play was of a nonsocial nature. A chi-square analysis of nonsocial versus social play by piece of equipment yielded a significant effect, $\chi^2 (4) = 88.71$, $p < .001$. So, although the modal level was social interaction play on each of the pieces (except the enclosures), the majority of dyadic play on traditional playground equipment was not social.

Discussion

Traditional playground equipment does indeed affect preschool children's play interaction. Several conclusions can be drawn from these findings. First, traditional playground equipment primarily promotes forms of play that are not social; second, with the exception of the enclosures, traditional playground equipment is very poor at facilitating social fantasy play.

The first conclusion is noteworthy because it suggests that the social and playful interaction of children on traditional playgrounds is not due to the equipment; in fact, it may be in spite of it. This is an especially surprising result because the children were observed in dyads, thereby increasing the likelihood of finding social play. The second conclusion is striking, given the prevalence of group fantasy play during the preschool years (see Rubin, Fein, & Vandenberg, 1983), especially when children play outdoors (Sanders & Harper, 1976). Taken together, these findings provide support for the claim that traditional playgrounds are best designed for gross-motor play (Frost & Campbell, 1977).

Although the traditional playground does not stimulate much social interaction, it does provide unique physical sensations. For example, children can experience the thrill from defying gravity by sailing skyward on the swings, or enjoy the brief but exciting whoosh down the slide. The gratification gained through conquering the challenge (quite formidable to the young child) imposed by the jungle gym also occurs. Thus obvious physical benefits, perhaps the greatest of which is the practice and mastery of sensorimotor skills, are offered by the traditional playground. However, this gross-motor exercise is not sufficient for the development of social and imaginative capacities.

The piece of playground equipment seems to shape or scaffold the kind of interaction occurring on it. The swings may be the most extreme illustration of how the design of equipment dictates the play (that is, how form determines function). The swings, with their specific function and limited range of uses—simply swinging back and forth—promoted play that was not at all social. Children typically swing to and fro, often without even looking at their nearby peer. The enclosures, on the other hand, actually brought children together and fostered social play, often with fantasy themes. This latter finding may be due to the enclosures providing a general structure for social interaction without limiting the quality of play themes inside them. Children were able to generate various fantasy scenarios and use the enclosure as a ''house,'' ''spaceship,'' or ''jail.''

The negligible percentages of social fantasy play on the other pieces of equipment corroborated previous findings (Frost & Campbell, 1977). The small portion of social fantasy play in the sandbox is surprising, though, in light of the malleable and adaptable sea of sand that surrounds the child. Although not specifically coded, much of the children's solitary play in the sandbox seemed to have pretense, suggesting that the sandbox may promote fantasy play but not with peers. The physical challenge and stimulation that the slide, jungle gym, and swings present to children may eliminate the possibility of and desire for social fantasy play. Most of the play interactions on these pieces were gross-motor exercises because the children were occupied with their physical engagement with the large, metal play structure. The slide seems to contribute to children's social skills, however, by making them realize the necessity for turn-taking.

Another approach to explaining the present findings is to consider the role of the complexity of the play environment. Children prefer play objects and environments that are high in complexity, defined as the potential to be used in a wide variety of ways by the child (Ellis, 1973; Gramza, Corush, & Ellis, 1972; Scholtz & Ellis, 1975; Unikel & Harris, 1970). Most traditional playground equipment cannot be manipulated by children, and as previous work indicates (e.g., Frost & Strickland, 1978; Johnson, 1935) children prefer adaptable, movable play equipment. As Ellis (1973) has suggested in his arousal-seeking theory of play, because the equipment cannot be adapted by children to fit their changing needs, the degree of complexity and interest offered by the equipment does not spiral upward with the children over time. The result is that the equipment becomes redundant and boring, and fails to function as a play environment that children return to. It is no surprise, then, that the typical visit by children to traditional playgrounds only lasts 15 to 20 minutes (Hayward, Rothenberg, & Beasley, 1974; Wade, 1968). Commenting on how children often ignore traditional playgrounds, architect Paul Friedberg (1970) grimly concludes: ''Playgrounds that offer no chance of manipulation; that are devoid of choice, complexity, and interaction will be empty of children—a dead ground'' (1970:27).

A bright spot in this otherwise bleak picture is the enclosure, which can be adapted by children to a greater degree than the other pieces of equipment. The enclosures thereby facilitate advanced levels of play interaction, including fantasy play among peers. The findings for the enclosures may have been due to the "sensory and visual discontinuity" (Gramza, 1970) provided by the encapsulation that the enclosures provide.

Finally, this study provides clear implications for playground design. If the objective of parents, communities, or playground designers is to promote primarily physical exercise play, then traditional playgrounds with their large, rigid, stationary objects are adequate. Even the thrilling sensations offered by these types of play environments appear to lose their appeal and cannot keep children for long (Hayward et al., 1974; Wade, 1968). If an alternative objective is to provide children with play environments that foster increasingly complex social and imaginative play as well as physical play, then adults should develop in their neighborhoods and communities playgrounds that can be adapted by children to fit their changing needs and desires (see Frost & Klein, 1979 for an excellent review of these nontraditional play areas).

The adventure playground is one kind of nontraditional playground that provides constantly changing challenges to children. Adventure playgrounds are fascinating areas filled with scrap metal, lumber, tires, bricks, and other construction-site refuse. Full-time adult play leaders direct the building of play structures that are modified often to guarantee the novelty and "discovery feature" of the play environment.

Although this kind of playground has been popular in Europe for decades, it has been slow to gain acceptance in the United States. This may be due to the prevailing belief, from early in this century, that play must be regulated and ordered for the good of the child and society, and the abundance of scrap pieces on the adventure playground does not seem to lend itself to order. The play leader, however, is responsible for organizing and maintaining order in the play area. These materials can be manipulated as playthings, and the adventure playground is a dynamic setting that embodies Nicholson's (1971) theory of "loose parts": the ideal play materials are those with which the child can truly interact and affect. These loose parts on the adventure playground make it a play environment that is "consumable" (Ellis, 1973:139). In contrast to this type of play area is the traditional playground, on which the only manipulable items are the sand in the sandbox and the enclosures. Although the traditional playground provides unique bodily sensations, in the consumable and adaptable play environment children can develop a greater understanding of their physical world, their peers, and themselves.

Acknowledgments

Portions of this paper were presented at the Annual Meeting of The Association for the Anthropological Study of Play, Washington, DC, March 1985.

References

Allen, M. (1968). *Planning for play*. Cambridge, MA: MIT Press.

Ellis, M.J. (1973). *Why people play*. Englewood Cliffs, NJ: Prentice-Hall.

Farrer, C.R. (1977). Play and inter-ethnic communication. In D.F. Lancy & B.A. Tindall (Eds.), *The study of play: Problems and prospects* (pp. 98–104). Champaign, IL: Leisure Press.

Friedberg, P.M. (1970). *Play and interplay*. New York: Macmillan.

Frost, J.L., & Campbell, S. (1977). *Play and equipment choices of second grade children on two types of playgrounds*. Unpublished manuscript, University of Texas, Austin.

Frost, J.L., & Klein, B. (1979). *Children's play and playgrounds*. Boston: Allyn & Bacon.

Frost, J.L., & Strickland, E. (1978). Equipment choices of young children during free play. *Lutheran Education, 114*, 34–46.

Gramza, A.F. (1970). Preferences of preschool children for enterable play boxes. *Perceptual and Motor Skills, 31*, 177–178.

Gramza, A.F., Corush, J., & Ellis, M.J. (1972). Children's play on trestles differing in complexity: A study of play equipment design. *Journal of Leisure Research, 4*, 303–311.

Hayward, D., Rothenberg, M., & Beasley, R. (1974). Children's play and urban playground environments: A comparison of traditional, contemporary and adventure playground types. *Environment and Behavior, 6*, 131–168.

Johnson, M.W. (1935). The effect on behavior of variation in the amount of play equipment. *Child Development, 6*, 56–68.

Nicholson, S. (1971). How not to cheat children: The theory of loose parts. *Landscape Architecture, 62*(1), 30–34.

Park, R.J. (1982). Too important to trust to the children: The search for freedom and order in children's play, 1900–1917. In J. Loy (Ed.), *The paradoxes of play* (pp. 96–104). Champaign, IL: Leisure Press.

Rubin, K.H., Fein, G.G., & Vandenberg, B. (1983). Play. In E.M. Hetherington (Ed.), *Handbook of child psychology: Vol. 4. Socialization, personality, and social development* (pp. 693–774). New York: Wiley.

Sanders, K.M., & Harper, L. (1976). Free play fantasy behavior in preschool children: Relations among gender, age, season, and location. *Child Development, 47*, 1182–1185.

Scholtz, G.J.L., & Ellis, M.J. (1975). Repeated exposure to objects and peers in a play setting. *Journal of Experimental Child Psychology, 19*, 448–455.

Sluckin, A. (1981). *Growing up in the playground: The social development of children*. London: Routledge & Kegan Paul.

Sutton-Smith, B. (1981). *A history of children's play: The New Zealand playground 1840–1950*. Philadelphia: University of Pennsylvania Press.

Unikel, I.P., & Harris, C.N. (1970). Experience and preference for complexity in children's choices. *Perceptual and Motor Skills*, **31**, 757–758.

Wade, G.R. (1968). *A study of free play patterns of elementary school age children on playground equipment*. Unpublished master's thesis, Pennsylvania State University, University Park.

Weilbacher, R. (1981). The effects of static and dynamic play environments on children's social and motor behaviors. In A.T. Cheska (Ed.), *Play as context* (pp. 248–258). Champaign, IL: Leisure Press.

The Strains of Idioculture:
External Threat and Internal Crisis
on a Little League Baseball Team

Gary Alan Fine

Each small group and every sport team have a unique culture of their own—a set of customs, rituals, behaviors, and meaningful images that constitute the way a team views itself. This I have termed the *idioculture* of a small group (Fine, 1979, 1982). Specifically, I claim that "idioculture consists of a system of knowledge, beliefs, behaviors, and customs shared by members of an interacting group to which members can refer and employ as the basis of further interaction" (Fine, 1979:734).

These idiocultures serve, in part, to regulate group behavior and typically to provide for a sense of cohesion. However, as I hope to demonstrate in this article, the existence of a small group idioculture does not mean the group will inevitably function harmoniously. Groups in disarray have group cultures as well, and these cultures will display lines of cleavage and hostility and may be used to promote additional disharmony. Yet, even here, the existence of the group's culture indicates to members that they have a view of the group in common and that they act on the basis of this shared perspective. I wish to demonstrate how group troubles are reflected in team traditions and the effects of these traditions in channeling members' behaviors. This disharmony is the inverse of some of the more positive functions that culture may have for promoting social integration. The depiction of conflict, though rarer, is as legitimate a cause of group culture as is a need for mutual support.

In the larger study of which this chapter is a part, I conducted in-depth participant observation with 10 teams in five Little Leagues in Massachusetts, Rhode Island, and Minnesota (for details see Fine, 1987). Here I focus on the development of the idioculture of a single team to demonstrate the effects of external forces on the creation and use of culture. Although any of the 10 Little League baseball teams could have been selected for a case study, I selected one group of preadolescent boys, the Sanford Heights Giants, a team whose record was fairly "average." Sanford Heights is a middle- to lower middle-class suburb of Minneapolis, consisting primarily of developers' tract homes. The League consisted of seven teams with 13 boys on each team; each team played all other teams three times during the season, which lasted from May into July.

In this chapter I shall examine the social structure of the Giants, the external circumstances with which they had to cope, the idioculture produced as a result, and the behavior that derived from this culture. I do not claim to have documented the whole of the Giants' culture, nor is this culture identical to that of any other team studied. The Giants were a team in some disarray, and I wish to examine how this disarray occurred and how it was shaped by and reflected in the Giants' idioculture.

Social Structure of the Giants

Because of a new coach, the Giants did not have any adult-created traditions from previous seasons. From a cultural perspective no team is typical, but at least the Giants did not appear especially competent or inept.

The Coach

The previous year the Giants had finished fifth in an eight-team league. Because their coach's son turned 13, the coach decided to resign his position to follow his son to the Babe Ruth League. Several weeks prior to the opening of the season two young men from the local community college (and former players in the league) agreed to manage the Giants. When they did not appear at tryouts, the league discovered to its dismay that the Giants were without a coach.

Fortunately, a league official recalled that Paul Castor, a father of one of the 10-year-olds at the tryouts, had coached youth hockey. Although he had once declined to coach a minor league team, the league asked him to fill in.

> GAF: Why did you decide to become a Little League manager this year?
> Paul: Mainly because my son made the team. They were hurting for managers, and they had asked me previously, and I had declined. . . . They called me the morning of the draft, and they said that Colin would definitely make the team, and they just didn't have anyone to coach, so I told them I'd do it. (personal interview)

Paul's story is typical in that often coaches are selected for convenience, not because of particular talents. The only way the league could promise that Colin would make the team is that the son of the coach *always* makes the team; to suggest (prior to the draft) that Colin had already made the team was shaving the truth. Because Paul had not attended the Little League tryouts, the man in charge of the minor league chose players for the Giants at the draft.

Paul's concern about coaching was the amount of time it would take; his job prevented him from being at the diamond before 6:00 p.m. (Games began at 6:30 p.m.) Because of his job he could not hold frequent practices. This constraint had a significant effect on the team's attitude toward him and on their culture.

Paul is an easy-going man in his 30s who appears genuinely concerned about his children and his community responsibilities. Although he had little baseball experience, he was a good athlete and tried to be fair to his players. He described his attitudes about the goals of Little League baseball as follows:

> [Little League] should teach the boys teamwork. I think they should have some respect for the coach's authority. The coach has got to get them to understand that they're playing as a unit, that they have to pay attention to what's going on, and if they don't have that attitude . . . if they come to horse around or screw around, then I don't think they should play the game. I mean there has to be a certain amount of competitiveness when you play any sport whether it be baseball, football or whatever, and I think that is very important because if they don't have that, if it's just something to do to pass the time, then they're hurting the other boys with that type of an attitude. (personal interview)

Yet, precisely these issues proved difficult for the Giants to deal with effectively, and this gave rise to important features of their idioculture.

Furthermore, most Little League teams have several adults in charge. Paul, however, had no assistant coaches and, as a result, had no one who could share the coaching burdens. Although the elder brother of one of the players did run three practices during the season (and in the process caused some difficulty for the coach), this boy was not an assistant coach.

The Players

Unlike most teams, the Giants at the beginning of the season were dominated by a high-status clique. The Giants had four 12-year-olds who attended sixth grade together, and who were close friends prior to the season. Two of these four (Rich Toland and Denny Malkis) were new to the team; the other two (Bill Anders and Rod Shockstein) were veterans. At the first practice, when asked to name their best friends on the team, these four boys named each other (see Figure 1). Not only was this group a tight clique, but they were also admired by their teammates. Five of the eight other boys completing questionnaires at this time named two of the four as best friends on the team; one other boy named one of the four as a best friend. Together these four boys received 71% of the friendship choices on the Giants.

Yet, the friendship structure of the Giants did not remain constant over the season. The number of friendship choices a boy received at the first

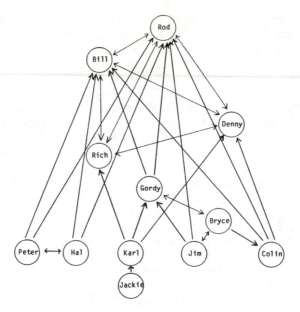

Figure 1 Giants sociometric analysis: first practice.

game of the season only correlated .28 ($n = 12$, $p = .19$) with the number of choices he received at the middle of the season—the lowest correlation for any team in the league. The Giants' social structure was less stable than any other team in the league, and a secondary core of leaders never developed beyond Rod. The change in the social structure of the Giants is evident in the status of two players, Denny Malkis and Karl Ruud.

Denny Malkis.   Denny began the season in the high-status clique; he was the third most popular boy on the team, behind only Rod and Bill. However, at some point in the 2-week period between the first day of practice and the opening game of the season, Denny's value as a friend declined dramatically. The other players, his former friends, spoke as if they had finally recognized Denny's "true character," and retrospectively reconstructed his biography. They claimed that Denny hung around with an ugly ninth-grade girl, insulted peers, beat up little kids, and was a crybaby (none of which I observed). One Giant colorfully expressed the collective sentiment of his peers: "He can lick where I shit." These boys created a new reality about this seemingly pleasant sixth grader, who apparently was not fully aware of what was happening to him.

Just before the first game of the season, the players completed another sociometric questionnaire. Only two players, both low in status, named Denny as best friend (see Figure 2). On the questionnaire distributed at midseason, no one named him as a best friend (see Figure 3), and in the final questionnaire, only a single player did so (see Figure 4). However,

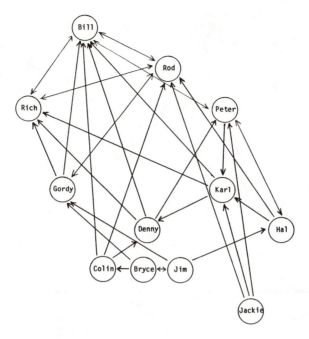

Figure 2 Giants sociometric analysis: first game.

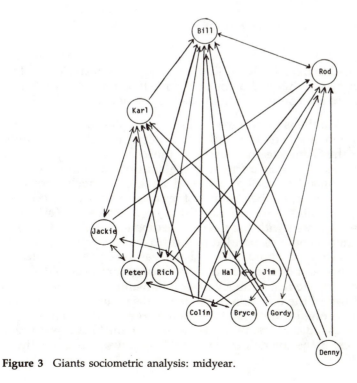

Figure 3 Giants sociometric analysis: midyear.

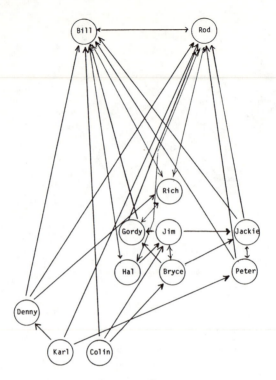

Figure 4   Giants sociometric analysis: final questionnaire.

Denny continued to perceive Rich, Rod, and Bill as his best friends. The change in Denny's status had a considerable effect on the behavior of the Giants toward each other and on the development of their idioculture.

Karl Ruud.   Another significant redefinition of a player's status in the Giants' social network is that of Karl Ruud. Because Karl was the only 12-year-old on the Giants' team from one of the local elementary schools, only one boy named him as a friend at the start of the season. By the first game, Karl, a good baseball player, received three friendship nominations and, at midseason, on the strength of his playing ability, he received six—second only to Bill Anders and Rod Shockstein. However, Karl eventually became disgusted with the Giants' mediocre record, and, unlike some team members who responded to this frustration by rebellion and subversion, Karl stopped attending the Giants' games regularly. His teammates scorned his poor attendance, and the friendship ties at midseason (which did not indicate real intimacy toward him and were more a result of the breakdown of the affection of the team) disappeared. By the end of the season no one on the Giants named Karl as a best friend.

These two cases indicate that the social network of the Giants was fluid, and an analysis of the idioculture of the Giants must recognize these changes in the team during the season. The Giants were a team with an inexperienced coach, two dominant preadolescent leaders (Rod and Bill), a disintegrating elite clique, no legitimate secondary leaders, and a lack of solid baseball players. Rod was a fine baseball player, batting .280, second highest on the Giants (though not one of the best players in the league—his batting average was 30th best in the 91-player league). Bill, however, was a mediocre player who batted only .121, poorest of any 12-year-old on the team, and was not particularly interested in baseball, although he was a peer leader.[1]

Effects of Team Structure

Each of the structural constraints within the team influenced the interaction of the Giants during the season and affected the content of their idioculture.

The Coach and His Players

The social order of Little League baseball relies on the power differential between adults and children. The adult has authority over his preadolescents. Although this power is present in theory, it must be negotiated in practice. Typically, adults believe they should "lay down the law" to preadolescents at the beginning of their relationship, so they can be more flexible later. If one judges by the first day of practice, Little League coaches seem to be a gruff, humorless lot; however, by the middle of the season most coaches have relaxed.

Despite his suggestions of the need for authority, Paul Castor started out by down playing his authority, telling the team he had never coached baseball before, and generally choosing to run informal practices. He commented in the postseason interview,

> A lot of the time [in practice] they just wanted to horse around. So the question is, is the coach gonna be a good guy, or is he gonna be a strict by-the-rule [coach]? For the first 20 minutes we're gonna do nothing but take infield practice and for the next 20 minutes we're gonna do this and this. . . . I find it hard in 10-, 11-, and 12-year-old boys to keep their interest that long. . . . In practices I would let the boys pitch to me. They seemed to enjoy that. Try to strike me out or whatever, and I tried to be kinda a pal to them, like one of the guys, rather than being a coach or a disciplinarian, and we seemed to get along quite well then. But then the practices are almost meaningless to a certain extent when you do that. (personal interview)

By his own admission Paul tried to be an equal with the boys. Those times when he attempted to have the team do relatively unpleasant activities did not last long. For example, Paul made the team do calisthenics (jumping jacks and touching their toes) at their first practice; however, after the second practice, at which players seemed bored by the exercises, the subject of calisthenics was not raised again. This lack of discipline and control was also evident after games.

> While the coach of the Phils insisted that his players clean up the dugout area before they get their free treats at the refreshment stand, Paul lets his players get treats, telling them that some of them (not naming anyone in particular) should return to clean up the dugout. None return, and when it is obvious that they will not return, Paul and I clean up the mess. (field notes)

In part, because of the lack of baseball training, the Giants, although finishing the season with an 8-10 record, had the lowest median team batting average (.157; the next lowest was .166), had fewer players who hit above .250 than any other team (two as opposed to four for the last place team), and the most players who hit under .050 (three as opposed to one for two other teams). The Giants were not noted for their fielding, nor did they have regular pitchers throughout the season. However, the Giants did win almost half their games, sometimes against the strongest teams in the league. The fairest characterization of their play is that it was erratic.

At the beginning of the season the Giants had a strongly defined hierarchy. Paul quickly recognized this and from the first practice he treated Rod like an assistant coach; the two developed a joking relationship, rare in coach-player relations.

> Paul is pitching batting practice and Rod is catching. After one pitch Rod asks him, "Is that a knuckle curve?" Castor answers cheerfully, "You bet." Rod says to the rest of the team, "I call him [the coach] the junk machine." Everyone laughs. "Junk" is a baseball term referring to off-speed pitches such as the curve, slider, and knuckleball. Rod's comment is made in a friendly tone of voice. (field notes, third preseason practice)
>
> Paul is pitching batting practice to Rod, and Rod tells him, "You bean me, I'm gonna repay. Right up the middle" [i.e., hit the ball so it hits him in the crotch]. Bill tells Castor, "He does that all the time to me. Up the middle right down low. Right in my nut cup." (field notes, practice, 2nd week of the season)

In addition to this joking relationship that characterized the beginning of the season, Castor gave Rod extensive responsibility for directing the team, as an assistant in Paul's presence and as the team leader in his absence. Castor commented at the end of the season,

> I relied on them [the team leaders—particularly Rod] a little more.
> GAF: Did you give them more responsibility?
> Yeah, I think to an extent, mainly Shockstein. (personal interview)

For part of the season Rod was responsible for bringing the equipment to the field. During practices he was as likely as Paul to give advice or shout encouragement to other members of the team. Sometimes it was difficult for the Giants to know whether Paul or Rod was running the team.

The rest of the players, sensing a lack of adult leadership, joked, and generally did not take the game seriously. This joking was light-hearted at the beginning of the season before the team felt pressure, but later became bitter. As Paul noted after the season,

> They didn't seem to have the desire that I'm accustomed to. . . .
> I think that a lot of the boys sloughed off, that it wasn't that im-
> portant to them. I had a lot of problems getting them to practice;
> they didn't really seem to care to practice. The same few would
> come. . . . We lost about four games because of haphazard plays
> or indifference, not hustling enough. (personal interview)

By the third practice, the Giants were behaving this way:

> Within an hour the outfielders were lying down in the grass and
> only running for an occasional fly ball. Whenever a poor player
> bats, all the outfielders move into the infield, and later when the
> last player is batting (another poor player), all of the fielders leave
> the field. During this, Paul says nothing. (field notes)

At one practice, late in the season, only three Giants (Rod, Bill, and Rich) even showed up. Perhaps, ironically, in light of this lackadaisical attitude—in part condoned by the coach—several players (particularly Rod) complained bitterly about the lack of practices. All four 12-year-olds interviewed at the end of the season agreed that the Giants did not have enough practices, that the practices were run poorly, and that they didn't like the coach. Paul was not entirely to blame for these problems, but the role and responsibility of the coach were a central focus for cultural creation.

The Disintegration of the Team Social Structure

In addition to the problems with the coach, strains developed among the players. One example was the hostility toward Denny Malkis that reached a point during the middle of the season when he was treated as a nonperson. His former friend Bill remarked to his former friend Rich, "Malkis isn't really a person," and Rich responded, "He's a thing. I hate him."

In addition, the team felt that Karl Ruud didn't attend enough practices; although he received several friendship choices at the middle of the season, these choices were not close friendships. At one game, toward the beginning of the season, Paul had Karl start at second base. Rich, who was not starting that game (and wished to), complained to Denny that

Karl shouldn't start because he attended so few practices. Denny agreed, saying, "Karl shouldn't be playing." Rich added, "It gets me so ticked." By the end of the season, players were openly sarcastic whenever Karl attended practice, and believed that he lied about the "conflicts" that made it impossible for him to attend. When up to bat at the end of the season, one Giant yelled to him, "Get a hit, Ruud, you're 0-for-27." When Karl eventually received a base on balls, and turned toward second base when he crossed first base (being in danger of being picked off), Rod warned him scornfully, "Ruud, what do you think you're doing?"

Even good players were attacked. Gordy Roolkis, the best hitter on the team (an 11-year-old), was accused of being lazy and asleep in the field. Once before practice Gordy said to the team, "Do you want to see a cool kid climb the fence?" and Rich retorted with scorn, "I only want to see a cool kid climb the fence, not a stupid one" (field notes). Later Hal told me to "write down that Roolkis is a faggot" (field notes).

During the 3rd week of the season, one Giant quit the team. Eddie Blair, an untalented 11-year-old, decided that he disliked his teammates, had no friends on the team, and didn't care for baseball. When the Giants heard that Eddie had quit, he was abused in his absence ("he just likes to quit things"), although he had been largely ignored when he was present. The Giants could have drafted another player to replace Eddie, but Paul never did, and for the rest of the season the Giants had only 12 players.

Finally there was Colin Castor, Paul's 10-year-old son. Although players were neutral to Colin at the beginning of the season, by the end they had become actively hostile. Like many father-coaches Paul overvalued his son's athletic ability, pitching Colin in games he would lose, and also starting him more often than two 11-year-olds and one 12-year-old. This apparent favoritism rankled several of the players, particularly Rich Toland, the 12-year-old who started less often than Colin. In one game toward the end of the season when Colin started instead of Rich, he commented to his friends, "God, our coach is dumb. God, he's dumb. Anyone's better than little Castor."

Related to the criticism received by these players (no one but Rod escaped hostile comments throughout the season) was the absence of secondary team leaders. The Giants had fewer boys who were named as team leader in the final questionnaire than any other team; aside from Rod, no Giant received more than three nominations as a team leader. Potential secondary leaders like Rich and Bill were mediocre baseball players, and both became disgusted with the team. Bill threatened to quit Little League, and Rich actually did quit the team at the end of the season. Only nine players attended the final three games, and the team was in a state of chaos because of the breakdown of discipline and the team social structure. The moral order on the Giants was oriented away from achievement.

External Pressures and the Development of Idioculture

The internal structure of the Giants provides the environment in which the team's idioculture developed. Yet, while recognizing these internal forces, we must consider how external social pressures directed the team culture. If the Giants somehow managed to triumph in each game that they played, the lack of practices or the fact that the coach decided to play his son more often than players on the team felt wise, would have meant little. If players are objectively winners, they are not likely to think of themselves as losers. Thus the definition of the situation that players accept and that shapes their idioculture is a consequence of stubborn realities—most particularly that the Giants were losing many of their games. This reality coupled with an inadequate authority structure and a disintegrating set of peer relations allowed for the development of their idioculture. Despite their troubles the Giants always considered themselves a team and developed an idioculture, even though its most salient qualities were negativistic and defeatist. They turned their structural difficulties into their culture.

Criticism of the Coach

The first and most obvious way in which the Giants reacted to their early defeats was to blame the coach for not holding enough practices. Paul rarely arrived at the field prior to 6:00 p.m., a 1/2 hour before the game, while other teams would begin practice at 5:00 p.m. This contrast with other teams was highly salient; blaming the coach was functional for removing the blame from the players' own lack of ability, and was appropriate sociometrically in that from the first practice, Paul Castor allowed himself to be teased and playfully insulted, while he down played his own authority. The recognition (triggering event) for the cultural symbol of Paul always arriving late for games seems to have first occurred before the third game of the season when the Giants had a record of 1-1. Rod brought the Giants' baseball equipment early and the players, led by Rod, began practicing informally without the coach. At about 6:00 p.m. Rod decided they should move to the field for their formal pregame warm-up. Although Paul arrived shortly after, and no negative comments were made toward him, this occasion gave rise to the group belief that he would always be late to their games and couldn't even be trusted to attend. The existence of this folk belief is evident at the next game when Paul arrived early (at 5:45 p.m.) and Rod commented sarcastically to some teammates, "Coach is early for once." Later in the season one player comments, when the coach has not arrived by 6:00, "Our coach never comes on time. You gotta take that for granted." On another occasion, Rod explained that Paul usually arrived at 6:29. On several occasions when Paul had not arrived by 6:00, players asked me if I would be willing to coach them if he did not show up. Despite this, Paul never failed to arrive by 6:30.

This cultural expectation about Paul's lateness was a consequence of the players' belief that practice is necessary for team success and that the team could have done better with more practices and more warm-ups. One means of explaining their losses and mediocre play (and the threat to their self-confidence) was to attribute the failure to the coach. For a coach not to attend games is to abrogate his most fundamental responsibility.

The criticism of the coach went deeper than simply complaining about his lateness and the lack of practices. Allowing his son to play, and particularly to pitch, was a constant source of irritation for several players, especially those 12-year-olds such as Rich, Denny, and Bill who were deprived of an opportunity to play. These complaints had some justice in that Colin batted only .037, second lowest on the team, and lower than every 12-year-old. It became a bitter joke that Paul would pitch his son, and the Giants would then be defeated. Once late in the season Rod and Bill secretly decided to quit the team if Paul pitched his son; because he did not at that time, the threat was not made public. Gordy commented, "The only thing the coach cares about is his son." In one crucial game 3 weeks before the end of the season, Colin started pitching in the third inning against the Phils, the best team in the league. Although the Giants were already losing by a considerable margin (6–0), the other players were angered at this decision. In the fifth inning Colin made an error while pitching, for which he was insulted by his teammates. His pitching that day was so poor that his father removed him as pitcher; Colin threw down his glove and ran from the field in tears as the game continued. Bill, who had been riding him hard, apparently feeling remorse, went over to where Colin was weeping bitterly and talked to him, calming him down by his tender words. On his return Bill insisted that he would "beat up anyone who criticizes Colin." For the remainder of the game Colin was treated considerately.

Despite this, the occasion became part of team lore as indicating Colin's lack of ability and how he was not able to take it. The account of that event became a team "memorate" and was used for the remainder of the season to justify Colin's low status and to explain some of the previous defeats. This occasion also served to remind the team of Paul's lack of fairness to the other players.

Negative Team Spirit

Perhaps the most striking feature about the Giants' culture was its self-degradation. Although most teams, despite evidence to the contrary, expect to win their games, this optimistic view was not characteristic of the Giants. This attitude by the players and the coach was evident in their behavior. After the third game of the season, which the Giants won, Paul reported to another adult, "We won 5–4. I couldn't believe it." After a victory later in the season, Peter Peyser, a 12-year-old, remarked, "We were lucky, lucky, lucky!" These comments contrast with those of coaches who tell their teams that they will win all their games and those of players who count on being undefeated. The Giants, contrasting themselves with other teams with more practices and better coaches and players, found it difficult to accept that they could be winners—even though they wished to be and thought they might be before the season began. Players readjusted their recall of their early expectations by the end of the season. Rod, for example, halfway through the season claimed that he had told me the Giants would be 9-9 for the season; his actual prediction was 16-2. Another Giant player said he put down 17-1, to which the coach sarcastically replied, "Oh, come on," as if to indicate that would have been impossible.

To cope with their disappointment at their poor first half (3-6), players regularly criticized their own team. By the 3rd week Rich was calling the Giants "a prange team." ("Prange" is a local insult in Sanford Heights meaning "rotten" with "homosexual" implications.) Once when the Giants were losing, I commented that their opponents "look strong," to which Rich retorted, "Not as strong as we look weak." These low expectations are reflected in the fact that players expected their teammates, even the better ones, to make outs. Thus with one out, Hal Brattle (a 12-year-old) said that he would not get up to bat that inning because the next two batters (the third and fifth best batters on the team) would make outs. Hal may have been correct in terms of the odds, but it is rare for a player to expect his teammates to fail, and, in fact, he *was* wrong. This lack of spirit is also reflected in that no members of the team wished to purchase a team picture (during the middle of the season), in contrast to other teams. The team image was that of an organizational failure. Although teams often adopt the mannerisms of professional baseball players in such things as wearing batting gloves, charcoal under their eyes, or batting in particular ways, the Giants only adopted one professional trait. By the middle of the season, players started to spit.

Unlike many teams in which the coach insists that the team pay attention to what is happening in the game, Paul did not attempt to discipline the team consistently. Most coaches refuse to allow players to buy refreshments during the game. Paul disapproved, but he did nothing.

> Denny is eating a lollypop and hands it to Paul to hold while he is warming up the pitcher. Paul comments, "You guys are here to play baseball or to eat?" Players ignore his comment and continue to eat. Paul doesn't do anything, as he holds Denny's lollypop. (field notes, 2nd week)

This same laxness is evident in other areas. In Sanford Heights teams must stay within the dugout while their players are batting; more often than not, the Giants were outside the dugout, watching the game or wandering around. Similarly, Paul allowed boys not on the Giants to walk in the dugout; girlfriends entered to flirt with their swains. Paul occasionally chased away these intruders, but they never stayed away long; the Giants more than any other team in the league had outsiders in their dugout. Paul's relaxed style—not setting or enforcing many rules—suggested to players that "anything goes." Even when he threatened to bench players for criticizing their teammates, the abuse continued. Unlike other teams, no player on the Giants was ever benched for his behavior and, while the Giants took advantage of this leeway, several players criticized Paul for not being strict enough.

The Giants did have moments of success, but even these occurred within the team's environment of failure. Consider the case of Jim Melton, an 11-year-old utility outfielder. In the previous season he had not gotten any hits, and was accused by some teammates of being asleep in the field. His low status was indicated by his nickname, "Smellton," and by the single friendship nomination he received from his teammates (from another low-status 11-year-old). In the fourth game of the season with the Giants losing to the Cards by a score of 7–1, Melton came to bat with the bases loaded. Much to the team's amazement, he hits a grand slam home run—his first hit in Little League baseball. Clearly, such a happening is a salient triggering event, and the story of Melton's miraculous home run was recounted frequently throughout the season, particularly when he came up to bat with the bases loaded or in a tight situation. Melton was given the game ball by the coach, even though the Giants lost the game 7–5; fellow players now called him "Jim" rather than "Smellton."

At the beginning of that game Bill had told his teammates that he would give a quarter to anyone who hit a home run; Paul topped him by announcing he would give a dollar, and Bill countered by saying that he, too, would give a dollar. Immediately after Melton hit his home run, I witnessed the incongruity of the coach handing a player money for doing what he was supposed to do *for fun*. When Jim came to bat again, Peter said he would give Jim $2.00 if he hit the game-winning home run (alas, he grounds out). The Giants had become mercenary; older players *paid* younger ones to go to the refreshment stand for them. Two games later Paul jokingly told the team, "I want some hustle. Anyone who's not hustling I'll give a $500 fine and a four-game suspension" (field notes). Economics had become a team tradition.

By the end of the season, team spirit had disintegrated to the extent that Peter claimed publicly, and was not contradicted, that Jim's home run had actually bounced in the field, but that the outfielders and umpires hadn't seen it bounce because they were turned the other way. Thus Peter claimed it was only a ground-rule double, depriving the team of their most memorable happening.

Idioculture and Behavior

Idioculture is a mediator or filter between both external threat and internal structure and the production of social behavior. Having examined some of the central themes of the Giants' idioculture, I now turn to how these major idiocultural themes shaped specific behaviors. I will focus on two important issues (a) the desire of the players *not* to play on certain occasions, and, (b) how the bitterness the players felt in defeat was expressed to teammates and the coach.

Lack of Desire

"Hustle" is an important part of coaches' moral repertoire. At the beginning of the season, Paul's rhetoric expressed this theme directly: "Hustle: Attack the ball. Always keep it in front of you" (field notes, week before season opener), and "You guys are dead out there. Let's hear a little chatter from you guys" (field notes, 3rd week of season). As the season progressed, the Giants were unlikely to heed these words and pay attention. This was indicated in their response to the National Anthem played before each game: During the early weeks of the season, the players stood quietly at attention, whereas toward the end of the season they were likely to embarrass their coach by fooling around, fidgeting, and hitting one another. Further, the Giants were increasingly likely not to play as "hard" as they could. On most teams, players wanted to pitch, considering this a sign of prestige. Yet, on several occasions Giants players, while reserving the right to criticize Colin when he pitched poorly, did not want to pitch themselves. For example,

> Bill and Peter are each supposed to pitch three innings against the Dodgers. Bill says that he wants to pitch the first three "to get it over with." (field notes, last week of season)
> Peter Peyser is scheduled to pitch against the Phils, but when he learns this he says: "Ish! I don't want to pitch." Later, before the game, he tells the coach that his arm hurts, although he didn't mention this when he first says he doesn't want to pitch. (field notes, 7th week)

This same lack of desire can be seen elsewhere.

> Before one game, Rod says he would "rather quit" than catch for more than three innings. He catches the first three innings and then tells Paul that his arm hurts from being hit by a pitch. (Field notes, last week of season)
> Rich, who has been complaining throughout the season about not playing much, tells me that he doesn't want to go in to play if Sid Copeland is still pitching for the Astros. The first time these two teams played (the first week), Rich did play for four innings against Copeland without complaint. (field notes, 4th week of season)

Unlike most teams on which the admission of fear or the lack of desire to play was inappropriate, for the Giants this sort of talk was legitimate, particularly by the 12-year-olds who were the team "leaders." This perspective, beginning during the middle of the season, developed from the belief that the team was lucky to win games and was not really competitive. This, in turn, was a consequence of the lack of leaders (beyond Rod) who were strong baseball players. Each time the Giants won a game (and they *did* win almost half of their games), they treated it as unexpected.

Even Melton's home run can be seen as consistent with this theme. The grand slam home run by one of the weakest players on the team served as symbol that chance was more significant than ability. For no team in the league did "hustling" mean so little, and by the 4th week even Paul was treating it as a joke by commenting (as noted above) that anyone not hustling would be fined and suspended. At the end of the season Paul admitted that many on the team were "lazy" and "didn't care." For the Giants, contrary to most other teams, past experiences and cultural perspectives legitimated their lackadaisical attitude.

Anger and Disgust

Although the Giants in some ways didn't appear to care how well they played, they did care if they won or lost, although each player was not personally willing to give extra effort to make the team successful. As a consequence of their idioculture and their personnel, players blamed those whom they felt were causing them to lose. With the exception of Rod, no player was immune to team anger. Most frequently, the coach was the source of the criticism.

> The Giants have just allowed the Phils to score five runs in the bottom of the third to lead 8-0, and the team is angry and bickering with each other. Hal Brattle throws down his glove in disgust and Rod holds his head in his hands, possibly in tears. Paul tries to reassert his moral authority by saying, "I'll do the bellyaching, not the players. You're a team. You got about as much spirit as a dead horse. Let's quit complaining." However, by now, Paul has almost no credibility and, after Paul finishes his talk, Rod whispers, "Fuck you" and gives him "the finger" to his back. Rich says about Paul, "Bite my bag." Bill adds sarcastically, "Let's put this game in the Hall of Fame" and refuses to coach the bases. (field notes, 7th week of season)

On the basis of the scorn for the coach's baseball abilities and lack of respect for his decisions, such a reaction makes sense. Further, the reaction is specifically legitimated by Rod who, for most purposes, exercises moral control on the team. Whereas at the beginning of the season Rod was supportive of the coach, as the season progressed he used his considerable influence to undermine Paul's position. This team aggression also was directed to opposing teams, coaches and umpires.

> The Giants are playing the Dodgers during the last week of the season, and the home plate umpire is calling a wide strike zone, meaning many pitches that players think are balls are called strikes. This is coupled with the fact that the Dodgers' pitcher is one of the best in the league, and the Dodgers have been leading the Giants since the first inning. In the bottom of the fifth inning (Little League games last six innings) Hal is called out on strikes on a pitch he thinks was high. Bill comments, "That ump is rotten.

I'm gonna throw up." Hal adds, "That ump's screwy." In the last inning with two outs, Bill is called out on what he believes is a ball, and throws his bat, looking as if he is about to hit the umpire, although he doesn't. He enters the dugout in tears. Rod calls the umpire "the professional dildo" and the Giants discuss attacking the umpire. When Dan Gregory (on the Cards) remarks "I thought [Bill] Anders was gonna hit him with the bat," Bill adds that next time he will. (field notes, last week of the season)

Although Bill's behavior was not unique in terms of Little League play (and was indeed more customary than the Giants' repeated self-degradation), it does indicate the emotional intensity of these boys who did not care that much about baseball. Indeed, Bill at one point in the season refused to pitch against the Dodgers because he was afraid of them. Losing to a team like that could hardly be surprising to the Giants but that did not allow them to be any more graceful in defeat.

What is significant is that the production of behavior is the result of the backgrounds of the players and a function of the team idioculture. Behavior is generated in a context in which the actor compares his situation to situations that are similar on relevant dimensions and acts in ways that are considered appropriate at those times. Thus behavior, in addition to producing idioculture (e.g., a narrative about Bill's attack on the umpire), is also a function of it.

Conclusion

In all groups, idioculture serves as a mediator or filter between the social structural features of the environment and the interactional components of behavior. Yet, this mediation can have quite different effects depending upon what stimuli are present outside the group and the attitudes of the members of the group toward each other. Although most research on groups has focused on harmonious, working groups, some groups find themselves in a state of disarray, and the idiocultures of these groups will reflect this disarray and likely reinforce it.

Sport serves as a particularly graphic example of an arena in which meaning is continually being generated. This meaning, because of the emphasis on "objective" victory and defeat, will often be highly emotionally charged. The stigma of perceived failure is often difficult to erase for participants. Thus sport teams may be particularly liable to the forms of disarray I have described in this article.

However, group culture based on external threat and internal crisis is surely not limited to athletic fields. Group culture can occur in any type of group environment in which dissatisfaction and failure are possible. Whenever evaluation exists, so exists the potential of moral defeat. Thus what happened to the Giants may happen to us all.

Note

1. The nicknames of these two boys indicate their different athletic abilities. Rod was known, at the beginning of the season, by a nickname that indicated his centrality on the Giants (the precise nickname refers to the actual team name); Bill, on the other hand, was known as "Doc" because of his talent at creating new words and preadolescent traditions—and it refers to his leadership outside of sport. Despite this difference, Rod and Bill remained good friends throughout the season.

References

Fine, G.A. (1979). Small groups and culture creation: The idioculture of Little League baseball teams. *American Sociological Review, 44*, 733–745.

Fine, G.A. (1982). The Manson family: Folklore and small groups. *Journal of the Folklore Institute, 19*, 47-60.

Fine, G.A. (1987). *With the boys: Little League baseball and preadolescent culture.* Chicago: University of Chicago Press.

Coping in Adversity: Children's Play in the Holocaust

George Eisen

The train slowly crossed the border, picking up speed toward an unknown destination. "Still, we had enough water for a while," the sole survivor of this transport later recalled in his memoirs.

> A little girl of about 9 looked up at her father and said: "Will there be schools and playgrounds there, Daddy, like there are at home? Will there be lots of other children?"
> For a moment, indeed, the wagon was quiet, subdued by the child's shrill voice. Then her father ruffled her hair gently and said: "Yes darling. There'll be schools and playgrounds . . . everything you want." (Vrba & Bestic, 1964:54)

Almost certainly, this little girl never came to the realization, even after the long march toward the tall chimneys, that for her no more play time was left. In fact, neither the diarist, nor the father, nor the little girl could have an inkling of Majdanek, where there was no place for children and the chimneys belching black smoke signified, diabolically, the end of the road.

This chapter is not only about this child; it encompasses millions of children who all wanted to play and perhaps played for a short moment but who died, and others who, although they survived, were forced to grow up prematurely in a hostile world. The chapter provides a historical overview of play activities of the young, the attitudes associated with them, and views of adult society, which made all attempts to salvage a familiar world, recreate a sense of normalcy through play, and construct islands of culture that would insulate the young from a world gone savage.

The topic of this chapter is a complex and emotional one. After all, hardly ever has a subject proved so gripping as the Holocaust. It defies in its scope, number, and magnitude the human imagination. For Western minds, trained to comprehend the world more in quantitative than abstract terms, the fact that over 1 million children were murdered is perhaps too shocking to digest—the power of this number almost numbs the mind. That from 15,000 children who passed through Theresienstadt (Terezin), euphemistically called a ghetto but what was in reality a forced labor camp, only an estimated 100 have survived is perhaps easier to comprehend (Dworzecki, 1958:58; Shoshnowski, 1962:70–75).

Children's play represents, inevitably, only a limited cross section of human experiences in the totality of the Holocaust. Nevertheless, its study harbors many of the same dilemmas and issues that are related or might be associated with historiographic problems inherent in the writing about this tragic period. One of the most complex questions comes from the fundamental realization that, in spite of an insulating distance that only time and space can offer, it is almost impossible to write about the Holocaust impersonally, and it is even harder to do so about children.

Also, children's play and the Holocaust confront the untrained observer with a perplexing contradiction in terms. The question as to whether death and play could exist side by side was as painfully pertinent to contemporaries as it is for us today. At first glance, indeed, the abyss between these two concepts seems unbridgeable. Perhaps the most mystifying thing about play is that, on the one hand, it is supposed to be disengaged from reality in a variety of ways, while at the same time it is credited with a great number of useful real-life functions. The concept of play, as it was defined by one of the earliest play theorists, Johan Huizinga, is a "free activity standing quite consciously outside ordinary life as being not serious" (Huizinga, 1949:13). Although his definition is a highly romanticized view of child play, it reflects common beliefs. The same term in the popular imagination also conjures a careless world of frolic and joy, void of purpose and rationale—a picture that, in turn, is hardly compatible with the tragic words of a Warsaw ghetto diarist.

> The streets resound with the futile screams of children dying of hunger. They wine, beg, sing, lament, and tremble in the cold, without underwear, without clothes, without shoes. . . .
> Children swollen from hunger, deformed, semiconscious; children who are perfectly adults, somber and tired of living at age five. (Keller, 1984:130)

It is almost impossible to reconcile wholly this paradox. Neither this paper, nor any other work for that matter, will be able to resolve completely this conflict of ideas between children's play and the evil of such an abysmal and depraved period. The only rationale that might suggest a solution to this dilemma, and the evidence will bear this out in the following pages, is that children's play was not only not divorced from reality, but, in fact, was reflective of it. Play also articulated skills for survival (Csikszentmihalyi, 1981:14–25).

The Holocaust Environment

Play is far from a frivolous activity. Play can take place, as the Holocaust demonstrated, even in the most hostile of environments. Beyond the inferno, or perhaps as a response to it, an epic of courage exists in a child's play that our civilization is not always willing or able to grasp. In a world pitching between excitement and utter despair, camp and ghetto prisoners tried to conjure a solution for this same dilemma; in Vilna, for example, a large segment of the population professed the view that "a graveyard is no place for entertainment" (Arad, 1982:321).

With the German invasion of Eastern Europe, where the bulk of European Jewry resided, more than 5 million Jews came under Nazi rule. German occupation commenced, with tragic regularity, with either the total physical annihilation of an entire community (by mobile SS units called Einsatzgruppen) or the introduction of oppressive legislation, excluding first the Jewish population from economic, social, and cultural life, and hermetically sealing them into ghettos later. The two approaches differed only in their temporal dimensions, for ghettos were also systematically decimated and destroyed parallel with their economic exploitation.

If degrees in misery existed, the most unfortunate victims were the millions of children, many of them orphaned or abandoned, whose struggle for survival was not only hampered by cold, hunger, and disease, but also by the fact that in the German scheme of things children were unproductive and therefore dispensable (Shoshnowski, 1962:71). To accomplish that, ghettos and camps were periodically raided, called "Kinderaktionen," and children and pregnant mothers were systematically carted off to extermination centers to be gassed or shot in mass graves. A description by a 12-year-old boy of the destruction of a maternity ward in the Lodz ghetto after his sister just gave birth to a baby girl typifies these methods and exemplifies the shock and trauma of a child learning about infanticide.

> Then as the next group of patients was being escorted to a waiting truck, we saw Esther. . . . She was pale and frightened as she stood there in her pink nightgown. . . . Soon the truck drove off and we knew we could never see our beloved Esther again. . . . There was silence for a moment. No one could figure what was going to happen next. . . .
>
> Suddenly, two Germans appeared in an upper story window and pushed it open. Seconds later a naked baby was pushed over the ledge and dropped to its death directly into the truck below. We were in such shock that at first few of us believed it was actually a live, newborn baby. . . .
>
> The SS seemed to enjoy this bloody escapade . . . the young SS butcher rolled up his rifle sleeve and caught the very next infant on his bayonet. The blood of the infant flowed down the knife onto the murderer's arm. (Edelbaum, 1980:91)

Once it was remarked that Nazism was more than an ideology; it was a system with ramifications. Even before the complete ghettoization, military governors and civilian representatives initiated a flurry of decrees all through Nazi-held Europe. They aimed to place all parks, playgrounds, swimming pools, and other recreational and cultural institutions off limits for the Jewish community. It is hard to construe these edicts in any other way but as deliberate attempts of psychological humiliation and physical repression. Suffice it to say that these measures brought immense health and psychological traumas in their wake.

A ghetto was a world unto itself, enclosed with its misery and pain. Outsiders looked in with awe and disbelief. People on the "Aryan" side, an inhabitant recorded, "gape curiously at the piteous spectacle presented by these tattered gangs [children]" (Keller, 1984:130). Nothing could ameliorate the dreary landscape for there were no trees, grass, or flowers. With intentional design, occupation policies saw to the exclusion of all parks and playgrounds from the ghettos. A diarist searching for parks, gardens, or flowers in the Warsaw ghetto had to admit that "such things do not exist here. Even my yearning for modest traces of green is in vain— all this has been eliminated through cunning measures." A popular song sentimentalized "For them the square and boulevards,/For me a place of misery" (Dawidowicz, 1975:200).

As for the Jewish community, among the many burning issues the rescue and shelter of children took precedence over all priorities. Valiant and desperate efforts were made to protect the young. "These had been our future," cried out a contemporary, "these broken little bodies, these cracked voices begging for bread" (Goldstein, 1949:82). Relief funds were collected, orphanages were built, children's kitchens were opened, and, in Warsaw, a "Children's Month" was proclaimed and posters spread slogans such as "Our Children Must Not Die," and "Children are Sacred." A few weeks before the final extermination of the Warsaw ghetto began, the head of the Judenrat (Jewish Council) even bravely launched a drive for the creation of ghetto playgrounds (Czerniakow, 1979:354, 363).

Many of the leaders apparently understood, intuitively for the most part, the practical and spiritual importance of parks and green areas in the dreary lives of the ghettos. This importance was based on the premise that the physical environment, combined with that of the psychosocial and operationalized in terms of trees, grass, sandbox, and the like, could influence the traumatized ghetto children positively. They adopted their views in the belief that playgrounds and activities could offer mental and physical health, social stability, and order in the face of crisis.

Ghettos, and more so the camps, were not healthy places. If one examines the extant child mortality statistics, specifically those caused by tuberculosis, the importance attached to these green areas amidst dirt and fetidness becomes readily apparent. They were to act, within rubble-covered eyesores, as "lungs for the ghetto," purifying its air and the spirit of its young. Kaplan's comment on the subject gives a fair record of the prevailing view in the community: "It is now three years since we have seen grass growing and flowers in bloom. Even before we were shoved into the ghetto we were forbidden to enter the city parks. Inside the parks there was space and breadth" (Kaplan, 1973:220).

Another primary rationale for the creation of playgrounds was "to give the ghetto children a sense of freedom" (Berg, 1945:89), as a young observer phrased it. The playground was intended to become a tiny oasis of peace, the games providing the children rare moments of joy, erecting symbolic walls against the harshness and ugliness of reality. The commanding impulse behind the playground was linked to the will of the masses to live and survive by every means. "Tzu iberleybn" in Yiddish, it promoted the belief that a people who were able to laugh and create in such an adversity would also be able to outlive their oppressors. In the words of Kaplan, who himself was not able to see the liberation, "A nation that can live in such terrible circumstances as these without losing its mind, without committing suicide—and which can still laugh—is sure of survival" (Kaplan, 1973:211)

Coping Through Play

Children's play constituted a part of this quest for survival. That this was a highly romantic, almost mythical, view of play is almost incidental. Jewish community leaders clung to these beliefs with a desperation, which could come only from a sense of powerlessness in dealing with the problems of the youth. In fact, the adults themselves needed these playgrounds to see playing children again. These children, guarantors of survival beyond the ghettos, engendered high morale and provided a faint hope for the future. An emotionally charged note by Adam Czerniakow, the Head of the Warsaw Judenrat (Jewish Council), reveals the anguish of a civic leader over the plight of the young. During the opening of a playground in 1942, when perhaps 50,000 children had already perished, he met with representatives of the gangs roaming the ghetto. "They are living skeletons from the ranks of the street beggars. . . . They talked with me like grown-ups—those eight-year-old citizens. I am ashamed to admit it, but I wept as I have not wept for a long time" (Czerniakow, 1979:366). The yearning for play, and consequently, a semblance of normalcy in the lives of the children resonates in a brief and emotional entry in the *Chronicle of Ghetto Lodz* as well.

> Just beyond the outer limit of the ghetto, on Urzednicza Street at the barbed-wire fence, an amusement park has been set up, as it was last year. The main attraction, the only one visible, is a suspension-type merry-go-around. Every day the children of the ghetto make a pilgrimage to this corner and gaze longingly at the activities on the other side of the fence. It is mostly children too on the other side, who are romping about and climbing into the small hanging boats of the merry-go-around. A radio amplifier broadcasts phonograph music. The ghetto children have never seen a carousel and have seldom heard music. They listen and peer at a curious, alien world, where children live in a sort of

never-never land. A merry-go-around, almost within reach, only
the barbed wire keeps them away. Children are children on either
side of the barbed wire—and yet they are not the same.
(Dobroszycki, 1984:352)

Alongside community leaders, educators, and citizens, parents also became concerned about the importance of play. Although all parks were
forbidden to Jews, courageous mothers slipped out of the ghettos, brav-
ing immediate arrest, and took their children to the forbidden paradise,
the city parks. "Mother insisted on going to the park. We needed fresh
air, and we were going to get it," a survivor remembered. "In the parks
Mother encouraged me to play with the children, but I was shy. Instinc-
tively I knew that we had nothing in common any more" (David,
1964:107–108). Several months later, the hermetic sealing off of the Warsaw
ghetto brought these clandestine excursions to the city parks to a halt.
The ever observant Kaplan noticed in Warsaw that "Jewish mothers have
already gotten used to their bad fortune, and in order not to deprive their
babies of the sunlight, they take their stand with their cradles wherever
there is a square or a vacant lot, or side walk covered with sunlight"
(Kaplan, 1973:220).

Even in the inferno of Bergen Belsen, all efforts were made to ameliorate
the children's lot by organizing play activities. One of the dedicated adults
rationalized her involvement in these efforts by commenting, "And I feel
it is an urge that springs from the soul of the children themselves, for
they follow my lead in their excitement, they show their desire to live, to
play, a desire stronger than they are themselves" (Levy-Haas, 1982:249).
Admittedly, play, an instinctual, almost atavistic activity, is embedded in
human consciousness. Children's adaptability, indeed, seemed remarkable. Oskar Rosenfeld recorded in Ghetto Lodz that cigarette boxes became prized treasures for the children.

Outside the ghetto, children receive beautiful and appropriate
playthings as presents. There is a great industry for manufactur-
ing them; artists and artisans invent new toys and build little al-
tars for children's hearts out of wood, cardboard, metal, silk, and
plaster. . . . A fantastic world emerges, and children go strolling
through it. The children of the ghetto, however, are not blessed
with such good fortune. They have to create their toys themselves.
Still, the Jewish child is talented enough to do without the fantasies of the toy manufacturer. Our children collect empty cigarette
boxes. They remove the colorful tops and stack them in a pile,
until they have a whole deck of cards. Playing cards.
And they play. They count the cards and deal them out. They
arrange them by color and name. Green, orange, yellow, brown,
even black. They play games that they invent for themselves,
they devise systems, they let their imaginations take over.
(Dobroszycki, 1984:360–361)

Not only new games were invented, but traditional ones assumed new meaning and rationale in the lives of the young, pointing to the detrimental role of a drastically altered environment. Games provided the children with powerful stimuli for "unconventional" social behavior. This suggests, in turn, that in an ecological setting created by the Holocaust, the external forces overshadowed any internal orgasmic determinants of behavior. The terror and desperation of the children in the ghetto is nowhere more disquietingly marked than in the journal of Emmanuel Ringelblum. "In a refugee center an 8-year-old child went mad. Screamed, 'I want to steal, I want to rob, I want to eat, I want to be a German'" (Halperin, 1970:134–135).

Behavior exhibited by children in a play setting was, then, eminently directed toward their needs and problems relating to the basic elements of survival. How a family hid for 2 years in a pit dug in a stable and covered with manure was described in graphic details by a young boy. The unbearable monotony, the fear of being discovered, the stench, and the danger of asphyxiation from lack of oxygen made life a veritable hell, ameliorated only by reading and chess. "We played almost all day long creating interest not only for the players but also for the kibbitzers. To make the games more challenging, we played for stakes, for a potato or a spoonful of soup, food being the most precious thing to us. The losing side had to yield part of the dinner, and we fought with bitter determination" (Eisenberg, 1981:169–170).

Chess also saved the life of a 15-year-old in Bergen Belsen. As a punishment, the Commandant took away the bread ration of the entire camp for 3 days, which was tantamount to the death penalty for many inmates.

> I tried to figure out how to get through the next few days. What could I do to get my mind off food? Then I got the idea; there was a fellow in my barrack who had a chess set. I went over to him and asked him if he wanted to sell it to me. Of course, I couldn't buy it with money; there wasn't any, and money was useless here. I managed to talk him into selling me his chess set for two rations of bread, which meant that I wasn't to get bread for FIVE WHOLE DAYS. I had my reasons. I took the set to my bunk, and for the next three days I did nothing but play chess with my friend, Walter. We concentrated on the game so intensely that we forgot all about our hunger, so the days went by quickly. (Spanjaard, 1981:131–132)

Building playgrounds and the organization of play days have not always received the approval of all segments of ghetto society. The moral question as to how play, games, and occasional merriment can coexist with destruction, death, and extermination flamed into heated controversies and soul searching. In Vilna, for example, a large portion of the ghetto, especially the working classes, disapproved of theatrical performances with the profound reasoning that "a graveyard is no place for merriment!" (Arad,

1982:321). Similar sentiments were raised in almost every area affected by atrocities and horrors of the war. Although somewhat more nebulous and muffled, critical voices about the prevalence of play, games, and dancing can be discerned in contemporary sources as well. Zelig Kalmanowitch's diary from Vilna raises this philosophical question in a dialogue. "The games are cheered loudly—as we were free. A road to man. My pious friend laments: 'So many mourn, so many died, and here merriment and celebrations!' " The only way these two ideas could be reconciled in his mind, as pious a Jew as Kalmanowitch had been, was through religion: "Such is life. But we must live as long as God gives life" (1953:25).

Almost inevitably, Adam Czerniakow from Warsaw was also subjected to severe criticism for his initiative to establish playgrounds and use them for festive openings. He deemed it necessary to jot down in his diary, with his characteristically terse style, that

> many people hold a grudge against me for organizing play activity for the children, for arranging festive openings of playgrounds, for the music, etc. I am reminded of a film: a ship is sinking and the captain, to raise the spirits of the passengers, orders the orchestra to play a jazz piece. I had made up my mind to emulate the captain. (Czerniakow, 1979:376)

Play as a Mirror of Reality

Although time, location, the socioeconomic situation of an individual, and of course the environment have played obviously crucial roles both in the organization, nature of, and participation in play, the children themselves perceived and voiced the importance of these activities in their lives. As mentioned earlier, for the young Dutch boy in Bergen Belsen chess play was a life-saving device. Mary Berg, a 16-year-old diarist from the Warsaw ghetto, also became keenly aware of this fact. She wrote in 1942, "The smiling rosy faces of the children were perhaps the best reward of those who had created this little refuge for the little prisoners of the ghetto" (Berg, 1945:147).

The sensitive words of the young adolescent Anne Frank reveals that the yearning and desire for play, games, and freedom transcended national, age, or social boundaries. "Cycling, dancing, whistling, looking out into the world, feeling young, to know that I'm free—that's what I long for" (Frank, 1967:140). These touching words, just like those of Czerniakow, suggest a clear grasp of powerlessness and anguish of civic leaders and children alike. One must recognize that the actual or purported benefits of efforts to create a sane, sheltered, and rational world for the children were short-lived at best. "With great sacrifice," a contemporary admitted, "we managed to perform pathetic wonders" (Goldstein, 1949:82).

In spite of all attempts, no playgrounds or other humanitarian endeavors could either arrest the rapidly deteriorating situation of the children or change the well-designed course of destruction. That is not to say that a community, geared for emergency, did not accomplish some psychological gains, ephemeral as they may have been. But with the backdrop of cold, starvation, and death, playgrounds or play activities could not provide more than temporary refuge. Jan Karski, a representative of the Polish government in exile, himself not a Jew, was smuggled into the Warsaw ghetto to see conditions and report to his superiors in London. "Everywhere there was hunger, misery, the atrocious stench of decomposing bodies, the pitiful moans of dying children," he noted in his report.

> We passed a miserable replica of a park—a little square of comparatively clear ground in which a half-dozen nearly leafless trees and a patch of grass had somehow managed to survive. It was fearfully crowded. Mothers huddled close together on benches nursing withered infants. Children, every bone in their skeletons showing through their taut skins, played in heaps and swarms.
> "They play before they die," I heard my companion on the left say, his voice breaking with emotion.
> Without thinking—the words escaping even before the thought had crystalized—I said:
> "But these children are not playing—they only make-believe it is play." (Eisenberg, 1981:345)

The deep and profound difference between the role and function assigned to play and games by ghetto society and their actual outcome, though shocking, are not surprising. The chronic crisis of the powerlessness of the ghetto administrations and more so of the concentration camp inmates, coupled with pervasive financial incapacity, rendered even the most genuine efforts marginal. Creating play settings, as a quasi refuge, had very little power of insulating the children from reality. After all, the Umschlagplatz (collection point for Warsaw Jews to be deported to death camps) was in close proximity to the playgrounds and courtyards where toddlers played in the sandbox. The frightening swiftness with which these two extremes alternated in the lives of the young ones can only magnify the inability of play to shelter them.

Janina David, in her early teens and an unofficial leader of the children in her courtyard, described vividly this tragic suddenness from serenity to fright and agony of children and mothers.

> When the raid started I was downstairs with them, watching the toddlers in the sand-pit we had built that summer.
> Suddenly there were shrill whistles in the street, panicky feet rushed past and the gate was slammed. We heard the lorries pulling up outside the house and commands shouted in German and Polish. In a moment the courtyard was empty. I was almost on our staircase when I saw one of our neighbors, a young woman, shrieking on her balcony and tearing her hair. She was on the second floor and her children, a baby of six months and a two-year-old girl, were still in the sand-pit. Without thinking I turned back, flew across the courtyard, grabbed the baby and, with the

terrified toddler clutching my skirt, reached the stairs just as the
front gate was opening and the "action squadron" marched in.
(David, 1964:151)

Similarly, in the unpredictable universe of concentration camps, where
life had to be lived for the moment because one never knew when it might
be the last, in a world alternating between hope and despair, play and
sport adjusted, like every other facet of life, to the surrounding uncertainty. "The chess contest has broken down completely and been for-
gotten," laconically recorded Philip Mechanicus, an inmate in the Dutch
transit camp in Westerbork,

firstly because people taking part had to go on the transports and
secondly because people's minds were very much taken up with
the cancellation of exemptions and the results of this as far as
deportation was concerned. (Mechanicus, 1968:87)

Fear had no escape—it had the power of asserting its presence into the
subconscious mind of every child. Mechanicus' words, resonating with
shock and sorrow, again reflect the helplessness and despair of the adult
population in sheltering the young from the surrounding world. "In the
night the little daughter of friends of mine dreamt that her doll had to
go on the transport" (Mechanicus, 1968:82). At best, play activities could
make the adjustment to this reality somewhat less painful.

Beside the suffering, the frequency and banality of death and its acceptance by society at large made an everlasting impression on the children's
psyche. Death assumed a grotesque, almost surrealistic dimension in which
corpses became mere objects, belonging to the streets, just like cobble-
stones and garbage. It was not the rejection of reality, it was reality itself.
As Borowski wrote in *This Way for the Gas, Ladies and Gentlemen*, in Auschwitz where even a swimming pool and soccer field existed, "Between
two throw-ins in a soccer game, right behind my back, three thousand
people had been put to death" (Borowski, 1976:84).

To accept reality, then, play and games of children facilitated a coping
mechanism at best. The term *coping* for psychologists investigating major
traumas on human psyche, connotes a "psychic numbing" that protects
one "from reality too hard to face and too chaotic to formulate" (Lifton
& Olson, 1975:122–123). The bewildered words of Janusz Korczack, one of
the leading pedagogues of his time, who chose to go with his orphanage to
certain death in Treblinka, gain new meaning and perspective with this
theory. He observed in one of his excursions that "the body of a dead boy
lies on the sidewalk. Nearby, three boys are playing horses and drivers. At
one point they notice the boy, move to the side, go on playing" (Korczack,
1978:121). Similar scenes were perhaps familiar to the youngsters of Tere-
sienstadt. When the funeral hearse was not carrying heaps of corpses to
the mass graves, it served the children as a toy, and many games were
invented for its use (Green, 1969).

Indeed, a fundamental transformation took place not only in the form but also the nature of the play activities, which more and more resembled reality. A survivor of the Kovno ghetto, Dr. Aaron Peretz, has described the effect of the executions on the children and the games they played.

> The children in the ghetto would play and laugh, and in their games the entire tragedy was reflected. They would play grave-digging: They would dig a pit and would put a child inside and call him Hitler. And they would play at being gatekeepers of the ghetto. Some of the children played the parts of the Germans, some of Jews, and the Germans were angry and would beat the other children who were Jews. And they used to play funerals. . . .
>
> The Jewish child was prematurely grown up. We were amazed to observe how children three or four years old understood the tragedy of the situation, how they clammed up when it was necessary, how they knew when to hide. We ourselves could not trust our ears when we heard small children, offered a sedative, say: "Doctor, this is not necessary, I shall be quiet, I shall not scream." (Robinson, 1965:122–123)

Conclusion

Although this and other sources convey to us a clear grasp of reality and a lack of illusion about its outcome, play reflected reality in a "bent" form, fitting one's existing level of cognitive functioning. Play, in this context, facilitated an accommodation process by which an organism, as J.H. Flawell postulated about the role of play in general, could negotiate the novel demands of an absurd situation. "The organism adapts repeatedly," he wrote in 1963, "and each adaptation necessarily paves the way for its successor" (Flawell, 1963:49–50). He also addmitted, and this is particularly true to children's behavior in the Holocaust, that this process cannot continue indefinitely.

These children played, hoped, and succeeded to ignore the ever present death for a moment, but they saw everything that grown-ups saw. Fear came to them as they could tell in their poems and diaries, knowing that they were condemned. Indeed, the constant accommodation was in itself no assurance that life and existence would prevail. Perhaps they were more honest and perceptive than adults, possessing the intuition of children. The toys or games were there for sharing the sorrow and anguish of the Holocaust, as the plaint of an anonymous little girl expressed in a brief poem, "I Sit With My Eyes."

> I sit with my dolls by the stove and dream.
> I dream that my father came back.
> I dream that my father is still alive.
> How good it is to have a father.
> I do not know where my father is.

> (Halperin, 1970:134)

References

Arad, Y. (1982). *Ghetto in flames*. New York: Holocaust Library.

Berg, M. (1945). *Warsaw ghetto, a diary*. New York: L.B. Fischer.

Borowski, T. (1976). *This way for the gas, ladies and gentlemen*. New York: Penguin.

Csikszentmihalyi, M. (1981). Some paradoxes in the definition of play. In A.T. Cheska (Ed.), *Play as context* (pp. 14–25). Champaign, IL: Leisure Press.

Czerniakow, A. (1979). *The Warsaw diary*. New York: Stein and Day.

David, J. (1964). *A square of sky*. New York: W.W. Norton.

Dawidowicz, S.L. (1975). *The war against the Jews*. New York: Holt, Rinehart & Winston.

Dobroszycki, L. (Ed.). (1984). *The chronicle of the Lodz ghetto*. New Haven, CT: Yale University Press.

Dworzecki, M. (1958). *Europa Lelo Yeladim*. Jerusalem: Yad Vashem.

Edelbaum, B. (1980). *Growing up in the Holocaust*. Kansas City, MO: n.p.

Eisenberg, A. (Ed.). (1981). *Witness to the Holocaust*. New York: Pilgrim Press.

Flawell, J.H. (1963). *The developmental psychology of Jean Piaget*. Van Nostrand Reinhold.

Frank, A. (1967). *The diary of a young girl*. Garden City, NY: Doubleday.

Goldstein, B. (1949). *The stars bear witness*. New York: Viking Press.

Green, G. (1969). *The artists of Terezin*. New York: Hawthorn Books.

Halperin, I. (1970). *Messengers from the death*. Philadelphia: The Westminster Press.

Huizinga, J. (1949). *Homo ludens*. New York: Routledge & Kegan Paul.

Kalmanowitch, Z. (1953). A diary of the Nazi ghetto in Vilna. *YIVO Annual of Jewish Social Science*, **8**, 9–81.

Kaplan, C. (1973). *The Warsaw diary*. New York: Collier.

Keller, U. (Ed.). (1984). *The Warsaw ghetto in photographs*. New York: Dover.

Korczack, J. (1978). *Ghetto diary*. New York: Holocaust Library.

Levy-Haas, H. (1982). *Inside Belsen*. Totowa, NJ: Barnes and Noble.

Lifton, R.J., & Olson, E. (1975). *Living and dying*. New York: Bantam Books.

Mechanicus, P. (1968). *Year of fear, a Jewish prisoner waits for Auschwitz*. New York: Hawthorn.

Robinson, J. (1965). *And the crooked shall be made straight*. New York: Macmillan.

Sells, S.B. (1963). An interactionist looks at the environment. *American Psychologist*, **18**, 696–702.

Shoshnowski, K. (1962). *The tragedy of children under Nazi rule*. Poznan, Poland: Zachodnia Press.

Spanjaard, B. (1981). *Don't fence me in*. Saugus, CA: B & B Publishers.

Vrba, R., & Bestic, A. (1964). *I cannot forgive*. New York: Grove Press.

PART IV

Play and Social Identity

Revival, Survival, and Revisal: Ethnic Identity Through "Traditional Games"

Alyce Taylor Cheska

Expressive culture, including games and sport, are embedded in the cultural context of an ethnic group; thus these physical activities help make up and reflect important identifiable values and meanings in that particular historic process. I contend that traditional games of an ethnic group's past cultural landscape may be renewed, continued, or modified from that era for furthering ethnic purposes within a contemporary dominant society. This paper addresses this thesis. Three basic questions are considered.

- How are the contrasting features of folk games and modern sports used selectively to reflect tradition?
- In what contexts and under what conditions have traditional folk games continued to exist?
- For what ethnic purposes are traditional games employed in contemporary societies?

Folk Games Versus Modern Sports—Selective Tradition

How are the contrasting features of folk games and modern sports used selectively to reflect tradition? Throughout much of the world sports have tended to replace local folk games. As a hegemonic expression of industrial dominant societies, so-called modern sports have contributed to confusion over the world concerning native populations' ethnic identity and worth. This powerful sociopolitical association carries the implicit message that modern sports are associated with modernity, economic progress, and internationalism, whereas indigenous "folk" games are attitudinally related to traditionalism, economic regress, and "tribalism" (Cheska, 1987). Elias (1978) contends that folk games are typical of a society's early stage in a civilizing process. Dunning (1973) contrasts properties of folk games belonging to the preindustrial era of Britain to the modern sports of industrial societies.

Table 1   Major Structural-Functional Characteristics of Folk Games and Modern Sports

Folk games	Modern sports
1. "Diffuse," informal organization, implicit in the local social structure.	1. Highly specific, formal organization, institutionally differentiated at local, regional, national, and international level.
2. Simple, unwritten customary rules, traditional legitimization.	2. Formal and elaborate written rules; worked out pragmatically and legitimated via rational bureaucratic channels.
3. Fluctuating game pattern; tendency to change through imperceptible "drift."	3. Patterns of change institutionalized through rational bureaucratic demands.
4. No precise limits on territory, duration, or numbers of participants.	4. Played on spatially limited area with clearly defined boundaries, within fixed time limits and fixed number of participants, equalized between the contending sides.
5. Strong influence of natural and social differences on the game pattern.	5. Minimization, principally through formal rules, of influence of natural and social differences on the game pattern; norms of equality and fairness.
6. Low role differentiation (division of labor) among the players.	6. High role differentiation (division of labor) among the players.
7. Loose distinction between playing and "spectating" roles.	7. Strict distinction between playing and "spectating" roles.
8. Low structural differentiation; several "game elements" rolled into one.	8. High structural differentiation; specialization around kicking, carrying, throwing, use of sticks, and so on.
9. Informal social control by players themselves within the context of the ongoing game.	9. Formal social control by officials "outside" the game who are appointed and certified by central legislative bodies and have the power, when a breach of rules occurs, to stop play, impose formally defined penalties, graded according to the seriousness of the offense.
10. High level of socially tolerated physical violence; emotional spontaneity, low restraint.	10. Low level of socially tolerated physical violence; high emotional control; high restraint.
11. Generation, in relatively open and spontaneous form, of pleasurable "battle-excitement."	10. Generation, in a more controlled and "sublimated" form, of pleasurable "battle-excitement."

Table 1   Major Structural-Functional Characteristics of Folk Games and Modern Sports

Folk games	Modern sports
12. Strong communal pressure to partici-pate; individuals' identity subordinate to group identity; general test of identity.	12. Individually chosen as a recreation; individual identity of greater importance relative to group identity; test of identity in relation to a specific skill or set of skills.
13. Emphasis on force as opposed to skill.	13. Emphasis on skill as opposed to force.

Note. From "The structural-functional properties of folk-games and modern sports: A sociological analysis," by E. Dunning, 1973, *Sportwissenschaft*, **3**, pp. 215–232. Reprinted by permission.

Cheska, Elias, and Dunning have each placed selective emphasis on modern sport as compatible with the dominant contemporary cultures, although folk games are not. This premise neglects potentially important uses of traditional physical activities in current societies. In the words of Williams (1977:116), " 'traditional habits' are isolated, by some current hegemonic development, as elements of the past which have now to be discarded."

If folk games, representative of tradition, are deemed inappropriate in modern culture, one must examine why they are present in today's societies.

Archaic and Residual Elements—Alternative Tradition

The second question is, In what contexts and under what conditions have traditional games continued to exist? In order to answer this question, certain assumptions are made.

- Traditional games do exist in contemporary societies.
- The features of these games are identifiable in their present state.
- Traditional games do serve contemporary function(s).
- These games function as ethnic identity responses to the hegemonic culture.

Tradition is selective; it depends on who is making the selection as to which traditional reality one ascribes. Williams (1977:115) contends "A selective tradition [is] an intentionally selective version of a shaping past and a pre-shaped present, which is then powerfully operative in the process of social and cultural definition and identification." Reaching back to those meanings and values created in actual societies and actual situations in the past represent areas of human experience, aspiration, and achievement that the dominant culture neglects, undervalues, opposes, represses, or even cannot recognize.

Certain experiences, meanings, and values that cannot be expressed or substantially verified in the dominant culture are nevertheless lived and practiced on the basis of the residue, cultural as well as social, of some previous social and cultural institution or formation. In this paper the two general categories of past human experiences as applied to traditional games are archaic and residual.

The first general category, *archaic*, according to Williams (1977:122), is any element of a culture's past that is wholly recognized as an element of the past, to be observed, to be examined, or even on occasion to be consciously revived, in a deliberately specializing way. A synonym for archaic in this chapter is *revival*.

The second general category, *residual*, according to Williams (1977:122), has been effectively formed in the past, but it is still active in the cultural process as an effective element of the present. Two forms of residual elements exist. One kind of residual element may have an alternative or even oppositional relation to the dominant culture. I call this kind survival, because the element continues as an actively lived and practiced residual, as distinguished from the archaic feature that is an element from the past deliberately revived. The difference between revival and survival is one of degree more than of kind. The other kind of residual I call revisal because the element may be wholly or largely incorporated into the present dominant society to fit or at least not conflict measurably with the primary culture. Williams has observed that a dominant culture cannot allow too much residual experience and practice outside itself without risk; therefore, it tends to incorporate the active residual (Williams, 1980:39). The term *revisal* refers to this incorporation. In various historic periods the traditional game, whether as a revival, survival, or revisal, may function in sequence and/or cycle as an alternative, opposition, or incorporation within a specific dominant culture.

Purposes of Traditional Folk Games in Contemporary Societies

For what purposes are traditional games employed in contemporary societies? I prefer not to translate the dominant/nondominant dialectic into a Marxian concept of class struggle, but instead to utilize the notion of ethnic identity. Ethnic identity in this context consists of self-ascriptive cultural qualities assigned and perceived by members to that group as distinctive from others. Folk games can serve as such ethnic signifiers and symbols in contemporary societies (Cheska, 1987).

The following ethnographic descriptions illustrate the use of traditional games in the dominant culture as

- *revival* of ethnic opposition to the dominant culture;

- *survival* as alternative ethnic values in a current society; and
- *revisal* as incorporating ethnic values within the dominant culture.

Archaic Revival: The "Northern Games" of the Canadian Inuit

The Inuit (Eskimo) of the Canadian Northwest Territory have increasingly experienced erosion of their cultural identity through introduction and insistence of "southern ways and schooling" by government agencies and personnel. Children are removed from their homes to distant boarding schools where educational knowledge is remote from traditional living. Jobs and government subsidies have created the urban Eskimo who have moved to distribution and job centers. Their ethnic culture increasingly includes more and more features of the dominant "southern" (that of southern Canadian) culture.

To preserve some of their fast-disappearing cultural uniqueness, the Inuit recently reached back to traditional folk ways to create in 1974 an annual summer festival called Northern Games, which grew out of and in opposition to the Winter Arctic Games, a rival Olympic-type winter sport festival organized and financed by the Canadian government that annually attracts some 2,000 to 3,000 Inuit, Indian, and Anglo athletes from several nations. Reflective of the modern sport competition found in the Canada Games, the Winter Arctic Games events include badminton, basketball, cross-country ski races, curling, figure skating, judo, shooting, volleyball, and wrestling. Other events that reflect the festival's northern location include snowshoeing, snowshoe biathlon, indoor soccer, and table tennis. Prizes for first, second, and third places in each sport are gold, silver, and copper *ulus* (traditional Eskimo knife) and the Games' flag (Paraschak & Scott, 1980). The modern Winter Arctic Games represent efforts of the dominant Canadian culture to further incorporate the Inuits within contemporary life.

In direct contrast to the Winter Arctic Games, the Northern Games are organized, financed, and participated in by the Inuit themselves, who gather from widely scattered points across the Canadian Arctic to socialize, share, and participate in indigenous Inuit activities. The "good woman contest" includes traditional living skills of bannock (biscuit) making, tea boiling, seal skinning, muskrat skinning, and fish cutting (filleting). The men's events include various sports of high kick (from one-foot, two-foot, and squat takeoffs), one-hand reach, ear pull, knuckle hop, rope gymnastics, musk-ox wrestling (head push from squat position), and head pull. (Although these are primarily Eskimo games, various traditional Indian games have also been included, such as stick gambling, mooseskin handball, and Indian blanket toss.) This event is an example of *archaic revival*, for these traditional Inuit (and Indian) activities have almost disappeared. In fact, the elderly Inuit knew better how to perform such activities and have had to teach the younger persons. A workshop at the University of Alberta, Edmonton, Canada identified and formalized rules for the Eskimo games across the Arctic, so future participants can practice the traditional games' style (Canadian Film Board, 1982; Paraschak & Scott, 1980). The Northern Games, by their creation, have revived attention to the old ways and archaic games and have strengthened Inuit camaraderie and identity. The archaic Northern Games are oppositional efforts by the Inuits to enhance their unique cultural identity by a conscious renewal of their traditional experiences in a significant, deliberate specializing way; thus the Northern Games are an example of *archaic revival*.

Residual Survival and Residual Revisal: Buzkashi of Afghanistan

Buzkashi of Central Asia is an equestrian game similar to polo, football, and rugby. The word *buz-kashi* is a combination of two Persian words, *buz* meaning "goat" and *kashidan* meaning "to drag" (Cuddon, 1980:183). Buzkashi is thought to date back to Alexander the Great's time. It is also associated with Ghengis Khan, growing out of aggressive tactics and maneuvers of the Mongol horsemen as they raided enemy camps and settlements. In these forays the riders snatched up women, animals, and plunder without dismounting. According to tradition, the game developed on the plains of Mongolia and Central Asia, where nomadic horsemen of the region are said to have used prisoners of war instead of goats or calves, dismembering the hapless creatures for the play (Dupree, 1980:208). For protection, the Afghans created a mounted defense against the Mongol raids. A common training practice was galloping at great speed past a ditch while attempting to pick up a beheaded goat or buz.

Buzkashi is a competitive horse race against opponents whose object is (a) to gather the "ball," a stuffed goat or calf skin from the ground without dismounting; (b) to keep control of the carcass by riding away from the crowd; and (c) eventually to drop the uncontested carcass, for which a reward is given. In this violent game the rider and the horse work as one unit displaying skill, agility, and courage. Buzkashi is played primarily in early fall and early spring starting near *nawruz* (March 21), the first day of the Afghan year. Today Buzkashi forms a major part of the extracurricular lives of the people of northern Afghanistan. Currently the game is played in two differing versions. One is the traditional Buzkashi called *Tudabarai*, meaning "emerging from the masses"; the other is modern Buzkashi called *Qarajai* meaning "black space," which describes the circle in which the carcass is dropped (Azoy, 1982:4).

Residual survival: Tudabarai Buzkashi.   The traditional Tudabarai form of Buzkashi is played in the northern Afghanistan provinces at the major festivity or *tooi* accompanying a rite of passage, either birth, circumcision, or marriage. Azoy suggests,

> The tooi as a whole, like a buzkashi it incorporates, exists for the sake of fun, friendship, and recreation. The anthropologist is quick to recognize it as a ceremony of integration; past is linked culturally with the present and men are linked socially with one another. (1982:44)

The main persons at a tooi are typically the Khans or local chiefs who use the game to enhance their reputations and popularity. These chiefs compete endlessly among themselves for prestige and dominance in every area: wealth, tribal leadership, land, hospitality, entertainment, wisdom, insolence to government officials, owning the best Buzkashi horses, and hiring the best riders or *chapandaz* (Balikci, 1978:54). Khans sponsor Buzkashi games. Each Khan stakes his own reputation on his chapandaz (master rider), who is hired to ride the Khan's specially prized Buzkashi horse against all others. As entrepreneurs the chapandaz sell their skilled horsemanship to the rival Khans.

The traditional game is relatively simple, loosely structured, and violent. The onlookers gather in an open area that has no precise boundaries. At the start of the game the goat or calf carcass is placed on the ground in front of the sponsoring Khan and his party. The individual riders or chapandaz, who in earlier days might total up to 1,000 horsemen, fight for position, try to outmaneuver their opponents, and try to grab and control the carcass. The aim in Tudabarai is to carry the carcass free and clear from everyone else by riding in whatever direction possible before letting it fall uncontested to the ground. The individual who does that is rewarded immediately with an enhanced reputation and material gifts, often money or a fine turban cloth.

According to the Northern Afghan, "In no other form of sanctioned activity are the cultural values of masculinity—courage, strength, dominance—so vividly embodied. As such, Buzkashi still serves as the centerpiece for traditional rites of passage celebrations in the northern region of the country. On these occasions a wide range of activities is combined into one interrelated experience that provides continuity across generations" (Azoy, 1982:11–12). Tudabarai is a residual survival that provides traditional values as alternative practices to those of the dominant culture as depicted in the nation's federalized political system.

Residual revisal: Qarajai Buzkashi. The sport of Qarajai is a team version of Buzkashi, combining both competition and cooperation. The players are divided most frequently into two equal teams of 10 players, but can range from 5 to 15 players. On the Qarajai field at one end is a middle circle measuring 12 to 15 feet across in which the carcass of a calf is placed (calfskin is more resistant to tearing than goatskin). On one side of this circle is a scoring circle for Team A, and on the other is one for Team B. At the other end of the field is a flag or post. In Qarajai, players seek to carry the calf around the flag and return it to their own team's scoring circle. The scores are systematically numerical: 1 point for carrying the calf around the flag; 2 points for dropping it in the scoring circle. Points are cumulative, and high score wins. The typical village contest is played on an open Buzkashi field ranging in size from 100 by 300 meters (Jones, 1982) to 400 by 350 meters (Dupree, 1980), around which the guests and visitors gather. The provincial centers commonly have smaller enclosed fields, and invited guests sit in a bleachered pavilion while the ordinary spectators observe from the sloped banks on either side or from outside.

The *wali* (provincial governor) is the honored guest whose every need is attended to by the *rais* (president) of the local Buzkashi organization. The nonplaying horsemen, who mingle on the field with the chapandazs before the game begins, dash to the sidelines after all the horsemen enmasse bow to the wali. He then blows his whistle to start the game. The neat field formation explodes in a moving blur. The two colorfully uniformed teams of chapandazs clash and spin in fast and freewheeling styles. The carcass is quickly grabbed from its circle, and with long gallops it is carried around the far flag and back toward the scoring circles. Here the agile technique of both the horse and rider rather than their sheer power is at a premium (Azoy, 1982:94). When a score is made, the pavilion spectators clap politely, while the anonymous onlookers on the earthen slopes respond more vigorously.

In a major sense, the Northern Afghan ethnic values are supported in a modified form compatible within the current dominant culture (centralized government, urbanization, and bureaucracy). In another sense the game provides a forum for resistance to the dominant hegemony. Under its cooperative surface of team play is the potential of unbridled competition—chaotic and uninhibited. The contest is a political event, a contest between rival leaders, taking place in a public arena. Two or three generations ago such rivalries would have been expressed by raid and counterraid (Jones, 1982). During the 1900s the central government of Afghanistan has become more powerful in controlling the warring Khans, so the Khans have increasingly used Buzkashi as a substitute for war, as a means of rivalry, and for political, economic, and social gain.

With its increasing popularity as an urban entertainment, Qarajai Buzkashi has become a political vehicle of the Afghan government in its efforts to consolidate the people. In a very real way, Qarajai is a residual revisal. The current U.S.S.R.–controlled Afghan politboro, based in the nation's capital Kabul, makes extensive use of the Buzkashi events for political propaganda. However, particularly in the northern provinces, the Afghan chapandaz are refusing to play and the Khan and people are absenting themselves from the games; thus Buzkashi is being used to oppose the central government. In one instance, opposition was expressed in the violent slaughtering of 50 Russians at a Buzkashi game (*Newsweek*, March 17, 1980:52). In a 1949 journey, subterfuge was used by the Kirghiz people of the northern Afghanistan high Pamir plateau, who used a Buzkashi game to capture a Chinese fort that blocked their return home. While the invited soldiers of the fort attended the Buzkashi game, Kirghiz fighters captured the fort with a single shot (Adams, 1985).

According to Azoy (1982), the two forms of Buzkashi correlate with two sorts of celebratory contexts. The traditional Tudabarai game is privately sponsored as part of a rite of passage, and in some sense is tribal in the preservation of ethnic identity. The Qarajai sport is publically sponsored as part of a government-organized holiday festival, and in some sense is official as evidence of incorporation in the dominant culture. Two cultural themes of ethnicity are reflected in Buzkashi: (a) survival, in promoting respect for the entrepreneurial past with its emphasis on assertively masculine values, and (b) revisal, as an active agent within current society that holds the political opinions of its participants.

Conclusion

This chapter points out that traditional games as features of the past culture are negatively perceived through selective tradition; yet, in fact, they continue to exist. Their presence in contemporary culture indicates that they indeed preserve ethnic identity in three ways: (a) archaic revival, (b) residual survival, and (c) residual revisal. The Inuit revival of their Northern Games and the two Afghanistan versions of Buzkashi, the traditional survival game of Tudabarai and the revisal game of Qarajai, verify the traditional games' value in ethnic identity as oppositional, alternative, and incorporative experiences within a contemporary dominant society.

References

Adams, N.M. (1985, March). Flight from terror on the roof of the world. *Reader's Digest*, pp. 216–240.

Azoy, G.W. (1982). *Buzkashi: Game and power in Afghanistan*. Philadelphia: University of Pennsylvania Press.

Balikci, A. (1978). Buzkashi. *Natural History*, **8**, 54–63.

Canadian Film Board. (1982). *The Northern Games* [Videotape]. Toronto: Canadian Film Board.

Cheska, A.T. (1987). *The role and place of traditional games and dances in West African nations*. Paris: UNESCO.

Cuddon, J.A. (1980). *The international dictionary of sports and games*. New York: Schocken.

Dunning, E. (1973). The structural-functional properties of folk games and modern sports. *Sportwissenschaft*, **3**, 215–232.

Dupree, L. (1980). *Afghanistan*. Princeton, NJ: Princeton University Press.

Elias, N. (1978). *The civilizing process*. New York: Urizen. (Original edition published in German, 1939)

Jones, S. (1982). Not work alone. In J. Cherfas & R. Lewin (Eds.), *Not work alone* (pp. 99–111). Beverly Hills, CA: Sage.

Newsweek. (1980, March 17).

Paraschak, V., & Scott, H.A. (1980). *Games northerners play—the Arctic Winter Games and the Northern Games: Reflections of one north or several?* Paper presented at the North American Society for Sport History meeting, Banff, Alberta, Canada.

Williams, R. (1977). *Marxism and literature*. Oxford, England: Oxford University Press.

Williams, R. (1980). *Problems in materialism and culture*. New York: New Left Books.

Play, the Development of *Kakada'*, and Social Change Among the Bulusu' of East Kalimantan

Laura P. Appell-Warren

The study of play among children in traditional societies is a relatively new field (see Lancy & Tindall, 1977:7; Norbeck & Farrer, 1979:vii; Schwartzman, 1980:7). A few ethnographies of Borneo peoples include mention of children's play (see, for example, Heppell, 1975), but there have been no in-depth studies of children's play, much less in relation to social change. However, many of the peoples of Borneo are currently undergoing rapid social change. This, I believe, is in turn causing change in patterns of children's play. In this chapter I examine traditional parental attitudes about child development and children's play among the Bulusu' of Indonesian Borneo and discuss the changes that are occurring in the socialization and development of children during a period of rapid social change.

The results of my research among the Bulusu' indicate that a decrease has occurred in the frequency and type of children's play due to a move to a resettlement village. The change in traditional play forms appears to be the result of (a) high temperatures in the resettlement village that the Bulusu' are unaccustomed to and that is due to a lack of vegetation; (b) the isolation of the nuclear family houses in the resettlement village; (c) the lack of jungle resources to create playthings; and (d) the stress of the resettlement village.

In addition I examine the difficulties that the parents and children are having adapting to their new environment and contrast my findings among the Bulusu' with similar research done among the Tulid Idahan Murut, whose culture, despite social change, is still rich in different forms of children's play.

The Bulusu'

The Bulusu' inhabit the Sekatak, Bengara, and Bataiyau river systems of east Kalimantan (Kalimantan Timur). Traditionally, the Bulusu' live in longhouses scattered along the banks of these rivers and on the small tributaries of these river systems. Their economy is based on swidden agriculture. The most frequently planted crops are dry rice and manioc. Maize is irregularly planted. In addition, the Bulusu' plant yams, a variety of vegetables, and fruit trees. Fruit is one of the more important Bulusu' crops, much of which is sold in Tarakan, a major commercial center.

The Bulusu' social organization is cognatic, and their kinship terminology is primarily of the Eskimo type. The major social units of the Bulusu' are the domestic family and the extended family that occupies a compartment (*lamin*) in a longhouse village. The Bulusu' are virilocal and a bride price of gongs and jars is paid by the groom's family (see Appell, 1983).

The Bulusu' maintain their traditional religion, which includes a creator god who is female. Each individual has multiple souls, the loss of any of which could cause illness and eventually death. A number of spirits dwell in rocks, trees, hills, earth, and springs and are potentially malevolent. The spirits (*karaganan*) can cause illness by stealing away one or more of an individual's souls. Parents are afraid that their children will become ill if they disturb these malevolent spirits. Thus they discourage any activities, including play, that may arouse the *karaganan*.

To cure an illness a religious specialist, called an *ulun gantu*, goes into a trance and calls his or her spirit familiars to aid in the search for lost souls. The ceremonies for curing involve trance dancing, gonging, and offerings of cloth, food, and drink to the spirits. These ceremonies can last for as long as 3 or 4 days.

The Bulusu' were formerly headhunters and once conducted elaborate ceremonies associated with the taking of heads. The vestiges of these ceremonies can be seen during the curing ceremonies of the present. The Bulusu' still perceive that the threat of attack by headhunters is real and constantly watch their children to see that they do not stray too far from their homes.

Social Change

In the late 1960s the Indonesian government first began a project entitled *Resetlemen Penduduk* (resettlement of citizens). Under this project the Bulusu' are being moved from their traditional villages into larger resettlement villages. The resettlement project was instigated to ensure that the Bulusu' would be continually available to the government officials who visit the area periodically, thus simplifying the process of census taking, dispensing of medicine, and schooling. Boundaries were placed around the resettlement village outside of which the Bulusu' are discouraged from cutting the jungle for their swiddens. Relocating the Bulusu' also serves to free the jungle for use by the lumber and paper companies that are moving into the Bulusu' area.

The resettlement village is multiethnic including Bulusu', Punan, Bulungan, and Tidung peoples, as well as a few representatives of other Indonesian ethnic groups such as the Timorese. The Bulusu' are thus integrated with members of other ethnic groups to a far greater extent than in their traditional villages. This integration has caused a great deal of friction and stress, and some interethnic fighting has occurred.

In the resettlement village land is scarce. With such a large, consolidated population, problems of sanitation arise because of the increased demand on the river for drinking, bathing, and for use as a latrine. In addition, an increased amount of contact with outsiders has occurred. Although the Bulusu' do not draw a connection between poor sanitation, contact with outsiders and illness, several adults did report that sickness has become more common now than in the past, especially among children.

At the time of our research the resettlement process had not been completely successful in the Sekatak River area. The Bulusu' still maintain, to the best of their ability, their traditional way of life by living in their longhouses as much of the time as possible. A few families live semipermanently in the resettlement village and attempt to cultivate in the surrounding marginal, less fertile areas. However, the majority of the population continues to live and cultivate in the longhouse villages, making periodic trips to the resettlement village when pressured by government personnel or when there is a hiatus in swidden activities. The distance that the Bulusu' have to travel varies, and these trips produce a fairly frequent turnover in the resettlement population.

Research Methods

The following discussion of Bulusu' parental attitudes and children's play is based on data collected over an 8-month period of residence in a resettlement village and over several short stays of 2 to 5 days in traditional villages, by participant observation (Adams & Priess, 1960; Wax, 1968), spot observation (Rogoff, 1978), and informal interviews with parents and children. One hundred seventy-nine observations on approximately 15 children aged 4 to 12 were made. Thirty interviews with adults and 14 interviews with children were conducted.

In addition, a short comparison study among the Tulid Idahan Murut of northeastern Kalimantan was conducted. The discussion of the Tulid Idahan Murut children's play is based on data collected over a 2-week period of residence in a resettlement village by participant observation and interviews. Thirty-five observations of 10 children aged 4 to 12 were made, and one interview with an adult was conducted.

Parental Attitudes Toward Children

The Bulusu' concepts of *jayil* (naughty) and *mabap* (crazy), as well as the practices of abortion and physical punishment, are aspects and reflections of what is reported to be the traditional Bulusu' parental attitudes toward children. Although these parental attitudes may be changing in the re-settlement environment, it was not possible to document these changes during this research period.

Table 1   Bulusu' Development Stages

Approximate age	Bulusu' development stages	English translation
Male and female		
Less than 1 year	lemaub	able to roll over
	timpun pangkor kamang	learning to crawl—pulling self along with arms only
1 year	timpun pangkor makow	able to crawl
	timpun makow	beginning to walk
2 years	ngimbol baloi	running in the longhouse
	lembabas	naked
3 to 4 years	nysagawan dungai lungud	carrying a small bamboo water tube
Female		
4 years	tumpun gatatapi	starting to wear a skirt
5 years	timpun pangkor nyiba beratakan awis	carrying a small basket (to help mother in field and carry cassava home in)
6 years	timpun gesesemandak	beginning to play at being a maiden (plays at wearing head beads)
8 to 9 years	timpun sinigod degagalu	starting of growth of breasts
10 to 11 years	timpun maiya' semandak laun	beginning to accompany sleeping parties of maidens
12 to 13 years	timpun nyamandak	beginning to be a maiden (characterized by the statement that the "body is full"—i.e., physical development is almost complete)
15 to 16 years	semandak laun	true maiden (physical development complete)

Table 1 Bulusu' Development Stages (Cont.)

Approximate age	Bulusu' development stages	English translation
16 years	kalap lumunan	able to start a family
adulthood	pongo lumunan	started a family
	or	
middle adulthood	nogom laki	has a husband
	pongo ganak	finished child-bearing
Male		
4 years	timpun gagabag	starting to wear a loincloth
5 years	timpun nyapok pompolu	starting to use a small blowpipe to kill birds
6 years	timpun muwayoi	beginning to be a young man
7 years	timpun titi timeru moi dandu	beginning to court the girls (mainly in play)
8 to 10 years	maiya' ngasu	follows father to hunt wild boars in the hills with dogs
10 to 15 years	timpun muyayoi laun	reaching manhood
15 years	moi dandu laun	seriously courting a girl (with the intention of marriage)
adulthood	ngandu	has a wife
Male and female		
middle adulthood	pongo berlaki *or* berdandu	children have finished getting a husband or wife
	nogon kupu naku	have grandchildren
late adulthood	nutok	pounding—i.e., the individual no longer has teeth and uses a mortar and pestle to make chew of betel and sireh

Concept of *Jayil*

Children are believed to be inherently *jayil* (naughty). When I mentioned a child in conversation or in an interview, an adult would interject a comment about how *jayil* that child was—it was a rare child that did not elicit such a response from adults. Play (*mengalan*) in general is perceived by the Bulusu' adult to be *jayil*.

The age at which naughtiness is first attributed to a child varies. When asked during interviews some adults said that a child begins to be naughty when he or she learns to walk; others said that children become naughty when they are 3 or 4. However, because Bulusu' stages of child development are demarcated not in terms of numerical years but in terms of motor ability and responsibility (see Table 1), the assignment of numerical ages is essentially meaningless to the Bulusu'. It is not uncommon for a mother to one day say that her child is 2 years old and the next day say that he or she is 4 years old.

A child is considered to be naughtiest when he or she wanders away from the house and when he or she plays outside the house on the ground for extended periods of time. The view that playing outside is naughty is linked to the fear that the child will become ill. It is believed that the "heat" (an undefined force that can cause illness) from the ground will rise and enter the body of the child and cause illness. Whether this fear is grounded in reality or not is unknown, but the parental fear of illness may be exacerbated by the high mortality rate among children.

Play in the rain is also considered to be extremely naughty. At that time the malevolent spirits that cause illness are believed to be more prevalent. If a child is found playing on the ground when there is a rainbow, he will surely die because a rainbow is believed to be the staircase of the *karaganan*. Also, tree climbing is considered to be naughty, as is over-exuberance around adults, playing with knives, destroying plants, harming animals, and too much playing in general.

Concept of *Mabap*

Children who play too much are not only *jayil*, but *mabap* (crazy). While all children are perceived of as *jayil*, not all children are perceived of as *mabap*. Only those children who play excessively and ignore the admonitions of their parents are considered to be *mabap*. Children who are *mabap* will most certainly anger the *karaganan*, malevolent spirits, and become ill.

Abortion

The mortality rate among children is extremely high. In 1978, 48 children in a nearby river system died from an outbreak of measles. By the end of the epidemic each family had lost at least one child. In the Sekatak River system a large number of children also died in this 1978 epidemic, but the exact figures are unknown. In view of this high rate of infant and child mortality, it is surprising that the Bulusu' perform abortions, unlike some people such as the Rungus Dusun (Appell, 1965). Although abortions are usually performed when a second child is conceived soon after the birth of another child, and is therefore perceived as a threat to the health of the firstborn child, they are also performed if the child is not wanted. Although the practice of abortion is common knowledge, only one known case of abortion occurred during the field period.

Physical Punishment

The Bulusu' believe that one should teach a child with words, and one should always include physical discipline in the learning process as well. A Bulusu' may walk into a room and see his or her spouse striking a child and say, ''*koh*'' (hit him or her again). A parent may also say, "I want to strike him or her also," when the spouse is observed in the process of disciplining a child.

It is said that one should hit a child until it hurts, but never until the child loses consciousness. Nevertheless, cases have been reported in the traditional villages of children being beaten until they lose consciousness, and in one extreme case until the child died. As yet no cases of abuse have occurred in the resettlement village, but the Bulusu' have resided in the resettlement village for only a short period. Generally, it is thought to be taboo to hit a child on the torso or head because this is where the soul resides. Despite this taboo, children are often beaten, or hit, on the torso or head. However, while physcial discipline is common, cases of child beating where severe injury occurs are rare. A child who is beaten by a parent is not totally helpless. He himself can, or an aunt, uncle, or grandparent can, demand a payment to *kotog lingu* (harden the soul), that as a result of the beating has been softened. This payment is in the form of a jar or brass box. It is not uncommon for children to go away to live with relatives until the fine is paid. If the fine is not paid, the child's soul will remain soft, and he will be particularly susceptible to illness and death.

In addition to the sanction of the fine to *kotog lingu* an aunt, uncle, or grandparent may remove an overly abused child from the parents. The parents who have had a child removed because of abuse of the child are looked down upon by the majority of the community, thus discouraging the abuse of children. (For an interesting discussion of more permissive discipline in another Borneo society, the Iban, see Heppell, 1975.)

Kakada' and the Emphasis on the Importance of Work

The negative view of play that the Bulusu' hold is in contrast to the positive view of *kakada'*, character. The characteristics of *kakada'* are calmness, quietness, responsibility, and the containment of emotions. It is also in this context that play is believed to be naughty. The spontaneity of play among children of any age shows a lack of self-control, which is in opposition with *kakada'*. Parents hope that their children will display *kakada'*, but it appears that the children are more eager to play. The children are, therefore, in opposition to their parents, a state that necessarily leads to tension between parents and children.

Kakada' is difficult to translate precisely, but it is a central concept to the Bulusu'. *Kakada'* is not explicitly taught. But, one gains and achieves *kakada'* by listening to the admonitions of an elder and by observing adults. A child begins to demonstrate *kakada'* when he is able to watch out for himself, care responsibly for a younger sibling, and help his parents in the garden without being asked. When a son makes his own garden, or makes a garden with his father, he is well on the way to achieving *kakada'*.

On the other hand, if he does not responsibly care for his garden, he has not fully reached *kakada'*. Also of importance to the achievement of *kakada'* among males is the taking on of the responsibility of his bride price. The most important achievement that signals the attainment of *kakada'*, by both sexes, is the ability to work hard. Thus a person with *kakada'* is a responsible, hard working, careful, thoughtful, functioning member of society.

Onset of *Kakada'*

Although the acquisition of *kakada'* is an ongoing process that continues into young adulthood, Bulusu' parents hope, and expect, that the acquisition of *kakada'* will begin in childhood between the ages of 8 and 12. However, this is not always the case, and therefore no set age is identified at which the Bulusu' universally achieve *kakada'*. Because individuals achieve *kakada'* at different times, it does not appear to be considered a set stage of development. As will be shown in the following examples *kakada'* may be achieved in childhood, but often *kakada'* is not achieved until after marriage, especially among males. Furthermore, not all adults are perceived of as having fully achieved *kakada'*. In this regard the concept of *kakada'* may be similar to the American concept of character—each individual's character is developed differently and at different times.

When asked, several people reported that Yasing, a young boy of approximately 9 years, "*sudah* **kakada'** *sebap jaga adik. Sebelum* **kakada'** *biar adik lari, biar tidak ada bapak dan mama.*"[1] (Yasing already has *kakada'* because he watches his little brother. Before he had *kakada'* it wouldn't have mattered if his little brother ran around alone [implying a potential for the younger brother to be hurt] even if his father and mother were not there.) On the other hand Idi, a young married man, about 18 years old, was said to "*belum* **kakada'** *sebap sudah besar dan kuat, tepi harus surulnya untuk apa apa.*" (Idid does not yet have *kakada'* because although he is already big and strong he has to be told to do everything.) Finally, it is also said that if a married man repays his father for *gama*, gongs and jars paid out on his behalf for fines, then the individual has *kakada'*.

Developmental Stages and *Kakada'*

Although *kakada'* is not a set stage of development the emphasis of *kakada'* on responsibility and hard work is reflected in many of the named developmental stages of Bulusu' children. For example, in Table 1 (which is derived from interviews with parents on how they refer to children of different ages), the following English translations for named Bulusu' developmental stages can be found: "carrying a small bamboo water tube"; "carrying a small basket"; "starting to use a small blowpipe to kill birds"; "follows father to hunt wild boars in the hills with dogs."

The named developmental stages contain references to social maturity, more specifically responsibility and hard work, as well as to physical maturity. This early reference to social maturity (beginning at age 3 or 4; see Table 1) may serve to encourage young children to work and thereby achieve *kakada'*.

Because work is differentially distributed between males and females, the developmental stages for boys and girls are different. Girls aged 3 or 4 to 5 have not yet achieved *kakada'*; nonetheless they are called *nysagawan dungai lungud*, "able to carry a small bamboo water tube." By age 5 or 6 the girls are referred to as *timpun pangkor beratakan awis*, "being able to carry a small basket to help mother carry food home from the gardens." A girl who is 6 or 7 is *timpun gesesamandak*, "beginning to play at being a maiden."

Boys around age 5 have also not yet achieved *kakada'*, but nevertheless they are called *timpun nyapok pompolu*, "beginning to use a blowpipe to hunt birds." By age 8 to 10 boys are referred to as *maiya' ngasu*, "able to follow father to hunt with the dogs." However, the Bulusu' report that it is not until boys are at least 10 to 12, and/or when they begin to help their fathers with their tasks, that it is considered possible for them to have reached the start of *kakada'*. This differential maturity of males and females is not only reflected in the developmental stages (see Table 1 for complete developmental stages) but in the age that actual work begins. By age 5 to 7 girls are observed sporadically helping their mothers. Girls of approximately 5 years can be seen weeding and practicing the replanting of torn-out weeds. They also carry water—an arduous task in the re-settlement village because many of the houses are far from the river. At 7 or 8 years they are pounding and winnowing rice, washing clothes, and caring for younger siblings. Young girls of age 5 or 6 follow their mothers to the garden and help; many girls have their own small paddles to aid in the paddling of the canoe to the garden area. Girls of 5 to 7 years are also left to guard the rice fields against the birds that ravage the fields.

By age 12 a girl is often said to have achieved *kakada'* and is helping full time with the adult female tasks, often doing the majority of the work for the household. This is especially true if the mother is pregnant or has a young child. Although a 12-year-old is capable of running her own household, Bulusu' girls do not usually marry until they are about 14 to 16 years old.

Boys who are aged 5 to 7 years also aid in the guarding of the rice fields and can be seen carrying small bundles for their fathers to and from the canoes. However, not until a boy is 9 or 10 does he begin to help his father with any regularity and has thereby begun to achieve *kakada'*. By age 12 he is helping more fully, although not to the extent that the 12-year-old girls are.

Children's Play

Despite the negative parental attitudes toward play, play does occur, bringing parents and children into opposition. Much of the play is non-competitive play that takes the form of imitative play (see Piaget, 1962), that is, play in preparation for adult life and the attainment of *kakada'*. In addition, the majority of the imaginative play, play in which objects are transformed into something other than what they are, takes the form of imitation of adult activities, as in the transformation of leaves into plates when playing at making a meal. In view of the fact that the parents encourage work and *kakada'*, it is interesting that the parents look scornfully upon the play that is essentially oriented toward the preparation for work.

Play Objects

The one plaything that all Bulusu' parents sanction is the small wooden boats (*padau rumot*) that all Bulusu' boys aged 4 to 10 play with. It is not uncommon for a father to carve one of these boats for either a son or daughter. These boats are played with in the sand or in the river. Fathers also cut small bamboo water-carrying tubes for their daughters aged 5 to 10 to carry water in, and will occasionally make, or have made, small machetes for their sons. Although these last two objects are functional, they are also considered, to a certain extent, toys.

Play Activities

The most popular activity of children of all ages and both sexes is swimming. Swimming occurs in both the traditional longhouse villages and in the resettlement village. The fact that more river play seems to take place in the resettlement village may be attributed to both the intense heat due to the lack of shade trees and to the lack of other activities for the children to participate in. Called *diu* (bathing), hours are spent in the river playing water games. These games include surface diving, making noise on the water's surface by slapping the water with cupped hands, which creates an air bubble that breaks with a noise (most often done by girls), and by clapping two rocks together under water.

The Bulusu' parents do not generally have any objections to play in the river, perhaps because of the amount of pleasure that they too derive from their evening baths. During this time a great deal of flirting, socializing, and adult play occurs. However, two cases occur in which water play is discouraged among children. Certain areas of the river are said to have crocodiles. Children who persist in playing in these areas are not only *jayil* (naughty) and *mabap* (crazy), but they lack *kakada'*. As in all cases of play, too much river play is *jayil* and children are told to stop and go home when they have overstayed an arbitrary amount of time that has been set by their parents.

Boys younger than 12 use slingshots made of a Y-shaped piece of wood and several rubber bands. They practice their aim on the birds in the rice fields using bits of manioc stems or small pebbles as ammunition. Boys aged 5 to 9 years practice their blowpipe skills using a small piece of hollow bamboo and clay pellets. By age 9 the boys are practicing with a real blow-pipe and are using clay darts as ammunition. Boys younger than 10 or 12 build small huts (*baloi tanah*) out of branches and bark. These are imitations of the temporary houses that are built near the gardens. While building these huts, the boys get practice in skills that soon will be necessary to their way of life.

Occasionally young boys will pretend that they are killing a wild pig. These pigs are scarce and killing one involves a great deal of skill. One boy was observed spearing a burlap sack with a stick and screaming "*Bakas! Bakas!*" ("Wild pig! Wild pig!").

The only competitive game that is played by the boys is soccer. Not an indigenous game, it caught on quickly when it was introduced by a school teacher. Although a real soccer ball is rarely available, large citrus fruits and potatoes are acceptable substitutes. In the resettlement village this game is often played with boys from several ethnic groups participating. The end result of these multiethnic games is often an outbreak of aggression and fighting.

Play occurs less frequently among the girls. Most of the girls tend to stay close to home and run errands or help their mothers. The girls are not allowed to wander far from home alone until they are 5 or 6, and by that time they are already beginning to work.

Solitary play among young girls is not unusual. Often they will "play house" under a tree or in the shade of a house. Older girls sometimes converse as they do household work together. Girls sometimes sit idly playing with flowers as they are resting by the river. They most commonly take flower buds and place them over their fingers. Small girls call them *sindulu buruwang* (claws of a bear). The petals of the flowers are also placed over the thumb and forefinger and then slapped; the result is a loud popping sound.

In the longhouse village the boys and girls occasionally play house together. This involves building a hut (*baloi tanah*) in the jungle near the longhouse, killing a few baby chicks, stealing some other food, and cooking a meal. While playing house in the jungle is *jayil* because it is play, killing baby chicks is a serious offense because the father of the child who kills the chickens must make restitution to the owner of the chickens.

Boys can also commit offense when they practice with their blowpipes. Upon occasion a poisoned dart will "stray" and kill a pig. Again the father of the child must make restitution to the owner of the pig. The replacement of a pig is a large expense and can cause a great deal of economic hardship to the family.

When not occupied with swimming or other play, the children are either doing some form of work for the household, sitting and talking in the shade, or aimlessly wandering around the village. When the children are unoccupied and wandering, conflicts and fights most often occur.

The Impact of Resettlement on the Bulusu' Children and Their Play

The Bulusu' are having difficulty adapting to the resettlement villages into which they are being moved. Although few people spend all of their time in the resettlement area, most of them are experiencing not only emotional stress due to continuous change and uncertainty but economic stress due to fewer and less fertile swidden areas. This stress is exacerbated by the new social situation in which several ethnic groups are living in close contact with each other. The Bulusu' who choose to remain in their traditional villages are subject to being called back by government officials to the resettlement area at a moment's notice. It is not unusual for a government official to arrive late at night and expect to see a full village by daybreak.

It is still too early for a full assessment of the cost that this life has had on the Bulusu', but the difference in children's play that has been reported by the parents is interesting to note. When asked, most parents agree that less play occurs in the resettlement village than in the traditional villages. The adolescents and children themselves also acknowledge the fact that less play occurs in the resettlement area than in the traditional villages. In addition, a large number of the play activities that are described by the parents and their children do not take place in the resettlement village but reportedly did (and still do to a certain extent) take place in the traditional villages.

Several differences in the physical environment of the two settings (the resettlement village and the longhouse village) may be responsible for differences in the level and types of play. Stripped of all trees and vegetation by government workers when the village was built, the resettlement area is now exposed to the sun all day. A substantial temperature difference exists between the resettlement area and the jungle where the longhouses are. Another possible cause of the lack of play is the physical layout of the resettlement village. In a longhouse all the compartments are contiguous and there is a common veranda area. Thus children can easily and safely form play groups. An adult is always present or in sight and will be able to watch the children. In the resettlement village the houses are all scattered dwellings, most commonly of nuclear families. In some areas the houses are relatively isolated. This makes it unsafe for children younger than 5 or 6 to wander in search of playmates because they will be out of sight of the parents.

Robert A. LeVine and Barbara B. LeVine, in their study of the Gusii of Kenya, also found that the physical isolation of the Gusii homesteads has an effect on the Gusii children's play. The Gusii children frequently do not come into contact with their peers from other homesteads due to this isolation (1977:152). This isolation coupled with herding activities results in a low frequency of play activities (LeVine & LeVine, 1977:153). On the other hand, when the homesteads are near to each other, or when pastures are shared, play groups form and children engage in limited amounts of play activities.

In the Bulusu' resettlement area the parents' fear of children wandering also curtails play activities, and can be explained by the fact that the resettlement environment is perceived to be a hostile one by the Bulusu'. The village is full of strangers and people of different ethnic groups. Because of this presence of strangers, the parents fear for the safety of their children. As was mentioned earlier, the fear of headhunting is still real. Thus if a child wanders to the area of the village where once hostile peoples now live, parents worry that he might lose his head. Parents are also afraid that their children will be kidnapped. Timorese workers from a nearby lumber camp often come to the village, and on one occasion took a child for a number of days.

When in the longhouse, the Bulusu' children also have the infinite resources of the jungle with which to create playthings and play situations. In the past, as was previously mentioned, the young boys and girls would build huts in the jungle and cook stolen chickens and manioc on small open fires. They could then sit and eat their plunder in the cool jungle.

Girls also frequently made dolls from banana stalks. These dolls were fairly elaborate and were made with small cradle boards in the traditional Bulusu' style. The dolls did not last long, but when they were ruined new ones easily made. In the resettlement area there is a lack of natural resources for the children to utilize in their play; consequently many of the playthings that could be made in the longhouse villages cannot be made in the resettlement village.

In addition to the hypotheses already offered, several more can be put forward as explanations for the decrease of play activities that parents report in the resettlement environment. First, the children, accustomed to life in the jungle, may be overwhelmed by the strangeness of the surroundings and by the interruption of normality, and, therefore, they may not have either the physical or emotional energy to play (see Appell, 1982).

Second, the parents may be reacting to the normless situation and may be harsher on their children because of their own doubts and fears. These doubts and fears stem from the inability to make successful swiddens in the infertile resettlement area, from the continual pressure placed on them by the government officials, from the increased need for money (instead of the customary trade items), and from the general strangeness and unpredictability of the situation.

In his study of Kpelle children's play during a period of rapid social change, Lancy also found that the Kpelle parents were critical of their children's play (1977:90). Although Lancy gives no reason for this criticism on the part of the Kpelle parents, he does suggest that "traditional playforms act to link the development of children to the technology of their parents" (1977:91). This suggests that the parent may be reacting negatively to the children because of the loss of traditional play patterns that serve to link the parents to their children. This may also be the case among the Bulusu'; however, further research is needed to confirm this hypothesis.

Finally, the case of the Bulusu' may also be similar to the case of American parents who, under stress, are more likely to abuse their children (Gerbner, Ross, & Zeigler, 1980:98). In addition, parents under stress may neglect their children to a greater or lesser degree. These products of stress are possibly at work in Bulusu' society creating a situation in which children, as a result of the parents' preoccupation with rapid change, are not playing as much as in the past.

These findings with regard to a decrease in Bulusu' children's play are in marked contrast with the findings of a short-term study among the Tulid Idahan Murut. The Tulid Idahan Murut are a group of swidden agriculturalists that live on the Sebuku and Tulid rivers of northeast Kalimantan. The Tulid Idahan Murut also live in resettlement villages; however, the attitude of the parents toward their children's play is positive. In addition the children are constantly playing and discovering new toys and games.

In a 2-week period of observation among the Tulid Idahan Murut the children created four new playthings. Among these playthings were stilts, two types of propellers, and saws from tin can tops. In 8 months among the Bulusu', two playthings were created by the Bulusu' children. This count of playthings refers to artifacts that take time and effort to create, not leaves, stones, and so forth that are picked up and played with.

Tulid Idahan Murut parents participate in, and encourage, their children's play. This never occurs among the Bulusu'. Like the Bulusu' children, the Tulid Idahan Murut children are expected to work; however, play is not considered in the negative terms that it is among the Bulusu'.

Because the research period among the Tulid Idahan Murut was restricted, a complete comparison between the Tulid Idahan Murut and the Bulusu' cannot be made. The Tulid Idahan Murut resettlement village is, however, well established, is not as hot or as crowded as the Bulusu' resettlement, has a larger percentage of fairly good swidden land available close to the resettlement (although some people still have swiddens in their old longhouse villages), and is not made up of several different ethnic groups. The Tulid Idahan Murut have also been missionized and have accepted Christianity to a far greater extent than the Bulusu'. Although the effects these differences in environment and religion have on the children's play and on the parental attitudes in the two groups are unknown, the differences in children's play and parental attitudes that do occur between the two groups are interesting.

The findings with regard to the Bulusu' children's decrease in play activities in an area of rapid social change are also significantly different than the findings reported by Anderson (1980) in her study of children's play in

Thailand. Although Anderson's study did not focus on social change, the area where Anderson's work was conducted was clearly undergoing change. Some examples of this change are the construction of roads linking the village where Anderson did field work to the city; the electrification of some of the houses; the acquisition of televisions by some of the families; more frequent school attendance in the city by the children; and more travel to the city to do marketing, and so forth (1980:23–70). This change in Thailand, however, is not as drastic as the change described for Kalimantan because the place of residence and the availability of subsistence areas are not affected by the change.

Despite the changes, Anderson describes a society rich in children's play. In fact, some of the games described have been played for several generations (1980:23). Although some minor changes have occurred in the play activities of the children due to social change (especially due to the introduction of television [1980:159]), a rich repertoire of play among the children still exists. This situation is in direct contrast to the Bulusu' children who have experienced a significant decrease in play activities due to social change.

Conclusion

Social change among the Bulusu' has affected the relationship between work, play, and the physical environment. In the traditional villages the environment of the jungle and the swiddens provided ample opportunities for the children to play and for the necessary subsistence work to be done by both children and adults. In the resettlement village the physical environment is not conducive to play, nor is it conducive to making swiddens. As a result both parents and their children have little swidden work to do. Less adult work activities are available for the children to imitate, and less work occurs for the children to do. Parents still perceive that their children are shirking their work duties by playing, and are therefore *jayil* and *mabap* and lack *kakada'*. What they do not seem to realize is that little work is available.

Because of the effects of social change and the inhospitable environment of the resettlement area, the children are also playing less than in the past. What effect this decrease in play activity will have on the Bulusu' children is not yet known. It is hoped that future research among the Bulusu' will be able to determine the long-term effects of social change on the children's play activities and development.

Note

1. This and the following quotes are in a mixture of the Bulusu' and Indonesian languages. All of the interviews were conducted in a mixture of the two languages because of the fluency of the interviewer and those interviewed in the *lingua franca* of Indonesian. Boldface words are

untranslatable Bulusu' vocabulary that are used regardless of the fact that Indonesian is being spoken.

Acknowledgments

I would like to thank Dr. David Pillemer of Wellesley College for all his useful comments, excellent advice and help. I would also like to thank Dr. M.M. Katz of the Harvard Graduate School of Education for all the time, encouragement, and excellent criticism that she gave me. Field work among the Bulusu' was undertaken in 1980–1981 under a grant from the National Science Foundation (Grant BNS-79-15343) with G.N. Appell, PhD, of Brandeis University, as principal investigator. I undertook independent research on the development and socialization of children among the Bulusu' when not working as research assistant to Dr. Appell. I am indebted to him for his guidance in this work both in the field and in the final preparation of this paper. We want to thank Lembaga Ilmu Pengetahuan Indonesia for their authorization of this research, and particularly Dr. Masri Singarimbun of Gadjah Mada University, Dr. Soestrisno Hadi of the Universitas Mulawarman, and Bupati Soetadji of Bulungan, for their many kindnesses and help.

This paper was presented at the 11th Annual Meeting of The Association for the Anthropological Study of Play, March 14, 1985, Washington, DC, as the first-prize winner in the 1985 TAASP Competition for the Best Student Paper on Play.

References

Adams, R.N., & Priess, J.J. (1960). *Human organization research: Field relations and techniques.* Homewood, IL: Dorsey Press.

Anderson, W.W. (1980). *Children's play and games in rural Thailand: A study in enculturation and socialization.* Bangkok: Chulalongkorn University Social Research Institute.

Appell, G.N. (1965). *The nature of social groupings among the Rungus Dusun of Sabah, Malaysia.* Unpublished doctoral dissertation, The Australian National University, Canberra.

Appell, G.N. (1982). *The health consequences of social change: A set of postulates for developing general adapation theory.* Paper presented at the National Conference on Social Stress Research held October 11–23, 1982 at the University of New Hampshire, Durham.

Appell, G.N. (1983). Ethnic groups in the northeast region of Indonesian Borneo and their social organization. *Borneo Research Bulletin, 15*(1), 38–45.

Gerbner, G., Ross, C.J., & Zeigler, E. (1980). *Child abuse. An agenda for action.* New York: Oxford University Press.

Heppell, M. (1975). *Iban social control: The infant and the adult.* Unpublished doctoral dissertation, The Australian National University, Canberra.

Lancy, D.F. (1977). The play behavior of Kpelle children during rapid cultural change. In D.F. Lancy & B.A. Tindall (Eds.), *The study of play: Problems and prospects* (pp. 84–104). Champaign, IL: Leisure Press.

Lancy, D.F., & Tindall, B.A. (Eds.). (1977). *The study of play: Problems and prospects.* Champaign, IL: Leisure Press.

LeVine, R.A., & LeVine, B.B. (1977). *Nyansongo: A Gusii community in Kenya. Six cultures series.* Huntington, NY: Robert E. Kreiger.

Norbeck, E., & Farrer, C.R. (1979). *Forms of play of native North Americans.* New York: West.

Piaget, J. (1962). *Play, dreams, and imitation in childhood.* New York: W.W. Norton.

Rogoff, B. (1978). Spot observations and examination. *The Quarterly Newsletter of the Institute for Comparative Human Development, 2*(2), 21–26.

Schwartzman, H.B. (1980). *Play and culture.* Champaign, IL: Leisure Press.

Wax, R.H. (1968). Participant observation. In D. Sills (Ed.), *International encyclopedia of social sciences: Vol. 11.* New York: Macmillan and the Free Press.

The Rugby Tour: Construction and Enactment of Social Roles in a Play Setting

Dan C. Hilliard

The game of rugby football developed in England in the 19th century, according to Dunning and Sheard (1979), as a consequence of certain developments in English social structure in general and certain changes within the English public schools in particular. A variant of rugby was imported to the United States before the turn of the century and gradually evolved into American football (Riesman & Denney, 1951). In the meantime, the original rugby game not only grew in popularity in England and the rest of the United Kingdom, but developed followings in other parts of the world, notably France, South Africa, Australia, New Zealand, and parts of South America. Throughout the 20th century, international rugby competitions have taken place in the form of "test matches" between national teams, and local rugby clubs have participated in international tours during which they have matched their skills against foreign hosts. Although rugby was quickly overshadowed in North America by American and Canadian variants of football, rugby continued to be played by small numbers of adherents in both countries, and a growth in popularity during the decades of the 1950s through the 1970s gave it the status of a cult sport. The United States began fielding a national team in the 1970s, and tours bringing foreign teams to the United States, as well as visits by American teams to other countries, became commonplace.

For the social scientist, one of the most interesting features of rugby is the "third half," an institutionalized period of sociability following the game during which the host team provides the visitors with food and drink, and the two teams engage in drinking contests, the singing of ribald songs, and so forth. Sheard and Dunning (1973) have described the rugby social scene as "a type of 'male preserve,'" which revolves around the breaking of taboos concerning violence, nudity, obscenity, theft, and the destruction of property. At the core of the rugby club culture are obscene songs that are transmitted from club to club and to newly initiated club members via an oral tradition. According to Sheard and Dunning (1973), these songs express disdain and contempt for women and homosexuals and thus become a means of expressing a strong value placed on traditional masculinity. Indeed, Sheard and Dunning argue that the male preserve developed as a response to pressures on the traditional gender roles of middle- and upper-class British males because of the movement to emancipate women. However, in recent years the "purity" of the male preserve has been diluted as women have gained entrance to the rugby club, both because of economic necessity and because of fundamental changes in attitudes concerning gender roles (Sheard & Dunning, 1973). Sheard and Dunning suggest that as the weekly social activities of rugby club members have become more conventional, the traditional forms of behavior emphasizing masculinity have been confined to special occasions, such as tours.

I have played rugby and been associated with rugby clubs in Texas since 1968, and when I first read Sheard and Dunning's analysis, I was struck by the degree to which their description fit American rugby social behavior. Over the course of time, the social activities of the club with which I am affiliated have also become more conventional. However, my impression is that this has been due not so much to changes in attitudes toward gender roles as to a kind of cohort effect in which the behaviors and expectations of club members have changed with their stages in the life cycle and corresponding occupational and family responsibilities. The similarities between the English scene described by Sheard and Dunning and the American scene I had observed gave rise to a number of sociological issues. I was thus eager to take the opportunity to participate in a club tour of England in August, 1984. By observing the behavior of tour participants I hoped to (a) compare English club rugby and American club rugby as indicators of cultural similarities and/or differences in the treatment of recreation and sport, and (b) develop an understanding of the significance of the rugby tour for its participants and for the club as an organization.

The Texas Rugby Tour

The tour party consisted of 38 individuals—32 players, 3 wives or girlfriends, and 3 nonplaying club members. The group flew together from Texas to London, where a chartered bus picked it up and carried it to its various destinations. The itinerary called for four stops during the first 2 weeks of the tour, with two games, a first-side game (involving the best players of both clubs) and a social-side game (involving less skilled or serious players), at each stop. Approximately half the group would remain for a third week during which two more social-side games would be played. At each stop on the tour, players were hosted by members of the host team, billeted in their homes, provided meals, led on sightseeing tours, taken pub crawling, and taken to other leisure activities. Some time was allowed for training sessions as well. I traveled with the group for the first week of the tour. During this time, field notes were produced from memory each evening.[1]

Dissociation from Dominant Roles

The rugby tour offers an excellent example of what Zurcher (1968, 1970, 1983) calls an "ephemeral role": "a temporary or ancillary position-related behavior pattern chosen by individuals to satisfy social-psychological needs incompletely satisfied by the more dominant and lasting roles they regularly must enact in everyday life positions" (Zurcher, 1983:135). Participation in the tour was voluntary, and tour participation removed the actors both physically and socially from their dominant roles and the settings in which they took place. This separation, which is a central element in play (Huizinga, 1955), is one of the major factors that makes ephemeral role enactment socially and psychologically beneficial. In his study of the friendly poker game, Zurcher (1970) found that the poker players went through a process of dissociation from their dominant roles, so that during the game itself outside statuses were suspended and irrelevant. In other words, temporarily the players came to be known by and acted toward only in terms of the role they played within the poker group. I want to argue that the rugby tourists also went through a process of dissociation from their dominant roles and that they then took on an "ephemeral role set" consisting of several interrelated roles. I shall now describe the dissociation process and the roles that make up the "ephemeral role set" of the rugby tourist.

Physical and social dissociation began with the boarding of the plane for the transatlantic flight from Texas to London and was largely complete by the time of the group's arrival. When the group disembarked at London's Gatwick airport, they were immediately identifiable by their dress. Virtually every member of the group was wearing some form of idiosyncratic dress—either rugby T-shirts or cowboy hats, boots, belts, and jeans, or some combination of the two.[2] The clothing was clearly costuming that served to set the individuals apart from their ordinary roles and mark them as members of the tour group. Several examples may serve to illustrate the costuming phenomenon.

- PW, by profession a municipal judge but known to his fellow players as "Wolfman," wore his teeth, which had been knocked out during a game some years before, on a chain around his neck.
- LM, a policeman of Puerto Rican descent who detests country-and-western music and Western chic culture, wore a tall straw hat; when asked about it, he said, "I only brought it to trade." From past experience with visiting English teams, the players knew that cowboy hats would be very popular items because they were consistent with the British image of Texans.
- During the first day on tour, the group stopped at a pub for a beer. Several of us were sitting outside when GK walked by dressed in a complete cowboy outfit—boots, jeans, rodeo belt buckle, red flower-print shirt, and black felt hat. Seeing him, a member of the group remarked, "I hope they [the English] don't mistake him for a real cowboy."

Costuming as a means of dissociation has been a part of Texas rugby tradition for a number of years since it was popularized by a Houston team that always dressed in flower-print Hawaiian shirts when they traveled.

In addition to costuming, the 11-hour flight itself served as an element of the dissociation process. On airline flights, and particularly international flights, one is in a suspended status (Zurcher, 1983:91–112), a kind of no-man's-land, which certainly reinforces other aspects of dissociation. On rugby trips, including the tour flight, the beginning of travel is almost always accompanied by drinking, and most of the tour participants were undoubtedly able to draw upon past personal experience or club folklore concerning previous trips to know that heavy drinking would be considered appropriate behavior. The following account of behavior on the flight over was gleaned from discussions at a "tour party" following the return to the United States:

> The players all sat together toward the rear of the aircraft. When the stewardesses offered beverages, the players immediately began drinking and in a short while had consumed the three cases of beer available on the plane. They then began to drink 7 liters of whisky purchased by several members of the group at the duty-free shop before departure. They also conspired to steal a tray of the small liquor bottles carried on the plane. They rapidly became drunk and began singing, harassing the stewardesses, and offending other passengers around them. It was said that the captain threatened to land in Greenland and put them off the plane. It was also said that when BW came over on the same flight a day later, the group was still the subject of conversation among the crew, and that one couple who had been seated near the group had been reimbursed the cost of their tickets to compensate them for their inconvenience.

Thus the physical separation from dominant roles and the suspended status of the international flight were combined with alcohol use, reducing inhibitions, and allowing the tour participants to begin to enact elements of the ephemeral role set that they might have perceived as deviant under ordinary circumstances. Although the players were extremely fatigued from the flight, and some were noticeably hung over, they enthusiastically boarded the bus and began to drink the cans of beer provided them by the tour organizer. Shortly after the bus had pulled away from the airport terminal, some of the group were asking when we would be making a "pub stop." Dissociation from dominant roles had now taken place, and the players took on tour roles, a transformation symbolized by the following incident.

> After about 30 minutes on the bus, one tour member took the bright orange, 100% polyester headrest cover from his seat back, placed it on his head, and yelled, "Tour hats!" Immediately

others joined him, and cries of "Tour hat! Tour hat!" echoed up and down the aisles. Within minutes almost everyone was wearing his headrest cover on his head, and we were all laughing hysterically.

The Ephemeral Role Set

During the next several days spent traveling to Lydney, sightseeing in England and Wales, and training and playing, the roles that defined the tour behavior emerged and received public expression. The ephemeral role set consisted of four major roles, each related but not necessarily complementary. These roles were (a) the macho role, (b) the rugby player role, (c) the American tourist role, and (d) the personal role.

Macho Role

The macho role is the role exemplifying the kind of behavior described by Sheard and Dunning (1973) in their paper on the traditional social life of the rugby club. The role is characterized by (a) derogation of women and focus on women as sexual objects, (b) expressions of disdain for homosexuals and homosexual behavior, (c) reward for excessive drinking and antisocial behavior accompanying it, and (d) theft. Each of these elements was found both in the conduct of individuals and in the public discussions and recountings of events during the tour.

The pursuit of sex was a major concern of many of the players, and discussions of sexual adventures were the most popular elements of the daily recountings of the previous night's activities. That women were perceived as sexual objects was illustrated not only by the continuous catcalls directed from the bus to women on the street, but also by numerous more specific incidents, a few of which are described here.

> The first morning in Lydney the team assembled for training, and the first of what became daily recounting sessions began. AS, an older player and tour leader with a reputation for chasing women, especially young women, walked up and another team member said, "Well, AS, this tour's off to a better start than the last one," a reference to the fact that AS had picked up a girl the previous night. Another fellow chimed in, "Yeah, and she was half his age." A couple of days later, this same woman was with another player for the night. When AS was told of this the next day, he said matter-of-factly, "I think we oughta auction her off."
>
> After our last night in Lydney, the group gathered to board the bus and depart for Worcester. Everyone wanted to know how BM had made out with the woman who was "hitting on him" the night before. Bruce promised to tell the whole story on the bus. He went home with her only to find that she shared her flat with her sister and brother-in-law, whose presence drastically altered

the potential of the situation. So, having "struck out," BM wandered the streets for an hour until he found his way back to the hotel. One of the English players accompanying us said for all to hear, "I can't believe it. She fucked two guys at once just last week." BM's response was, "Oh, God, I've been turned down by a nympho." To add insult to injury, this woman showed up at the hotel at 10:30 the next morning to collect the T-shirt BM had promised her. AS quickly decreed, "No shirt given until after the act," which BM immediately shortened to, "Hump, shirt! Hump, shirt!" (a takeoff on a scene from a Monty Python movie).

On the team's first evening in Worcester, our hosts had arranged a boat ride on the Severn River with drinks, a band, and local women invited. By the time the ride ended about midnight, many of the Texas players had paired up with English women. Many of them went to a pub and stayed until early morning. When the team assembled for training the next morning and JB arrived, one player greeted him with, "Hey, Bardahl, I hear you got a blow job last night." JB responded, "Well, almost, but she had to go throw up." He then proceeded to explain that the woman had gotten extremely drunk, in fact, so drunk that when they were still at the pub she passed out in the women's room and he had to send someone in to revive her. Nevertheless, he had gone home with her and they had engaged in sex. He added that he had tried to get her to "do it" again the next morning, but she was too hung over to be interested.

LW, the youngest member of the tour party, was reputedly a virgin, and one of the group's goals was "to get LW laid." On the last night of the tour, he did have sex with an English girl. Back in the States, when he was asked how it was, he replied, "She was just like a jar of mayonnaise," repeating a phrase that was popular on the trip. His use of the phrase not only indicated the level of derogation of women but also showed that he had been effectively socialized into the macho role.

Derogation of homosexuals was less pronounced, perhaps because the group had no direct contact with known homosexuals. References to homosexuality took the form of self-mocking, with certain members of the group singled out for extra attention. For example:

When the group first boarded the bus, our English tour director, Mike Robbins, discussed the arrangements, mentioned the hard work AS had done in organizing the tour, and asked AS to take a bow. When AS stood in the aisle of the bus, instead of receiving applause, he was greeted by chants of "Blow job! Blow job!"

Later the same day, the group was tired from the exhausting flight, and players were beginning to doze off on the bus. The club president, LG, announced, "You'd better sleep while you can. This is about the only time you'll be safe with TG around."

Such comments were repeated daily during the tour.

As mentioned previously, heavy drinking had begun as soon as the flight from Texas was under way, and pub crawling was part of the daily schedule throughout the tour. On any given day, players would have a pint of beer at noon, a couple of pints at pub stops during the afternoon, and begin drinking more heavily after dinner, with some players continuing until almost dawn. Tales of drunken excess were repeated with almost as much delight as tales of sexual conquest.

> On the team's last night in Lydney, after the game had taken place and the party at the Lydney RFC clubhouse had ended about midnight, a group went to the Feather's Hotel bar and continued drinking. They drank until they finished all the beer in the bar about 5 a.m. BH passed out in the hotel corridor and was awakened at 8 a.m. by two maids. They were standing over him while one asked the other, "Do you think he's all right?" AS appeared at the field limping and with a gash on his face. The other players assumed he had been in a fight. As it turned out, he had been injured by his own roommate, SW, who threw him out of bed and then dropped the bedpost on his ankle. AS, SW, and others who were involved described with relish how they had "trashed out" the hotel.

Theft is institutionalized in rugby culture, but is generally restricted to objects belonging to opposing teams or individuals that have symbolic significance. A rugby player is likely to steal the kit bag of an opposing player or the flag of the opposing club, but he is unlikely to steal street signs or other public items, to shoplift, or to steal personal property from a host's home. The Texas players recognized that they could be victimized, and their tour kit bags were never left unguarded. These thefts are in addition to a great deal of bartering of mementos between individuals and institutionalized gift exchanges between host and visiting clubs. During the tour, the Texas players conspired to steal the flags of two host clubs from their clubhouses, and the players involved delighted in telling how the thefts had been accomplished. Members of the Worcester club also took great delight in showing us a whitetail deer head they had stolen from a Texas bar when they had been on tour in the United States.

Rugby Player Role

The rugby player role, the second element of the ephemeral role set, has to do with the individual's responsibilities and performance as a member of the athletic team. Although American teams touring England do not expect to go undefeated, they do expect to be competitive, to give a good account of themselves, and to win some of their games. Rugby football is a game that requires a high level of physical fitness, a considerable degree of specialized skill at passing, kicking, and tackling, and a willingness to be involved in physical contact. During the tour, the team held 1- to 1-1/2-

hour training sessions on days when they were not playing. Frequent discussion among the players was about rugby strategy, about what we could expect from the opposing teams, and about the selection of players for each game.

Successful performance of the rugby player role was complicated by several factors. First, not all members of the tour were regular club players, and thus the ideal level of teamwork was not present. Second, players were called upon to play a relatively large number of games in a short period of time, on the average of a game every fourth day, which increased the number of nagging injuries and hindered performance. Third, the fatigue produced by the tour and the lack of a regular daily routine made it somewhat more difficult to prepare psychologically for the games. As a result, performance on the field is not emphasized as much on tour as it is during the regular season at home, but each player is still expected to give his all on the field and to play his position competently.

American Tourist Role

Members of the tour are aware that they are representatives of their club, their state, and their country while traveling abroad. Because numerous English teams have toured Texas and been exposed to "Texas hospitality," the players know they will be hosted well, and they are obligated to participate enthusiastically in the planned events, even if they are tired, hung over, or injured. For many members of the group, the tour is their first trip outside the United States, and they feel some personal obligation to make the most of it, in other words, to expose themselves to the tourist attractions of the area and to learn something about British culture. In addition, tour members want to be well thought of by their personal hosts; they want to be good guests, not offensive, demanding "ugly Americans."

Personal Role

Each member of the group developed a personal role, that is, a set of behavioral expectations that applied to him alone, based on the group's knowledge of his personality and personal history. This personal role tied the individual to a nontour identity, but identity is related to characteristics relevant to rugby and the rugby club, and not to occupation or other dominant roles. Thus AS is a hell raiser and chaser of women, TG is a bad ass likely to get into fights, JB is the song leader, and GK is "a brick shy of a load." The individual in question may accept this role and incorporate it into his identity, or he may seek to refute it, but the set of behavioral expectations remains, and his behavior is judged accordingly.

Playing the Roles

Each member of the tour party must simultaneously enact each of these four elements of the ephemeral role set, although some elements may be more important to some individuals than to others. In other words, some tour members may place the greatest emphasis on drinking and chasing women; others may be concerned primarily with the rugby games themselves; still others may especially enjoy the sightseeing and meeting non-rugby-playing locals. Nevertheless, regardless of personal emphasis, the structure and schedule of the tour requires that each individual pay at least some attention to each of these elements.

Although these elements combine to form a role set, they are not always complementary. Indeed, certain conflicts are inevitable within the role set. For example, the macho role may conflict with both the player role and the tourist role. Although the rugby saying "Try by day, score by night" indicates a congruence between the macho and player roles, obviously too much drinking and late night carousing will interfere with fitness and playing ability. An example follows:

> On the club's first full day in Worcester, we gathered at the Worcester RFC grounds in the morning for training. We trained seriously, being aware that the Worcester teams were not as strong as Lydney's and that we could win the games if we played well. After practice we had a beer at the clubhouse, then loaded on the bus to go to Stratford-on-Avon. After only a few miles, we stopped at a pub for a "mandatory beer stop." Mike Robbins, who was our local guide for the day, bought a round of beer, and we all drank because "you never turn down free beer." Then we proceeded to the Bell Pub in Shottery, just a few blocks from Anne Hathaway's house, where we had lunch and more beer. After two hours in Stratford-on-Avon, we returned to Worcester in time for happy hour at the Guifford Hotel bar. We then went to still another pub for a predinner drink and to another pub for dinner. After dinner many of the players went pub crawling for a couple more hours. We suspected that we were the victims of "coarse rugby," the practice by which nonplaying club members entertain their guests to excess, rendering them incapable of playing well.

Thus the relationship between the macho role and player role is a complicated one. They are partly complementary and partly in conflict. Playing well proves one's masculinity and provides access to women, but too much attention to women and drink reduces one's ability to play well. This complicated relationship exists outside of rugby as well. Gileau (1984) has described another athletic subculture with an exaggerated element of machismo—the weight room. Her observations of serious weight lifters, many of whom used competitive bodybuilders as role models, indicated that heavy drinking and drug use were common even though they were known to interfere with athletic performance. Indeed, in the weight room as on the rugby field, one's manhood was proven by one's ability to push oneself through a difficult workout in spite of the fact that one had spent the previous night drinking heavily and chasing women. Likewise, Mitchell

(1983) reports that English rock climbers consider climbing with a hangover a praiseworthy activity.[3]

The macho role may also conflict with the tourist role, for in acting according to the standards of machismo, the player may offend locals and earn the moniker of "ugly American." One incident from the tour makes this conflict especially clear.

> In Lydney, AS and AA had already begun to try to get LW laid. They had found two English women who agreed to take LW home, but the women later changed their minds and began to drive away. AS screamed at them through the car window, while AA sprawled across the hood and made grotesque faces at the driver. The driver said to the other girl, "My God! He looks just like a bloody ape." Later the two girls were overheard talking about the incident. The first said, "I hate all Americans." The second replied, "I don't. I just hate AS."

Likewise, the player role and the tourist role may result in conflict because the individual's desire to perform well may lead him to seek solitude and rest in order to prepare both psychologically and physically for the upcoming game, which may be interpreted at least as lack of interest and possibly as rudeness. On the other hand, the player who participates fully in the sightseeing provided by the hosts may feel unprepared for competition, as my field notes reflecting my personal feelings attest.

> On our first full day in Lydney, we began with a lengthy training session in the morning, followed by a bus trip to the Boat Inn on the Welsh border for a pub lunch. On the way back to Lydney we stopped to see the ruins of Tinturn Abbey and Chepstow Castle. We returned to Lydney only one hour before the Social XV were to play their match. I had to change clothes and walk from my host's house to the club—about a 15 minute walk. I arrived at the clubhouse only about 10 minutes before game time. The team was in the dressing room discussing strategy, stretching, running in place, and "getting fired up." When we ran onto the field I felt dizzy and completely unprepared to play.

Setting Role-Playing Priorities

The potential conflicts between these various roles were managed through a system of prioritizing; while each individual may have had his own set of priorities, as mentioned previously, group discussions and activities produced a set of group priorities.

During the tour itself, neither the macho role nor the player role was clearly more important than the other. Indeed, what was clear was that both were important and that the macho role would not be subordinated to the player role. No curfews or other rules regulated the behavior of the players. However, the players did regulate their own behavior somewhat, reserving their most excessive behavior for nights following games and for the final night in a particular host city. An example of this self-regulation is provided from field notes.

> On Saturday morning the team assembled at the Worcester Guild Hall to be formally welcomed by the Mayor. Both teams were to play against Worcester RFC at 3 p.m. Although we had been drinking most of the previous day, and I knew some of the players had been out late the night before, there was virtually no discussion of the night's activities. Everyone was neatly dressed, well behaved, and attentive—quite subdued as a group. I think most of the players had their minds on the upcoming games.

In retrospect, a number of indications showed that by the time the tour was complete, the macho role had taken precedence over the player role. First, the club president occasionally announced fines that had been assessed against members of the tour party. Fines were never assessed for poor play; rather they were always assessed for behaviors relating to the macho role. For example, the first fines levied were as follows, even though both sides had been beaten badly in Lydney:

> Several members of the club were fined for sleeping on tour. SW was fined for his excessive drunkenness on the flight. BS was fined for "trying to get it on the plane, and failing." BM was fined for "messing up a sure thing." And JB was fined for "the crime of bestiality," a reference to the physical appearance of the girl he had been with in Lydney.

Another indication of prioritizing appeared at the tour party that took place approximately 1 month after the group returned to Texas. A central feature of this party was the showing of large numbers of slides taken by members of the group. The slides consisted of group portraits at various locations, photos of landmarks and scenery, photographs of social activities, and action photos of the games. The reactions to the slides and commentaries on them indicated the greater significance of the macho role.

> The photos that received the loudest comments, including greater laughter, were those that touched on the macho role. Photos of players with English women invariably drew whistles, laughter, and so on. Often the remarks were humorous insults to members of the group, such as the laughter when CP was pictured talking with a fat woman, or even self-deprecatory, as when AS remarked about a photo of a woman both he and LW had laid, "Yeah, LW and I had a lot in common on this trip." Photos of animals always elicited comments concerning bestiality, for example, the pictures

of GK and JB riding a donkey. Photos concerning the rugby action were never commented on in terms of skill or strategy, even when they pictured the Texas team on the attack. Rather, they elicited comments about homosexuality whenever two or more players were stopped by the camera in what appeared to be a compromising position.

It is not clear whether this emphasis on the macho role was a kind of rationalization of the club's failures on the field (the club's record on tour was 3 wins and 7 losses, and many players felt we should have won at least 2 additional games) or the result of socialization that took place during the tour, during which the players learned from their English hosts that the macho role was supposed to be more important than the player role. That the latter is a strong possibility is suggested by a humorous book written by former British Lion captain Mike Burton, which summarizes the accomplishments of a fictitious English club as follows:

Season 1981–82:

Hotels wrecked 11, police helmets captured 4 . . .
Pissed 34 times, hopelessly pissed 52 times, don't remember 36 times . . .
Arrested twice, Chinese runouts 17, Indian runouts 19, sent off once, Legovers 23 . . .

We've *got* to do better next year! (Burton, 1981)

The tourist role was clearly subordinated to the other two roles, particularly the macho role. Our hosts were apparently aware of the potential conflict between these roles, having themselves either participated in rugby tours or hosted previous rugby tourists, and they seemed ambivalent about their role in helping us to develop an appreciation for their history and culture. One method for managing this potential conflict was to focus on sightseeing that was related to the macho and/or player roles. Country pubs were frequently on the itinerary. When we went to Cardiff, we drove by Cardiff Castle, but we spent two hours at Cardiff Arms Park, home of the Welsh Rugby Union and one of the great rugby stadia in the world, and the Cardiff RFC and their museum, where we saw the jerseys of great players and were reminded of rugby history. Another method of dealing with this ambiguity was to mention something of cultural significance and then make light of it, or reinterpret it in terms consistent with these other roles. While I observed numerous instances of this tactic during the tour, one example stands out.

After we had eaten our lunch at the Bell Pub in Shottery, Mike Robbins encouraged us to tour Anne Hathaway's cottage just a few blocks away. When a number of players indicated their preference for another pint of beer at the pub, Robbins explained that Anne Hathaway had been William Shakespeare's mistress, and said, "When you see the little bench where he did it to her, it's quite remarkable, really."

For their part, the players took active and polite interest in seeing and hearing about local history and culture. Although I got the impression that many of them were genuinely interested in this aspect of the tour (for instance, many took numerous photographs and purchased reading material related to historic sites), they were careful to publicly conceal their personal interest. For example,

> We stopped at Tinturn Abbey outside of Lydney, and everyone piled off the bus to walk through the ruins and take photographs. JN remarked for all to hear as we unloaded, "Holy shit! It's even older than the Alamo."

Publicly, then, by the end of the tour a hierarchy of tour roles had been established, with the macho role being most important, the player role somewhat less important, and the tourist role least important. Given this hierarchy, I would argue that the macho role has the most shared meanings attached to it, and it is on this role that I will focus in trying to explain the significance of rugby tour participation as an ephemeral role.

English Club Rugby and Dissociation From Dominant Roles

To recapitulate, Sheard and Dunning (1973) argue that the rugby club as a male preserve developed as a defense against the increasing emancipation of middle- and upper-middle class women in British society. Also, the exaggerated machismo of the rugby social life gradually dissipated because of (a) the economic needs of the clubs requiring the integration of women into club activities, and (b) more general changes in attitudes regarding gender roles. Sheard and Dunning (1973) also hint that the rugby tour provides an opportunity for the original form of rugby behavior to reassert itself, saying,

> It is true that obscene songs and rowdy behavior still occur in rugby circles, but increasingly, they are being limited to special occasions. The "hot pot suppers" and Eastern tours are, in most cases, the only situations where the rugby club still tends frequently to get out of hand. (p. 22)

Drawing on my limited observation of English rugby and the Texas tour, I would like to comment on the declining rowdiness of rugby behavior in general and on the special place of the rugby tour.

Although Sheard and Dunning are undoubtedly correct in linking changes in rugby club behavior to economic and gender role factors, I would like to suggest another factor that is involved, one directly related to the enactment of "ephemeral roles" and indirectly related to the growth and institutionalization of the game of rugby football. That factor is the structure of the community and the degree to which it allows rugby players to dissociate themselves from their dominant roles. A comparison of the Texas tour party's experiences in Lydney and Worcester will serve to illustrate this factor.

Lydney is a town of approximately 8,000 people, located in far western England on the Severn estuary and very near the Welsh border. Lydney gives the visitor the impression of being a large village; one can easily walk across it on foot, and when I walked through town with my host, he greeted many persons on the street by name. The Lydney RFC is located very near the center of the town, adjacent to the Cricket Club and a large public park, and clearly the rugby club is an important recreational facility, not just for its members, but for the community as a whole. Our games had been advertised informally by placing hand-written posters throughout the town, and the Texas players were recognized and greeted wherever they went. The games were played on Tuesday and Wednesday evenings, and on each occasion the clubhouse was packed and there were constant lines at the three bars in the club. Local women had been encouraged to attend by advertising the postgame parties as "Grab a Yank Night," a band was provided, and on Tuesday evening the "world's champion beer chugger" performed for charity. My impression was that most of those in attendance were not really rugby fans; the atmosphere was more like a community festival, similar in mood to a public street dance in a Texas town. *None* of the behavior traditionally associated with rugby parties (i.e., bawdy songs, games, etc.) was evident at the Lydney clubhouse, although, as has already been shown, levels of alcohol consumption were very high and sexual matchmaking was active.

In contrast, Worcester is a "county city" of over 100,000 people, decidedly urban in lifestyle, with heavy traffic, modern shopping, and a faster and more impersonal pace. The Worcester RFC grounds are located at the outskirts of the city, several miles from downtown; they were newly built there about 8 years ago when the club sold its valuable inner-city property. Although the games were announced and subsequently reported in the local newspapers, very few people seemed to know much about them, and virtually no spectators were present at the Saturday afternoon games. When the games ended at about 5 p.m. a lull of about 2 hours occurred before many of the nonplaying club members arrived. When the partying got underway, it contained all the elements of traditional rugby culture—bawdy songs, obscene mimicry, drinking games. Gradually, these gave way to a more conventional party pattern as a band began to play around 9 p.m. Most of the women in attendance were the wives, girlfriends, or daughters of club members, or women that had been invited by the Texas players. The social scene here, in contrast to that at Lydney, clearly took the form of a private party.

A number of factors, including the economic and gender role aspects mentioned by Sheard and Dunning, could account for the vastly different social scenes found in these two rugby clubs. First, Lydney has a history of recent rugby success, whereas the Worcester club has been relatively weak in recent years, and this may account for the varying degree of community support. Second, Lydney is immediately adjacent to the area of South Wales, which is the producer of many excellent rugby players and clubs and where the fans follow rugby with religious fervor (Bale, 1982; Gammon, 1976). The Lydney RFC play many fixtures against Welsh clubs, and the Welsh approach has likely influenced them to some degree. However, I would argue that in addition to these factors the social behavior of the rugby club is related to the role of the club in the larger community, which is in turn related to demographic characteristics of the community itself.

In Lydney, the rugby club has assiduously cultivated for itself a place as a community recreational center. In part this is a matter of economic necessity. In a small community the critical mass of rugby players necessary to support a club on dues alone is probably not available, so wider community support must be developed, either in the form of social memberships or through attendance at parties where alcohol is sold, raffles conducted, and so forth. However, in another sense the Lydney rugby club probably had little choice but to become a public resource. In a closely knit community of this size, where overlapping organizational memberships are many and one's status as rugby player (or cricket or soccer or tennis player) is a significant element of one's overall position in the community, the kind of complete dissociation from dominant roles that would allow one to engage in traditional rugby behavior in a completely uninhibited way is impossible to achieve. On the other hand, in Worcester, which is larger and more impersonal and where one's status as a rugby player has little bearing on one's larger status in the community, relatively complete dissociation is possible, and the rugby social behavior manifests itself in its more pure form. Thus we find that the meanings attributable to a given recreational behavior may be contingent on the ability to separate that behavior both spatially and socially from other behavior patterns (Hilliard & Zurcher, 1978).

This situation suggests that the declining purity of the traditional rugby social behavior is associated with the increasing institutionalization of the sport. As more emphasis is placed on winning, and as local players gain stature as representatives of their club and community in regional, national, and international competition, the role of the rugby player shifts from that of an ephemeral role to that of a dominant role. Both players and administrators then become concerned about the reputation of the game and hope to solidify its place as a serious athletic endeavor. That this is important not only in the United Kingdom but in the United States as well is indicated by the remarks of a Texas club president.

> The USA Union has really been coming down on roguish behavior. Clubs are changing the image. Partying, unfortunately, is what goes in the press. It's hard for people outside the sport to under-

stand. You're there for the sport. It's a sporting fraternity, but it's also a social atmosphere. (Schwartz, 1984:165)

Symbolic Aspects of the Macho Role

The dissociation from dominant roles, or lack of it, that is so important to ordinary rugby social behavior also helps explain the special place of the rugby tour in rugby social life. Because of the relatively complete dissociation from ordinary roles, the rugby tourists are able to emphasize the macho elements of rugby culture. Yet the question remains, What purpose is served by the public sharing of these macho themes?

The conduct and certainly the discussions of the rugby tour participants are similar to that found in other all male settings—military barracks, lower-class street corner hangouts, and fraternal lodges—that are common in both American and British cultures. Thus a full understanding of the significance of the rugby tour would have to be developed within the context of this category of "male preserve" activities; this is a larger analysis than I wish to undertake at this time. In any case, in spite of their similarities, each male preserve has its own specific argot, ritual, and meaning. The rugby tour is a form of male preserve, participated in primarily by single, college-educated, white-collar and skilled blue-collar men aged 20 to 35. I would argue that the rugby tour offers these men an excellent opportunity to express concerns and experiment with new gender roles closely associated with the gender roles they are experiencing in their everyday lives.

These men increasingly find themselves involved in a new style of gender relations in which, in contrast to the traditional macho role that cast men as sexual aggressors and women as sexual objects, both men and women may become either pursuer or pursued.[4] These changing gender relations are likely to produce a certain amount of ambivalence, particularly among those older players who went through adolescence when the more traditional norms were still in force. The rugby tour, then, becomes a stage on which the players may express their understanding of the new gender relations, both to one another and to the rest of the tour participants. The constant references to homosexuality, bestiality, and so forth may serve to reinforce the notion that the traditional macho role is no longer the norm.[5] The tales of sexual conquest that relate to the traditional macho roles are balanced by self-deprecating tales of sexual failure, which serve both to remind one of the risks involved in the new gender relations and to remove women from their pedestals and represent them as deceitful, manipulative, and untrustworthy.

At the same time, the tour offers individuals an opportunity to experiment with these new gender relations in a suspended, and therefore virtually risk-free, environment. On the rugby tour, the sexual marketplace is open, the needs of the players complement the needs of sexually aggressive local women (brought to the parties by advertisements of "Grab a Yank Night"), and potential emotional complications are minimized by the "here today, gone tomorrow" nature of the tour. Thus the rugby tour becomes a kind of caricature of sexual relations in the larger society, intensified by the short duration of the tour and purified by the suspension of ordinary roles.[6]

The representation of gender roles through the rugby tour parallels other cases observed by anthropologists such as the Balinese cockfight as a representation of kin and status networks (Geertz, 1973) and the cricket festival with its attendant betting as an expression of the underlying political structure of Bermuda (Manning, 1981). In the Bermudan cricket festival, the carnival atmosphere and its lowering of inhibitions allows for a temporary inversion of the status system. Similarly, the dissociation from conventional roles during the rugby tour allows the player both to experiment with new social roles and to express their understanding of those roles, but in a playful way and in a setting where one is not accountable for one's behavior according to ordinary standards.

Notes

1. My wife and I met the group when they landed in London and accompanied them for the first week of the tour, during which the party made stops in Lydney and Worcester and played two games at each site. Although I had not played regularly with the club for several years, my wife and I were known to most of the tour participants, by reputation if not personally. The fact that I played in two games and that I was a long-time member and former leader of the club helped confirm my status as a legitimate member of the group. However, I did not have complete access to all the happenings of the tour, for two reasons. First, because the tour participants were split into smaller groups for billeting, it was impossible to observe all the groups simultaneously; that is, periods during each day occurred when the tour was split into numerous small groups. However, there were also periods during the day when the entire group was assembled together, namely training sessions and bus travel, either for sightseeing or to our next destination. Each time the group gathered, there was ''time to kill'' as we waited for those who were late; this time turned out to be an excellent opportunity for members of the group to share experiences from the previous evening and to make observations and comments, which gave an indication of the meanings they attached to the tour. Indeed, during these times tour culture was most visible, in the sense that shared meanings appeared and were reinforced. My analysis will be based as much on observation of these recountings and discussions as on observation of behavior per se. Indeed, I would argue that it is this sharing and recounting that gives meaning to the behaviors of various tour participants. The second limitation on my opportunity to observe tour behavior is related to the first and concerns the presence of my wife on the tour. Because attempts were made to match hosts and guests for billeting, and because it was assumed that married couples would be somewhat more sedate in their leisure preferences, we were excluded from some of the wilder

late night drinking and carousing. This was not a serious problem, as the tales were routinely retold the next morning. A more serious potential problem was that the behavior I was able to observe directly would be biased in some way by the presence of a woman companion, given the kinds of themes Sheard and Dunning (1973) attribute to rugby culture. I do not believe this was the case to any great degree. First of all, because two other women were present, tour participants very quickly developed a mechanism for dealing with their presence—they were treated as if they were "one of the guys." As I shall indicate in the body of the paper, no attempt was made to protect the women on the tour from exposure to drunken excess, open discussion of sexual experiences, and so on. On the other hand, as best I could tell, no attempts were made to exaggerate these factors to "gross out" or otherwise influence the women. Their presence was taken in stride and did not appreciably alter the behavior of the tour participants.

2. It should be mentioned that each member of the tour, as part of the tour package, received two game jerseys, a number of T-shirts, a warm-up suit, a kit bag, and several insignias. These mementos served both as personal souvenirs and as articles to be bartered with members of English teams. The role of souvenirs in the construction of meanings associated with recreational activities is discussed in Mitchell (1983).

3. This pattern is reminiscent of Feldman's (1968) analysis of heroin use in black neighborhoods dominated by the "stand-up cat" as an ideal social type. Feldman argues that the "side bet on becoming a stand-up cat" by proving that one can handle a drug that has disabled other "stand-up cats" leads to the rapid spread of drug use in such neighborhoods. In a culture where competition for status according to traditional standards of masculinity is extreme, perhaps it is not enough to be an outstanding athlete or a heavy drinker; perhaps one must be both. This factor may even be an overlooked reason for the reported very high levels of drug use among professional athletes.

4. An interesting commentary on the new gender roles is provided in a recent segment of the television movie review program "Sneak Previews." Discussing the new sex symbols of the 80s, the hosts compared such female stars as Kate Capshaw and Kathleen Turner to earlier stars like Marilyn Monroe; they suggested that today's female stars can be openly aggressive, unlike the previous era's, who had to be seductive, yet vulnerable. Similarly, it was argued that while earlier male stars such as Clark Gable were seen as attractive because they were strong, fearless, and so forth, many of today's new male stars such as Mel Gibson are attractive first and foremost in a physical sense.

5. In 17 years of playing rugby, I have never been approached by a homosexual at a rugby function, nor have I ever heard any stories about male homosexuals involved in the rugby scene, though it is widely asserted that a high incidence of lesbianism occurs among female rugby players. Thus I seriously doubt that the references to homosexuality express concern about homosexuality per se.

6. While some players took a much more active part than others in the sexual marketplace, none attempted to establish an alternate cultural form for the tour, I heard no complaints about the active players' behavior, and everyone seemed eager to hear the tales and participate in their retelling. In this respect, the active players were analogous to the "jailers" in John Irwin's (1970) study of California prisons, who participated actively in the inmate economy and status system and, as a result, had an inordinate amount of influence on the prison subculture.

Acknowledgments

Portions of this paper were presented at the annual meeting of The Association for the Anthropological Study of Play in Washington, DC in March 1985. I am indebted to Louis A. Zurcher, Jr., Gwen K. Neville, T. Walter Herbert, and two anonymous TAASP reviewers for their criticisms of an earlier version of this paper.

References

Bale, J. (1982). *Sport and place*. Lincoln: University of Nebraska Press.

Burton, M. (1981). *Tight heads, loose balls*. London: Queen Anne Press.

Dunning, E., & Sheard, K. (1979). *Barbarians, gentlemen, and players*. New York: NYU Press.

Feldman, H. (1968). Ideological supports to becoming and remaining a heroin addict. *Journal of Health and Social Behavior*, **9**, 131–139.

Gammon, C. (1976, November 1). Feed me till I want no more. *Sports Illustrated*, pp. 36–39.

Geertz, C. (1973). *The interpretation of cultures*. New York: Basic Books.

Gileau, J. (1984). *The Nautilus experience: A study in interactions*. Unpublished manuscript, Southwestern University, Georgetown, TX.

Hilliard, D., & Zurcher, L.A., Jr. (1978, October). The temporal segregation of activities and their meanings in leisure sports settings. *Leisure Today*, 26–30.

Huizinga, J. (1955). *Homo ludens: A study of the play element in culture*. Boston: Beacon.

Irwin, J. (1970). *The felon*. Englewood Cliffs, NJ: Prentice-Hall.

Manning, F. (1981). Celebrating cricket: The symbolic construction of Caribbean politics. *American Ethnologist*, **8**, 616–632.

Mitchell, R.G. (1983). *Mountain experience*. Chicago: University of Chicago Press.

Riesman, D., & Denney, R. (1951). Football in America: A study in culture diffusion. *American Quarterly, 3,* 309–319.

Schwartz, M. (1984, September). Blood brothers. *D Magazine,* 163–166.

Sheard, K., & Dunning, E. (1973). The rugby football club as a type of "male preserve": Some sociological notes. *International Review of Sport Sociology, 8*(3), 5–24.

Zurcher, L.A., Jr. (1968). Social psychological functions of ephemeral roles: A disaster work crew. *Human Organization, 27,* 281–297.

Zurcher, L.A., Jr. (1970). The "friendly" poker game: A study of an ephemeral role. *Social Forces, 49,* 173–186.

Zurcher, L.A., Jr. (1983). *Social roles: Conformity, conflict, and creativity.* Beverly Hills, CA: Sage Publications.

Contra Dance in New York: Longways for as Many as Will

Judy Levine

In New York City, with its mixture of cultures, what type of shared cultural experience can a folk dance be? Contra dances are the basis for an active social community in New York; this study explores the expressive ordering of the New York City contra dance experience, and attempts to identify what in the contra form itself contributes to the behavior I observed. Contra dance in New York is centered around dances sponsored by the Country Dance and Song Society in the gymnasium of Duane Methodist Church in Manhattan on Friday and Saturday evenings. This study is based on 6 months of observation and participation in that experience. Judith Lynne Hanna writes that "because dances tend to be integral parts of their host sociocultural systems, dances in urban areas manifest urban patterns of social differentiation and interaction" (Hanna, 1979:237). Contra dancing is not a particularly urban form, but it has found a comfortable niche in New York City. What is its appeal?

History

Contra dancing is a geometrical dance form in which movements are done with a partner in a line. John Playford's *The English Dancing Master* (Dean-Smith, 1957) was the first time community dances, usually learned by watching or doing, had been published (he continued publishing new editions, with his sons, until 1728). According to Nevell, author of *A Time To Dance* (1977), Playford's book "changed the very nature of country dance, by turning it into a commodity. For the first time in history, this simple part of English folk life became salable [sic]" (Nevell, 1977:24). The rise in popularity of the contra, or longways,[1] form, can be traced by the increasing proportion of contras to other forms in Playford's manuals; each edition contained more than the previous one (Wood, 1949). Playford's publishing made the contra form accessible, and, therefore, survivable. Accessible also meant accessible to the dancing master, or teacher, who slowly changed the form into one of a more genteel nature (Wilson, 1811). The dual nature of the contra as the dance of the peasant and the dance of the nobility provides historical precedent for the issue of contra's adaptability and survival potential. After the War of 1812, most of America denounced any traces of English culture and turned to the French quadrille (later to become the American square dance). Contras survived in America mainly in small rural pockets in New England (Holt, 1907; Page, 1976).

In 1915, Cecil Sharp came to America. Collecting old English music and dances, he inspired several Americans to form the English Folk Dance Society, centered in New York City. In 1940, this society was renamed simply The Country Dance Society, and it remains the foremost center for country dancing in the United States (Horosko, 1965). Sharp used Playford's published manuals as a guide to reviving contra dances but warned that "our aim in reviving these dances should be to keep them fresh and natural and, to this end, to avoid the use of elaborate steps, together with the tricks and mannerisms of the theatre or of the drawing room" (Sharp, 1924:23). Differing from Sharp's point of view, but equally insistent about reviving the "old" dances was Henry Ford. Ford despised jazz, as well as what he considered to be "ultra modern dancing" (Nevell, 1977:63). He coauthored a book in 1926 with Benjamin Lovett on country dancing, and went on a lecture tour of the United States, determined to champion the pure form of innocent enjoyment he considered country dancing to be. However, according to Nevell, "Ford's sources were clearly not the original folk dances of this country but rather the updated, sophisticated versions of the country dances that emphasized morality and manner more than exercise and community spirit . . . he failed to understand that the nature of the dancing he liked so well was originally far more spontaneous and free than he allowed" (Nevell, 1977:65).

Contra dancing has been able to change and bend with the times and contexts within which it is done (Gadd, 1937a, 1937b, 1956, 1957, 1958, 1959). On the simplest level, the dances that are done now (as opposed to in the Playford era) are simpler forms with stronger rhythms. American contras are not as sedate or refined as contemporary or old English contras. American contras were described to me as rowdier, with more stomping and fancy moves, and as much more relaxed than the English dances. Contras have had a flexible evolution in the process of traveling from Playford's England to current America (Rosoff, 1977); this flexibility is one of the factors in contra's openness of response to the needs of an urban environment.

Form and Description

In 1956, Ricky Holden, author of *The Contra Dance Book*, defined a contra as "one of the six geometric forms of the American Folk Dance, in which the dancers form in 'sets' of two parallel lines as for the Virginia Reel, and go through a certain sequence of figures, repeated over and over. Each repetition results in some of the dancers' progressing toward one end of the set and the others' moving toward the other end. If the sequence is repeated enough times every dancer eventually progresses to each end and finally back where he started" (Holden, 1956:1). This definition contains all of the elements of the contra form. The repeatable figures (figures refer to the movements that are the basic contra steps) and progressions down (or up) the line, as well as the form of a double line itself, combine to create a dance that is simple, accessible, and social.

Contra lines are composed of active and inactive couples, either alternating active and inactive, or having a ratio of one active couple to two inactives. Generally, all men stand in one line facing women in another line, but in some dances every other couple switches lines so that men and women alternate in the same line. Dances are generally phrased to 32 bars of music, with each figure taking either 4 or 8 measures to complete. Then, the entire 32 bars are repeated again and again.

Lady of the Lake is a typical and well-known contra (Tolman & Page, 1937:86), and I quote it here for its expression of the simplicity of movement units, easy management of the progression (during castoff one changes places with the couple below), the example of dancing with not only your own partner but the one next to you as well, and the walking down the center and back, at which time you get to see everyone in your line and they get to see you.

Lady of the Lake
music: Speed the Plow

Contra Formation.................six or eight couples in a set

First couple cross over, balance and swing the one below	8 bars
First couple balance and swing partner in the center	8 bars
First couple down the center and back	8 bars
Cast off, right and left	8 bars
Third and fifth couples also start the dance	

In the longways for as many as will form of contra, sets are not limited to an arbitrary number of couples, but expand to fill the entire length of the room. Curt Sachs felt that "the entire dance was based on the smooth interweaving of the figures and the harmonious co-operation of the couples" (Sachs, 1937:421). The geometrical aspect of a contra dance, that of figures interweaving, is one that is not seen by the dancers themselves, but it has great significance for the sociability contained in the form.

Contra dances are run by callers. The caller is the orchestrator of the evening; he or she not only teaches the steps, patterns, and geometry of the dances, but by the tone of his or her voice he or she also gives dancers the energy to dance. A caller influences the way people new to contra dancing feel about themselves. Callers give hints of preferred style to newcomers—styles of communication as well as styles of dance. At the same time the caller encourages experienced dancers to maintain an open policy of helpfulness to new dancers. One caller I observed stopped in the middle of an evening and announced, "Contra dancing is not like brain surgery. Here, if you make a mistake, it's okay." This dictating of attitudes to others is important in maintaining the open sociality that is at the heart of contra dancing.

At the end of a longways dance a caller will ask people to pick another partner and re-form the lines. By having to switch partners (most people do follow the caller's instructions), dancers get to meet many different people. In the longways formation itself, a dancer is able to visit all along the line, and several figures involve walking down the line, turning, and coming back.

Contra dancing evolved as a social dance. American dancing, I was told by a caller, "is a very social thing. We're not as worried about the technique of it." The fact that sociability is unquestionably more important than technique is an important factor in contra's appeal. Historically, contras were a way of courting and getting to know a person. Checking out how a potential partner danced was important, and even today several dancers talk about finding someone they moved well with, and the electricity that goes on between them. In a contra, a dancer can meet and have contact with any number of people as he or she goes up or down the set. In the longways form, lines are broken into sets of four (two couples), which are constantly changing as the progression changes your place on the line. Only your partner remains the same. This can give those so inclined an opportunity to flirt with almost everyone in the line. The weaving in and out of the figures with members of the set is also a form of social interchange. One dancer felt that dancing with everyone on the floor alleviated the tension of "picking up" a person and that it was a good way to meet women. Another dancer articulated the interrelationship of dance form and social desire: "The pure form makes it workable, but people go there to meet people. The form allows that to happen."

Form and Sociability

The element of one-on-one contact within a group is an important factor in contras (Page, 1953). Within a contra dance, a dancer can maintain the autonomy of his or her own partner without the type of sexual tension of a disco. As well, one-on-one contact with strangers is less threatening than one-to-group contact. Having a partner provides a personal stability, and, conversely, having contact with a line within a partner format makes the partner relationship less intense. Contra dancing is not the dancer within a crowd; rather, it is the dancer in a series of constantly shifting one-on-one dancing relationships.

The contra dance figures themselves are often concerned with greeting. Several are modified handshakes with steps or turns added (the allemande and balance). In one figure, the lines themselves go forward and back and greet each other. The swing, a modified waltz position in which a couple turns together at great speed, involves a deepening of that greeting, and I have been told that a dancer knows a lot about another dancer by the way that they swing together.

One New England caller feels that "each movement or change is a communication between dancers that has a specific meaning" (Nevell,

1977:129). Contra dance is very involved with communication, both visual and sensory. One dancer said, ''The people you don't want to dance with are people who don't really touch you.'' Dancers also talk about giving weight, which involves leaning slightly away from one's partner, so that each person can feel his own weight and that of his partner. I feel giving weight is a metaphor for the social relationships and cooperation between dancers that contra requires. One caller felt that giving weight expressed reassurance, attraction, and acknowledgment. Another caller said of contra dancing: ''It is a social dance, and if you're doing a social dance you establish contact in some way with the person you're dancing with. . . . You are dancing with *someone*. When the first corners change places, you're changing with some *person*, not just from point A to point B.'' This quality of truly dancing with everyone in your line, built into the form by opposite couples and active and inactive formations, leads to the feeling as one dancer told me, that ''it's not just dancing, it's part of a community.''

Part of the attraction of contra dancing is that it is a group experience. This group experience differentiates contra dancing from couple dances, as well as from discos where the focus is on the individual or the individual and partner. In a contra you are constantly meeting new people and dancing with them. Square dances, on the other hand, are a finite unit, and tend to be much more cliquish (Rossoff, 1977). In a square, you can choose the people you will dance with, and that allows each set to be exclusive. Squares also tend, by the nature of their figures, to be more individual partner-oriented. In Balkan and other ethnic folk dances the circle formation is prevalent. The circle tends to be less anonymous, because the dancer can be seen by the entire group all of the time, but also less personal, with a lack of one-to-one contact.

Because of this one-to-one contact with many dancers, one caller felt that contra dancing breeds tolerance and open-mindedness. Due to the progression, the dancer must learn to enjoy his opposites and not just his partners. ''When you're dancing with a whole line of people, you'd better find something to enjoy with everyone your dancing with,'' she said. She also talked about the relative lack of class in contras. ''Once you commit yourself to a contra dance, you have no choice about who you dance with as they come along.'' This commitment to whomever comes along is a central feature in not only the sociality of contras, but in the attitude toward strangers as well. Newcomers feel that the experienced dancers help them out and do not make them feel inadequate. Within a contra line, the breaking up into immediate sets of four makes social interchange manageable, and in New York City that is no small feat among strangers.

Community

The dances that I observed in New York were open dances. A diversity of people was present, very few of whom had a real idea of one another's background. One caller told me, ''There's no necessity of identifying people beyond the fact that you dance . . . you aren't required to have any particular credentials. It's the most relaxed way you can meet people besides a folk music club, but there is a lot more at stake in performing well. Here you can be quite a mediocre performer and still enjoy it." The contra dances I saw also cut across age levels, and very few social activities exist in New York City that those in their 20s and those in their 60s can do with equal ease. At a contra dance, one doesn't have to come with a partner, and many people don't.

If, as Hanna says, "Dances in urban areas often provide adaptive vehicles for coping with personal or group need" (Hanna, 1979:227), what are the needs of New York City residents that these social aspects of contra dancing fulfill? For one thing, this activity breaks up the city into manageable groups of strangers. People are encouraged to enjoy themselves openly, and the sociability and tolerance provide a place of belonging. Contra dancing supplies a home with warmth in the middle of New York, and several people used the image of a family when talking about contra dancing.

The main identification in contra in New York City is with a social setting. One dancer described "a clear, brightly lit hall, and everything's visible, right there. There's something 'pure' seeming with contra." A caller talked about urbanization and specialization, feeling that life was becoming so technical that the feeling of community was lost, especially in New York City. She felt that "this is a response to it—those of us reaching out to feel this, who have had it or haven't had it." The dancers in the church gymnasium are mostly white, and range in age from their 20s to their 60s. Another caller talked of contra dancing not starting that way, but representing "democracy in action. . . . Today, the fact that you can come to this open place, with easy access, operate on your own level, and be a part, is really an essence of democracy." Through its interrelationships and open-door policy, contras have the potential of being a true "mixer" dance form, ideal to the intercultural diversity of New York.

It is instructive to see how contra dancing treats misfits. Misfits are generally those who have been coming for a while and have never managed to get the basic rudiments of dancing. Another group of misfits are known as "sexual wolves"; those who take the sexuality and flirting further than most people are comfortable with. Contra dancing accommodates misfits by tolerating them, dancing with them, and hoping they will someday learn by example. Misfits, on the other hand, sometimes feel that people are stuffy, but they do have a good time. Contra dancing also tends to attract people who would be misfits in other social environments such as the disco. One dancer told me that contra was "the only thing I know of that is an unconditional acceptance of all levels and all social behaviors at one place at the same time . . . of all places in the world, it's something unconditional and warm in the middle of New York City." In a way, this unconditional acceptance ties back to the fact that no prior credentials are needed for contra dancing. The dependence on everyone is crucial to the social tolerance in contras, and that, in turn, is crucial to its appeal to New York City as a diverse cultural environment.

The contra dance community in New York has, according to one caller, a "tremendous diversity of education, social background, skills, and all the rest of it, but somehow the community has something for everyone at a level they can enjoy it." This diversity is different from membership-oriented club dances, which are exclusive in terms of the desire to dance with people of similar experience and the selection of people for their ability. In New York contra dancing, there is a core of regulars, and many other people who come in and out. The regulars are, on the whole, fairly welcoming. A certain cliquishness exists, but most new people find that they are invited in, and that the regulars are helpful rather than nasty. The progression of lines also helps to ensure a certain mixing of regulars and newcomers. One of the regulars and I talked about the underlying tension between those for whom dancing correctly is important and those for whom the pluralism of the form is important, and she said that though she might ask mostly "good" dancers to dance with her, if someone asked her to dance, she would never refuse. Making mistakes is better tolerated if the person gives weight. One caller said to the crowd, "Those of you who are new to dancing, if you make mistakes, they'll forgive you, if every time you touch somebody make sure you give weight, so they can feel, too."

Learning and Assimilation of Strangers

Skill is not needed for a contra dance as it is, for example, in tennis. The entire dance is built around a few basic figures. In traditional New England contras instruction was minimal, and people who came in were absorbed into it. Contras have a fairly simple basis, and the way these basics are put together makes one dance different from another. One of the strongest initial attractions to contra dancing is the speed with which a dancer can become familiar with the dances. At the first dance that I went to, the caller invited new people to dance at the very beginning of the evening. "Get a partner right away and learn by experience," she said, and the fact that one can and does learn by experience is an attractive factor in contras. Here dancers are dancing in the very first dance, and do not have to stand in the background as they might in another dance form. In contra dancing, one does not have to know what to do with one's feet, and one does not have to know any intricate rhythmic or foot patterns. The movement is very simple, and is done in an almost "Simon Says" type of way. This allows the form to be one in which almost anybody can join.

Other folk dances are perceived by contra participants as being too specialized, and the perception is that it would take too long to learn them. In Balkan dancing, for instance, an importance is placed upon which foot one puts down at what time, whereas in contra you just walk. One contra dancer told me that in other types of dancing, his arms could go, but that his feet just would not do it. If the contras get confusing, someone is always there to help or push you along. The figures in contra dancing are people-oriented figures; right and left matter only in terms of interacting with different people, or as directions for walking in a circle with people.

The rapid assimilation of strangers that I have been discussing is another important factor in contra's adaptability to New York. Figures are simple and taught, and the very title of Longways For As Many As Will (the title given this form in Playford's manuals) implies an open figure with emotional space for all to join. A caller gives all of the figures with time to walk through them and ask questions, and during the dance he or she will call the figures slightly before the action. The fact that only four or five basic actions are repeated during the entire dance leads to mastery of the dance within the time of the dance itself. Thus after four or so repetitions, a caller is able to stop calling and step in only if there is any trouble. The way the dance is structured, with a breakup into sets within the line, leads to divisions of first and second couple roles. The first (active) couple is the most difficult part, and the second couple is able to watch and learn from them. This division of labor within a dance, as well as the changing of partners between dances, makes access to the form easy for newcomers. Sets must also be mixed for self-preservation; if a set occurs in which everyone is new and doesn't know what is going on, it has the potential for falling apart and then, through the progression, messing up the entire line.

Several levels of learning exist within the same dance. That is part of what makes contra dancing special; it can accommodate several levels of dancers and all types of people within the same dance. More and less difficult dances exist, but there are levels of skill to sustain interest in the same dance for the highly experienced as well as the neophyte. The first level is that of learning the figures, or movement units; this is the basic level of learning the mechanics of the contra form. The next step is becoming musical and aware of other dancers. Timing and balance also come into play at the second level. With a good teacher, the first and second levels of learning can be associated, but they are often assimilated separately. The third level is adding style. Contra dancing has a correct style, but it is beyond the scope of this essay to delve into the rudiments of that style. Giving weight, which I have discussed, is part of style, as is grace, rhythmic precision, and phrasing. The fourth and final level is innovation. Contra is open to change by personal invention. However, very few people get all the way to the fourth level of learning. Personal style comes in somewhere between the third and fourth steps. Most people get stuck at one level or another of this process and never go further, but, most importantly, they still enjoy themselves no matter at which level they end.

Urban Life and Contra

In 1923, Violet Alford wrote, "The Country Dance is for anyone who wishes for a little amusement and exercise. As long as you get into your right place you may pretty well do what steps you please" (Alford, 1923:62).

Form in contra dancing is so simple that a dancer can invest his or her personal flow into it, and have it become a personal statement of being. According to Royce, "Dance is a powerful, frequently adopted symbol of the way people feel about themselves" (Royce, 1977:163). What does contra dancing, especially the idea of contra as play, express? If we see leisure activities as a choice of what a participant wants to do with his or her life, what values are implicit in contra dancing to make it attractive? How do these values relate to urban life in New York?

Dance in an urban environment can serve as a mechanism to cope with urban transience. Many people who started dancing contras elsewhere continued to dance when they moved to New York because contra was an activity they could become part of right away. Thus contras can provide stability, with New York simply becoming a regional variation in a non-regional dance form. Many people travel from dance to dance, not only within the New York area, and contras can become a place of belonging outside of a particular geographical area. For people who no longer go to church, contras and the philosophy that go along with them can form a type of "religion of peers," as one dancer put it.

Contra dancing, even in New York, retains the flavor of a community dance. I see the room in which a dance is given as being a frame for a community, with communication structured by the dance figures and given meaning by the sharing of weight, rhythm, and space. Within the line, going down the outside of the line and back establishes your place in the community, and when a caller is calling this figure he will tell you to come back to your place by telling you to come back home. Also, going down the center and back becomes a showing of oneself to the community, as in "Here I am." Such is the strength of this community that a waltz is always done at the end of a contra dance evening. This serves to break up the "small town" community into couples, and to prepare people to go into the "outside" world.

Another couple dance, the schottische, is done toward the end of intermission and serves the opposite purpose of gradually forming the individuals (who have been talking during intermission) into couples, and then back into a cohesive community. In New York, juice and cookies are served during intermission, and this "old time" small town informality serves, I feel, to establish and reestablish the contra dance community as pleasant and nonthreatening in as many ways as possible. When compared with the New York City environment just outside of the dance room, the dichotomy between the two becomes quite strong.

This dichotomy of urban versus small town is aided by the play function of bracketing the inside and outside frames of the activity. Many people do not see any of the other dancers outside of the dance site. Dancers have also spoken to me about being able to lose outside pressure while within this community. The focus on community is strengthened because, for almost all of the people doing this activity in New York, contra dancing is not something they grew up with. As one dancer put it, "It's a form I actively sought to make my own."

Contra as Play

Contra dancing is sociality without threat. This brings in the issue of play framing, and how this framing allows for the expression of sexuality. A good deal of touching and eye contact occurs in contra, but because of the play factor this contact is generally not threatening. One dancer felt that it was a legal outlet for flirting, and that dancers generally ignored wedding rings on the dance floor. A married dancer said, "It's a place where I can let myself get attracted to other men and let it stay on the dance floor." Historically, these play framing aspects of contra dancing can be seen in this quote from an old manual on ballroom etiquette: "An introduction in a public ballroom must be understood by the gentleman to be for that evening only, after which the acquaintanceship ceases, unless the lady chooses to recognize it at any future time or place" (Tolman & Page, 1937:45). This is codified play framing, but the act of dancing itself frames an experience of physicality.

According to Royce, "Dance provides one of the few opportunities in the modern world for displaying the body that is accepted by society" (Royce, 1977:160). The use of the body is itself a factor in the potency of communication, and adds to the sensitivity of those dancing together. One older female caller who has been dancing for many years spoke with me about this, and when I questioned the wholesome image of contra dancing versus the sexuality involved in the dances, she retorted, "Are you saying that sexuality isn't wholesome?" She went on to say, "Dancing is a sexual activity, and that's part of the delight of it. It is flirtatious, and that's part of the enjoyment of it." The play frame of contra gives this expression of sexuality an innocence and takes away any element of commitment within it.

Restoration of Behavior

Play can give order to a disordered world and that is important in the attraction to contra dancing. Contra dancing is to some degree a restoration of an "American folk culture," although to discuss that concept in depth is beyond the scope of this essay. The attraction to contra as an American dance form, as opposed to other ethnic dance forms such as Israeli, Balkan, or International Folk dancing, is part of the initial attraction for a new-comer to the contra community. The creation and imitation of a New-England-type small town within the dance environment, as restoration of behavior, "offers to both individuals and groups the chance to become someone else 'for the time being' or . . . to rebecome what they never were" (Schechner, 1981:3). One of the essential differences between New England community dances and New York City dances is that in the New England dances, dancers do all know each other, and the play element involving role playing brackets an activity that is with people with whom you have an outside relationship. In New York City, dancers act as if they all know each other and were a community outside of contra, and then bracket the role playing. Thus an extra element exists in New York that is tied to the restoration of a small town community.

Contra dancing, in New York and elsewhere, is a combination of restored behavior and a live, evolving tradition. This combination is part of its widespread appeal. I have found that often the reasons for someone's initial interest in contra dancing are not the same as what eventually keeps them interested in continuing. An American search for roots (Hareven, 1978), as well as the back-to-nature movement of the past 20 years, have contributed to the interest in contra dancing, but I think that people stay because they enjoy the dances. Historical precedent is evident in Ford and Sharp's interest in innocent, "natural" American-heritage type of dances, but once a person gets to contra dancing, the physicality, accessibility, and sociability involved in contras are what make them stay.

Contra dancing is ideally suited to Csikszentmihalyi's (1975) conditions for an activity that involves flow, most importantly in the fact that dancers can interact with the environment on a level at which their skills match the opportunities available. Music helps a great deal in this level of involvement in the activity. One of the advanced skills of contra is matching the dance phrasing to that of the music. In a certain way, music provides a frame for the aesthetic activity of contras; that goes along with the acquisition of style.

Contras may indeed be more enjoyable when one has a personal style and a certain level of ability, but the beauty of contras in relation to New York City lies in the geometry of the form and the social interrelationships that it allows. Watching a contra from above, as from the balcony above the dance floor, the space itself becomes alive and moves around, becoming its own metaphor for a town or home-like place. Dancing as specifically physical enjoyment holds an important place in our generally sedentary culture. Contra dancing, by virtue of its simplicity, accessibility, and management of diverse performance levels, is able to deal with New York as a multicultural center. All are able to dance together with varying levels of cultural knowledge, and built into that dancing is a very high level of social interchange. Contra dancing is truly social dancing and occupies a much-needed place in New York.

Note

1. Longways simply refers to the two long lines that are the geometrical form contras take. In this essay when I refer to longways I am speaking of the physical structure, as opposed to any social or emotional components. Basically, the two terms are synonymous.

Acknowledgments

Judy Levine is a dancer, choreographer, and doctoral candidate in the Performance Studies Department at New York University. Her specialty is movement studies, and she is a Certified Laban Movement Analyst. This paper won second prize in the 1985 TAASP Competition for the Best Student Paper on Play.

Special thanks to the dancers and callers who contributed time and energy to this study, especially Sue Dupre, Kristeen Helwig, Susan Levitas, Jody McGee, Julian Rubenstein, and Genny Shimer.

References

Alford, V. (1923). *Peeps at English folk dances*. London: A and C Black.

Csikszentmihalyi, M. (1975). *Beyond boredom and anxiety*. San Francisco: Jossey-Bass.

Dean-Smith, M. (1957). *Playford's English dancing master 1651*. London: Schott and Co.

Gadd, M. (1937a). The folk dance as a social dance. *Dance Observer*, 4(9), 114, 116.

Gadd, M. (1937b). Folk dance in America today. *Dance Observer*, 4(8), 95.

Gadd, M. (1956). History of the country dance society of America. Part 1. *Country Dancer*, **12**, 20–21.

Gadd, M. (1957). History of the country dance society of America. Part 2. *Country Dancer*, **12**, 40–42.

Gadd, M. (1958). History of the country dance society of America. Part 3. *Country Dancer*, **12**, 15–16.

Gadd, M. (1959). History of the country dance society of America. Part 4. *Country Dancer*, **12**, 27.

Hanna, J.L. (1979). *To dance is human*. Austin: University of Texas Press.

Hareven, T.K. (1978). The search for generational memory: Tribal rites to industrial society. *Daedalus*, **107**, 137–149.

Holden, R. (1956). *The contra dance book*. Newark: American Squares.

Holt, A. (1907). *How to dance the revised ancient dances*. London: Horace Cox.

Horosko, M. (1965). [Interview with May Gadd]. WNYC Radio Profiles.

Nevell, R. (1977). *A time to dance*. New York: St. Martin's Press.

Page, R. (1953). On the contra trail. *American Squares*, 8(10 and 11), 6–7, 26, 10–11.

Page, R. (1976). *Heritage dances of early America*. Colorado Springs: The Lloyd Shaw Foundation.

Rossoff, M. (1977). *Hoedown heritage*. Sandusky, OH: American Squaredance Magazine.

Royce, A.P. (1977). *The anthropology of dance*. Bloomington: Indiana University Press.

Sachs, C. (1937). *World history of the dance*. New York: W.W. Norton and Company.

Schechner, R. (1981). Restoration of behavior. *Studies in Visual Communication, 7*, 2–45.

Sharp, C.J. (1924). *The country dance book. Part II*. London: Novello and Company.

Tolman, B., & Page, R. (1937). *The country dance book*. Brattleboro, VT: The Stephen Greene Press.

Wilson, T. (1811). *An analysis of country dancing*. London: J.S. Dickson.

Wood, M. (1949). English country dance prior to the 17th century. *Journal of The English Folk Dance and Song Society, 6*(1), 8–12.

PART V

Play and Modern Technology

Social Impact of Video Game Play

Steven B. Silvern
Mary K. Lang
Peter A. Williamson

Statistics gathered regarding the money and time spent on the phenomenon of video games indicate that they are having a significant influence on children and society (Adilman, 1983; Shapiro, 1983). Researchers have noted that the trend in video game content has been toward violence, and they have questioned the impact that these games may have on the subsequent social behavior of the user (Brooks, 1983; Lynch, 1983). Aggression in particular is a theme that has been addressed by researchers only briefly in regard to video games (Favaro, 1984; Silvern, Williamson, & Countermine, 1983; Winkle, Novak, & Hopson, 1984).

Existing studies that have examined aggressive behavior following video game play show a general lack of agreement in their findings. These findings may be the result of variability in the types of video games used in the studies and also of the diversity of the population sampled. They may also be explained by examining the context surrounding video game play and the stimuli involved in the environment following video game play.

Favaro (1984) examined whether video game play caused adult subjects to feel more or less hostile after they played. In this investigation he compared video game playing to television watching and dart game playing in college students. He manipulated the amount of time people spent playing the games as well as the level of aggression shown in the activities. For example, to increase the aggressive content of the dart games, he changed the target from a simple bull's-eye to such images as people in cars. He also selected television shows and video games based on their aggressive content so that each task was comparable to the other.

Favaro used six different measures including a self-report and a psychological projection test to determine the levels of hostility, anxiety, and aggression after subjects performed each task. Based on these self-reports he found that any activity—playing video games, television viewing, or dart game playing—when performed in the more aggressive version, caused an increase in reported hostility. Of all three activities, however, video games caused the least amount of reported hostility. Video games rated as ''high'' in aggressive content caused less feeling of hostility than the television and dart game that were rated as "low" in aggressive content.

Winkle et al. (1984) examined the relationships in early adolescents among personality factors, physiological arousal, and aggression after playing video games. The effects of the aggressive content of the games on subsequent aggression was also assessed. The two independent variables consisted of subject gender (males vs. females) and video game content (very aggressive vs. aggressive vs. nonaggressive). The dependent measures included subjects' responses to a personality inventory, physiological arousal (heart rate), and aggressive behavior. The method to determine aggressive behavior was a modification of a research paradigm that consisted of subjects deducting monetary rewards from a confederate, rather than delivering electric shocks.

Video game content was rank ordered according to levels of aggressive content, which ranged from very aggressive to not aggressive. The greater the number of human figures and the longer the duration of destructive events occurring in the game, the more aggressive the game content was thought to be. Winkle et al. found that the aggression cues or the content of the video game (i.e., aggressive vs. nonaggressive) does not affect the subsequent behavior of the user. Furthermore, they found that the aggressive nature of the video games employed in the investigation did not lead to increased psychological arousal.

In a preliminary investigation of video game playing and aggression in young children, Silvern et al. (1983) compared the levels of aggressive, imaginative, and prosocial behavior in young children after video game play with levels of the same behaviors after television viewing and at baseline. During the video game condition, pairs of subjects played "Space Invaders," a game of violent content in which one of the subjects attempted to blow up aliens on the screen while the other subject observed. In the television condition, subjects viewed a Road Runner cartoon. Video tapes of play sessions following the three different treatment conditions were coded for aggression, fantasy, and prosocial behavior using a modification of the coding system developed by Greer, Potts, Wright, and Huston (1982) for their television studies.

The findings of this investigation indicated that aggression after viewing television and after playing the video game was significantly greater than aggression at baseline. No difference occurred in levels of aggression between television and video games. No main effects were found for order of involvement, and boys were significantly more aggressive than girls.

Results of the investigations that have shown a change in prosocial behavior following video game play have been explained by various models that have previously been used as explanations for behavioral change in television research (Greer et al., 1982). These models include the catharsis model, the social learning model, and the arousal model.

Silvern (1986) defines each of these models in a discussion on emotional affect and arousal in relation to television and video game research. The catharsis model is based on the hypothesis that individuals have drive states that, when fulfilled, decrease that drive. Aggression is one possible drive state. Given the opportunity to experience aggression, cathartic experience takes place, and the subject experiences a decrease in aggressive feelings. In the social learning model, children model behaviors that they observe and that are socially sanctioned. Therefore, when children witness behaviors and observe rewards or no punishment for the behavior, the likelihood is increased that children will perform the behavior witnessed. The arousal model is based on the reactions of the sympathetic nervous system as described by Schachter (1964). Essentially, when children experience generalized arousal (evidenced by increased sensitivity, increased respiration, and increased heart rate) they lack the cognitive ability to identify why they are aroused and tend to associate the feelings with the last behavior observed. If the most recent experience was violent, children would most likely feel antagonistic.

In the context of video games, the arousal model explains the player's reaction to the various events on the screen during the game-playing activity. Reacting at an almost instinctive level to the video game excites the sympathetic nervous system of the player so that the player begins to feel a non-specific emotional affect. Schachter (1964) found that individuals in a state of generalized arousal could be readily manipulated into a variety of emotional states, depending upon the contextual cues that were surrounding them.

Conflicting findings in the above reported studies would suggest that future investigations are necessary to establish a consistent notion regarding the effects of video game playing on the subsequent social behavior of the user. The appropriate model used to explain these findings may also be indicated by examining the content and design of the video game used and the nature of the activity involved in playing the game. The stimuli surrounding the game playing activity and following the game might also be important.

Apparently, if the social learning model were a possible explanation for the subsequent social behavior of the video game player, then the above reported studies would have found that aggressive behavior follows playing video games containing violent themes or aggressive content. This was not the case for two of the reported studies. If the arousal model was used to explain the subsequent behavior of video game players, then the nature of the game playing activity or stimuli implying a cooperation factor in the game would determine the effect it might have on the social behavior of the user.

Video games have been suggested to be the most appropriate medium for testing the three models mentioned above. Specifically in relation to the hypothesis that games with aggressive content produce aggressive behavior in the user (Silvern, 1986), the interactive quality of video game play allows the investigator to control for the effects of both content (i.e., violent vs. nonviolent games) and interaction (i.e., cooperative vs. competitive interaction). These two separate variables must be examined in order to determine and explain the social effects following different types of video game play.

The purpose of the following investigation was to test the hypothesis that video games containing violent content cause subsequent aggressive behavior in children. In this investigation the video game content (i.e., violent content) and quality of interaction required during the game (i.e., cooperative vs. competitive interaction) are controlled in an effort to identify the most appropriate model that might explain the resulting social behavior emitted by the user.

Method

Subjects

The subjects were 46 children between the ages of 6 and 9 years. All the children were white, came from middle-class families, and lived in a rural college town. Mean age of the subjects was 7 years, 1 month; all but 4 of the subjects were boys.

Materials

The materials consisted of two microcomputer-operated video games and a play area. Each of the games was selected because of the potential to induce either cooperative play or competitive play.

Cooperative video game.   The cooperative video game was called "Star Wars." The video display consisted of a gunner's cross-hair (sighting device) and a moving space ship (presumably one of the "Empire's" fighter ships). The players must center the enemy ship in the cross-hair and fire on the enemy ship. The cross-hair was controlled by two game paddles. One paddle controlled horizontal movement and one paddle controlled vertical movement. Each child in the dyad had a paddle; in order to successfully play the game they had to coordinate the movement of the cross-hair using the paddles.

Competitive video game.   The competitive video game was called "Boxing." The video display showed two boxers in a boxing ring. By turning the paddle control one boxer moved toward or away from the other boxer. Pressing the fire button causes the boxer to punch at the opponent. Each child in the dyad used a separate paddle to control a boxer. The object of the game was to knock down the opponent's boxer.

Play room.   An area of 20 ft by 20 ft was marked by masking tape within a larger room. Inside the tape boundaries were the following toys: unit blocks, Raggedy Ann, Raggedy Andy, plastic zoo animals, play money, a Fisher-Price airplane and a bus with wooden doll pieces, two stick horses, a baby doll, a Nerf ball, and an inflatable doll designed for hitting (generally referred to as a bobo doll). Toys were included that would allow for a variety of kinds of play and matched the set of toys used by Greer et al. (1982).

Procedure

Same-sex, similar-age dyads were taken to a play area three separate times on three separate days. One session consisted of playing the competitive video game for 5 minutes and then immediately moving to the toy area and playing for 10 minutes. One session consisted of playing the cooperative video game for 5 minutes and then immediately moving to the toy area for 10 minutes. One session consisted of 10 minutes in the play area without prior video game arousal. The order of play session was randomized across dyads.

Prior to playing each video game, the subjects were shown how the paddles worked, and the objectives of the game were explained. Upon entering the play area the subjects were told that they could play with any of the toys in any way that they liked, but that they had to stay within the tape boundary. The experimenter stayed outside of the play room. During computer play the experimenter was available to respond to questions or to prompt the players if the game stalled.

The subjects were audiotaped during video game play and were videotaped in the play area.

Two raters coded the videotapes for

- physical aggression—striking a child or physically threatening to strike (e.g., raising a clenched fist);
- object aggression—striking or throwing one of the play objects;
- verbal aggression—name calling or verbally threatening another child (e.g., ''I'm going to get you'');
- collaborative aggression—engaging as a dyad in a nonfantasy aggressive activity (e.g., playing baseball using the stick horse as a bat and striking the Nerf ball);
- solitary fantasy aggression—one child in the dyad using pretend play in an aggressive way (e.g., striking the bobo doll and saying, ''Take that, bad buy'');
- collaborative fantasy aggression—both children engaged in aggressive fantasy (e.g., playing cops and robbers and hitting the bobo doll);
- fantasy play—for example, playing store;
- solitary play—manipulating toys; and
- verbal interaction—talking together that does not involve fantasy theme.

The category collaborative aggression was added to the categories already identified by Greer et al. (1982).

Behaviors were coded for 15-second intervals with 5 seconds for coding. In a 10-minute observation 30 codings were recorded. Interrater reliability was determined by dividing the number of agreements between raters by the total number of observations. Interrater reliability was 0.80.

The audiotapes were coded by two raters on six categories of utterance. All utterances were coded. The categories were

- inquiries concerning how to play—asking the experimenter about the game;
- inquiries about play—requesting information or action from the other player;
- comments on play—statements or commands to the other player;
- laughter and onomatopeia;
- announcements—statements about the game not related to actual play (e.g., "I got 27"); and
- other—communications not falling into the above categories.

Interrater reliability, calculated in the manner previously described, was 0.89 for all categories. Because some dyads may have been more verbal than others, all utterances are expressed in percent of total utterances.

Data Analysis

All play categories were entered into a multivariate repeated measures design. Utterances were analyzed using a chi-square statistic.

Results

The multivariate analysis of variance was significant at the .05 level of confidence. Four variables contributed to the multivariate design: physical aggression, object aggression, collaborative aggression, and fantasy play. Means for the three play sessions are reported in Table 1.

Physical aggression was greater after playing the cooperative game than after playing the competitive game or in the play-only session. No difference in physical aggression occurred between the play-only and competitive game sessions. Object aggression was greatest in the play-only session, and more object aggression was in evidence after the cooperative video game than after the competitive video game. Collaborative aggression was

Table 1   Mean Incidence of Behavior Reported by Behavior Category and Play Condition

Behavior	Play condition		
	Play only	After cooperative video game	After competitive video game
Physical aggression	0.21	1.00	0.26
Object aggression	3.07	1.76	0.96
Collaborative aggression	7.30	9.04	8.73
Fantasy play	17.74	18.35	20.44

greatest after the cooperative video game, and more collaborative aggression was observed after the competitive video game than in the play-only session. Fantasy play was greatest after the competitive video game. No difference occurred in fantasy play in the other two sessions. All pairwise differences were at the .05 level of confidence.

The utterances emitted during game play were significantly different from chance ($\chi^2 = 130.16$, $df = 5$, $p < .001$). During the cooperative game 73% of the utterances were comments to the other player about how to play the game. Laughter and onomatopeia accounted for 10% of the utterances and the remaining 17% of utterances were equally distributed among the other four categories. In contrast, 41% of the utterances emitted during the competitive game were laughter and onomatopeia. Announcements accounted for 24% of the utterances; comments on play accounted for 17% of the utterances; 10% were inquiries of the other player; and 8% were inquiries and other utterances.

Discussion

Given that both video games contained violent content, social learning theory would suggest that more aggressive behavior would be found after video game play than after the play-only situation. The results here seem to be mixed. The cooperative game elicited the most physical aggression (although an average of one incident in a 10-minute period is extremely low), play only elicited the most object aggression, and both video games elicited more collaborative aggression than the play-only condition. At this point it is more important to consider the operational definitions of "object aggression" and "collaborative aggression." Object aggression was coded when a child simply struck an object. Collaborative aggression was coded when children were engaged together in a nonfantasy aggressive activity. The emphasis here might be on collaborative aggression; in other words, the children were playing together. We might observe aggressive activities (e.g., baseball, football, soccer, and even rough and tumble play) and note that the children are playing together, not that they're being aggressive. Playing an adaptation of baseball for two is qualitatively different from striking the Nerf ball with a stick simply for the sake of striking. Based on this analysis, the children were less aggressive and more collaborative after playing video games than in the play-only condition. These findings support Favaro (1984) and Winkle et al. (1984).

The findings of this investigation, as well as those of the other reported studies, would lead one to question the efficacy of the social learning model. If the social learning model were a viable explanation for subsequent behavior, playing video games containing violent content would increase aggressive behavior. Other reasons to reject this model were discussed by Silvern (1986). These include the notion that in order to model behavior, the behavior must be reproducible. Thus the abstract nature of the action depicted in video games is generally irreproducible. Also, whereas television heroes engage willingly in violence, many video games like Frogger,

Donkey Kong, and Pac-Man encourage the avoidance of violence. A more suitable explanation would be from a model that can increase the likelihood of behavior that is different in kind from behavior shown by the model.

Other possible explanations might include the catharsis model or a model of generalized arousal. The arousal model suggests that once an individual is in a general state of arousal whether that state is directed or undirected, being aroused will make a difference in the outcome of the behavior. This model indicates that aroused children who lack direction tend to be aggressive. Using the arousal model as a theoretical basis, one might conclude that a prosocial effect in young children might be produced by making sure that when children are in a generalized state of arousal, situational factors direct them to behave in a prosocial manner. Thus the arousal model forces us to examine the nature of the play activity during the investigation as well as the situational factors that follow the play behavior.

The current findings suggest that possibly, generalized arousal occurred during the treatment conditions of the studies involving dyads, but this state of arousal was directed toward prosocial behavior (i.e., playing together) resulting in a decrement of aggressive behaviors following the treatment condition. In both treatment conditions the children were involved in organized play, although the content of the stimuli used in the play setting was violent. Thus, apparently, the organizational activity of the play environment had an overriding effect on the content of the stimuli involved in the play environment (i.e., a video game). Indeed, the organizational activity may be the critical factor operating in all of the reported studies if the arousal theory can be used as an explanation of the results.

The findings from the verbalizations during video game play are important here. In both cases (cooperative and competitive games) the children are playing together. Yet, based on the high percentage of laughter and onomatopeia in the competitive game, more camaraderie seems to be in the competitive than in the cooperative game. This camaraderie may be an indication that even though the features of the game may be competitive, the action of playing a game may be focused on playing together.

A reduction in aggression possibly occurred as a result of cathartic experience. Silvern (1986) suggests that this reduction of a drive is based on an appropriate vicarious experience. This notion would readily account for the findings of the reported studies that used both single subjects and dyads (i.e., pairs of subjects).

Caution is necessary in interpreting these findings because of two limitations. First, an overwhelming proportion of subjects was male. Findings should not be generalized beyond young white boys. Second, only two games were used, and findings may not generalize beyond these games.

Future investigation in this area should continue to consider the importance of the game design variable when designing investigations to support or reject these theoretical models. The components that make up program design may be found in television research. Regarding content of television programs, researchers have found that program form can be influenced by such variables as setting, frequency of change of setting, length of verbalization, frequency of change of speakers, number of characters, uncertainty of setting change, amount of camera movement, and amount of physical movement by characters (Greer et al., 1982; Silvern, 1986). These variables as well as the type of video games used (i.e., arcade vs. video games), context of observation (arcade vs. laboratory), length of time spent playing games, and the nature of the content (i.e., violent vs. nonviolent) are also important considerations.

References

Adilman, G. (1983). Video games: Knowing the score. *Creative Computing,* **9**(12), 224–232.

Brooks, B.D. (1983, May). Untitled paper presented at the Harvard Symposium on Video Games and Human Development: A Research Agenda for the '80s, Cambridge, MA.

Favaro, P.J. (1984). How video games affect players. *Softside,* **7**(1), 16–17.

Greer, D., Potts, R., Wright, J.C., & Huston, A. (1982). The effects of television commercial form and commercial placement on children's social behavior and attention. *Child Development,* **53**, 611–619.

Lynch, W.J. (1983, February). *The contribution of video games to computer-assisted cognitive training.* Paper presented at the annual meeting of the American Psychological Association, Anaheim, CA.

Schachter, S. (1964). The interaction of cognitive and physiological determinants of emotional state. In L. Berkowitz (Ed.), *Advances in experimental social psychology* (Vol. 1, pp. 49–80). New York: Academic Press.

Shapiro, L. (1983). What are children learning from video games? *Popular Computing,* **2**(4), 121–124.

Silvern, S.B. (1986). Video games: Affect, arousal, and aggression. In P.F. Campbell & G.G. Fein (Eds.), *Young children and microcomputers* (pp. 61–72). Reston, VA: Reston.

Silvern, S.B., Williamson, P.A., & Countermine, T.A. (1983, April). *Video game playing and aggression in young children.* Paper presented at the annual meeting of the American Educational Research Association, Montreal, Canada.

Winkle, M., Novak, D.M., & Hopson, H. (1984, April). *Personality factors, subject gender, and the effects of video game content on aggression in adolescents.* Paper presented at the annual meeting of the Southwest Psychological Association, Houston, TX.

Will Video Games Alter the Relationship Between Play and Cognitive Development?

David F. Lancy

Although the question of what functions are served by play, especially the play of the young, has a respectable history (e.g., Groos, 1898), an answer is not close at hand.

> The . . . functions of play can be classified into three categories: those involving motor training, socialization, and enhanced cognitive abilities. But surprisingly, while such functions may and probably do, exist, there is little hard, non-controversial evidence for any of them. (Burghardt, 1985:7; see also Smith, 1982)

Many functions have been proposed, but for our purposes here, I want to focus on the conflict between Piaget's assertion that play serves mainly a practice function and Sutton-Smith's (1967, 1983) counterassertion that cognitive skills are not only illustrated and consolidated in play, they are *developed*.[1]

Needless to say, this conflict has spawned a great deal of research, which has been dominated by two broad concerns. First, numerous studies have been conducted in which children are given an opportunity to play with objects and then tested to see if this activity facilitates problem solving, divergent thinking, and associative fluency (for example, Cheyne & Rubin, 1983; Dansky & Silverman, 1973, 1975; Koehler, 1927; Sylva, 1977). The results of these studies have generally shown positive effects for play experiences; however, they suffer from a number of methodological weaknesses (Simon & Smith, 1983; Smith, 1985). One of the most damaging criticisms is that investigators in these studies failed to differentiate between play and exploration, a distinction that is critical both for Piagetian theory (e.g., Piaget, 1951/1962) and to the question of whether learning occurs during play (Hutt, 1966). Furthermore, with respect to the gains in problem solving and so forth, "It is unclear . . . whether play, exploration or both was responsible for these gains" (Christie & Johnsen, 1983:103).

The second major line of research, initiated by Smilansky (1968), focuses on the functions of sociodramatic or make-believe play. In the cognitive area the benefits of sociodramatic play include creativity, role playing, perspective taking, and so on (for example, see Burns & Brainerd, 1979; Fink, 1976; Johnson, 1976). However, definitional problems also weaken the validity of these studies. In particular, many of the studies that have shown the most marked effects involved a great deal of adult intervention that could have turned "play" into "instruction" (Krasnor & Pepler, 1980). In studies where adult intervention and management are not present, the research designs tend to be correlational rather than causal-comparative (for example, see Lancy, 1983b).

As Sutton-Smith (1980) points out, the study of play in early childhood has been dominated by developmental psychologists, whereas the play of older children has more often been studied by sociologists and anthropologists. This has meant that when researchers look at the functions of games or sport they are more interested in examining the contributions of play to society, the band, the culture, the civilization, and so forth, than in examining the contributions to the child's own cognitive development. Inspired at least in part by Jack Roberts's work in this area (e.g., Barry & Roberts, 1972; Roberts & Sutton-Smith, 1962), I undertook a study of play and cognitive development among the Kpelle of Liberia, which focused heavily on games. I conducted both correlational and experimental research (Lancy, 1977). Both approaches yielded positive but not earth-shattering results. The experimental work, in particular, indicated that cognitive gains were modest insofar as very little generalization of skills apparently was acquired in play (Lancy, 1974). One of the reasons that games may not stimulate the transformation and development of cognitive abilities is that children can generally get by with playing the game at a level at which they are intellectually comfortable. Among the Kpelle, children first act as spectators; when they have a general idea of how to play, they join in but can count on being treated leniently for rule transgressions; they can expect to be "coached" by other players as the game progresses; and so forth. This observation is comparable to Piaget's observations (1932/1965) about children playing marbles. Children can "play" marbles without following the "rules of the game"; in fact, many may not even have a very good grasp of the whole notion of the arbitrary rules that are supposed to govern game play. It brings to mind my own recent work in Papua New Guinea where we observed very few games that could be called intellectually taxing. I explained this by reference to the fact that Papua New Guinean villages/hamlets tend to be very small with populations of 500 people or less. Consequently, play groups span a fairly wide age range; thus games must be no more demanding than the physical and intellectual capacities of the youngest player (Lancy, 1985).

Unfortunately, no other research that I am aware of addresses the impact of game involvement on development. Lack of empirical support for this relationship has not dampened the enthusiasm of educators for play, of course (e.g., Block, 1984; Maxwell, 1983); but I, for one, had been willing to accept Piaget's "null hypothesis," at least until recently. That hypothesis is that play, generally, and games, in particular, provide children with opportunities to practice and perfect emerging cognitive, sensorimotor, and social skills. However, this practice is an incidental benefit to the individual because such practice could, if necessary, be obtained in other ways (Smith, 1982).

The Nature of Video Games

My interest in the cognitive impact of video games was prompted by the discovery of "Star Raiders." The game cartridge came as a "bonus" when I purchased the Atari 800 computer. I was completely overwhelmed at first—it seemed incredibly complicated. The game is a simulation of some elements from the recently popular space films. You pilot a Starship and try to destroy the entire Zylon Fleet before they surround and destroy your Starbases. At one level you just aim and shoot, and it thus has much in common with many other video games. However, you can alter speed, direction, sector, and so forth. You can also refer to several distinct information screens including the Galactic Chart, the Long Range Sector Scan, and the Attack Computer Display that shows the status of the ship's vital functions, its location, the location of enemy ships, and so forth. Furthermore, a great deal of arithmetical estimation is involved. Just reading and understanding the manual took me several hours. Despite many complications and the lengthy training period, "Star Raiders" is one of the most highly acclaimed and popular computer (as opposed to VCS or arcade) video games. Thus the game was likely being played by thousands of average American children. I, like Greenfield (1983), felt that something was going on here that deserved investigation. Let us briefly examine what all this excitement is about.

First, as I have noted, video and computer games represent a very high degree of complexity—they would top just about anyone's game hierarchy (e.g., Sutton-Smith, 1976). Mastery for even the most rudimentary games may take hundreds of hours (Sudnow, 1982; Surrey, 1982).

Second, most video games can be played at several levels of difficulty. The game, "Miner 2049er," for example, has 10 levels, and the player must complete them in exact order of increasing difficulty. The kinds of sensorimotor skills required are relatively constant throughout the game even though the amount of skill required increases. Strategic or problem-solving features of the game increase exponentially from level to level, however. Level 1 has only about three things to "figure out"; at Level 2 at least three new "twists" are added, and so forth. The "rules of the game" are simple at first but get increasingly demanding as one progresses. This means that a player can be fairly inadept and yet gain entry to the game and begin practicing and improving.

A third and closely related point is that like traditional games, one can learn to play video games by reading a guide, observing games being played, and by being taught. Unlike traditional games, however, one can learn to play many video games by trial and error as well. Trial and error may not be very efficient, but any parent who has been rebuffed by the words

"I can do it myself!" knows that it is the preferred learning tactic of young children.

Fourth, video games incorporate built-in opponents, score keepers, timers, playing props, and, in many cases, coaches. In short, most of the major impediments that might prevent a child from enjoying the benefits, if any, of an intellectually challenging game have been removed in the video game. Take chess, for example, a game that has been used to represent the epitome of cognitive skill (Simon & Chase, 1973). To play chess, you need to know *all* the rules; you can't move the knight at whim until you have learned what its legal moves are. You need a board, chess pieces, and an opponent. We would no sooner expect an 8-year-old to learn to play chess by "messing around" with the board and pieces than we would expect a chimpanzee to write *The Carpetbaggers* while pecking away at a typewriter. Video games have the same mass appeal as television. More people learned to play Pac-Man in its first year of existence than have learned to play chess in the several millennia of its existence.[2]

Video games share some other characteristics with traditional games. Unlike other kinds of play, games provide constraints that keep the player "on task." As we have seen earlier, sociodramatic play's virtues may be considerably diminished were we to remove adult supervision and guidance. Unlike other activities that require concentration, learning, and persistence to master, games are fun, playful, and *intrinsically motivating* (Loftus & Loftus, 1983). Not surprisingly, students spend 50% more time with a fraction exercise when it is presented in a video game format than if it is presented in a computer drill format (Lepper & Malone, 1985).

To summarize, although video games are intellectually very demanding, they are also extraordinarily seductive. The net effect of this combination may well be to accelerate the cognitive development of children who have access to them.

Some Tentative Inquiries

The study that I would like to have done would have taken a fairly large and diverse cohort of children and carefully logged their video game play over several years and simultaneously monitored their performance on various measures of cognitive, academic, and social development. For various reasons, not the least of which was the lack of financial support in the form of a grant, I was not able to undertake such a study. Hopefully someone is doing it because, as was the case with television, the opportunity to control the "amount of exposure" variable is extremely limited (Liebert, Sprafkin, & Davidson, 1982). Consequently, I have had to make do with small-scale studies that yield several firm hypotheses but no firm conclusions.

The first study was undertaken 3 years ago in Arizona. Essentially we (Lancy, Cohen, Evans, Levine, & Nevin, 1985) compared the social and cognitive effects on sixth-grade children of prolonged engagement with two video games, "Star Raiders" and "Missile Command." Star Raiders, as I have indicated, is intellectually quite demanding. Missile Command is a much simpler game, requiring only hand-eye coordination and two to three strategic insights. Twenty-four students were assigned randomly to either the Star Raiders or Missile Commanders after-school computer clubs. Students were then further assigned to triads (there were four Atari 800 stations), although later they were free to choose new partners. We pre- and posttested the students on a variety of measures of cognitive development, mostly with a Piagetian flavor. None of these measures yielded significant differences between the two groups, so we had to accept the null hypothesis that the intellectual challenge inherent in computer games does not lead to gains on conventional broad measures of intellectual functioning. However, our participant observer notes yielded many fascinating insights (cf Lancy et al., 1985). For example, students avoid reading the documentation or instruction manuals unless absolutely necessary; they want to play, and reading directions is work. Cooperation was the rule in both clubs but especially so with Star Raiders. A few of the brighter, more experienced students learned to play and then taught the others. Girls deeply resented being grouped with boys, feeling that they didn't stand a chance. Their scores, however, equalled or exceeded those of the boys in both clubs. But this fact did not lead to a reversal of attitudes because the girls tended to compare their current scores to their own previous best scores rather than with other players' best scores (as the boys did).

In the second study (Hayes, Lancy, & Evans, 1985), our focus was considerably narrower. Students in the experimental groups were exposed to a sequence of increasingly more challenging "fantasy adventures,"[3] whereas the control group played video games of the aim and shoot variety. Approximately 30 students participated, ranging in age from 9 to 12, with a dyad at each computer (mostly Apple IIs) station. Our objective this time was to determine the effect of computer gaming on information processing (e.g., note taking, organizing, and summarizing skills). We were unable to achieve definitive results because the test we used as a dependent measure, the Wisconsin Test for Reading Skill Development (Stewart, Kamm, Allen, & Miles, 1973), was too easy and we got a pronounced ceiling effect. One result did come through quite clearly, however. In addition to reading, fantasy adventures require the use of maps (ready-made, or, in some cases, constructed as you play), lists of items found, lists of words the computer understands, and so forth. If a student could play the game without doing one or more of these activities, then they did so. Again, these activities were viewed as burdensome extracurricular tasks. Also, older children were more likely to maintain appropriate records and were, consequently, more successful than younger children.

In our third and fourth studies we have gotten even more closely focused on specific types of computer play and the potential effects on children's cognition. We have (Forsyth, 1986) done a study of how children use maps to find their way around Winnie the Pooh's "Hundred Acres Wood." This game is a fantasy adventure that utilizes A.A. Milne characters and story line and the graphics from the Disney film. The object is to explore the

Hundred Acres Wood, find 10 objects, and return them to their various owners and/or proper locations, all the while avoiding hazards such as being bounced by Tigger. There were various experimental conditions and numerous independent and dependent variables; however, we essentially found that (a) all children (some 120 subjects in the fourth and fifth grades) got deeply engrossed in the game, and (b) deeper involvement (e.g., greater exploration, interaction with characters, etc.) with the game and greater use of the map were associated with greater success on the various posttest measures of place-location recall.

We are now engaged in a developmental study of "interactive fiction."[4] Our subjects range from fourth to eighth graders, and the fantasy adventures (also called interactive fiction) they are involved with span a wide range of difficulty. Difficulty here reflects the reading level of the prose, the number and type of problems to be solved, the type of communication with the computer (e.g., multiple choice, words, and whole sentences), and so on. We have observed that all students progress from elementary to higher levels in the sequence (the sequence includes about 12 games of gradually increasing difficulty). However, all but the oldest students reach the upper level of their ability, tolerance for frustration, and willingness to take notes, make maps, and so on without having reached the most difficult games in the sequence. The games seem to have the power to drive children to the outer limits of their capacities but not far beyond, at least not in the short run.

Some Tentative Conclusions

From the standpoint of meaningful and conclusive results, we must back off and plead "work in progress." Nevertheless, as a parent and as an educator I am confident that the cumulative impact of hundreds of hours of video and adventure game play on children's thinking will be substantial and positive. Although an initial flurry of concern was expressed over the potential negative consequences of video games, research has shown this to be completely unwarranted (Brooks, 1983; Egli & Meyers, 1984). In fact, one obvious positive contribution is the attendant reduction in television viewing (Mitchell, 1983).

The enormous motivating power of video games is increasingly being harnessed to support instruction in basic academic subjects (Chaffin, 1983; Dunne, 1984; Lepper, 1985; Malone, 1981). Although video arcades disappear from the shopping malls and manufacturers go under, whole new categories of computer games keep appearing on the scene. My own research in the immediate future will continue to focus on "interactive fiction" (Adams, 1985a; Strehlo, 1984; Unwin, 1983) and "construction kits" (Adams, 1985b; Ardai, 1985; Burbules & Reese, 1984). These new play forms retain video game features, colorful graphics, sounds, contingencies, and feedback, but add plot, storyline, feminine themes, greater control and flexibility, and the ability to "save" the game to return to repeatedly over an extended period. The net effect of this increasing diversity will be to ensure that regardless of age, gender, or setting (e.g., school, home, or office), individuals in the industrialized countries will be able to find opportunities to engage in computer play and will do so enthusiastically. Schools, especially, will find many opportunities to use computer games (Lancy, Evans, & Forsyth, 1985).

Meanwhile, individuals who do not have access to video games and computers will be further "deprived" of the kinds of experiences (e.g., formal education, television, and the stimulus-rich industrial/commercial urban environment) that have opened an almost unbridgeable gulf between, for example, the real estate salesmen of Palo Alto, California and the rice farmers of Gbarngasuakwelle, Liberia. As I have previously argued (Lancy, 1983a), cognitive development beyond the age of about 6 is largely a function of the need to process information that varies in amount and need for critical judgment. If an individual is confronted with large amounts of information that cannot be ignored, he or she will develop various cognitive skills and strategies to process it more effectively. Video games certainly do present enormous quantities of new information, and unlike television, most, if not all, of this information must be processed in order to succeed at the game. Thus I would argue that video games will be as significant as formal education in shaping what we think of as "advanced" thought. Alas, Piaget is not able to tell us what he thinks about video games. I suspect he would not be overly impressed. As a practical matter, however, determining empirically the role of play or video games in cognitive development has become increasingly difficult since Piaget's death because of our decreasing certainty over what is meant by "cognitive development." Play has always eluded firm definition, but, for a time in the 1960s and 1970s, I think we felt (largely thanks to Piaget) that we could get a good grip on cognitive development. This confidence is no longer the case, at least with respect to the end point or significant milestones of the developmental process.

I believe that the most productive line of research will be to examine the relationship between very specific game categories (e.g., "interactive fiction" and "maze chase") and very specific skills (e.g., map reading and visual tracking). However, I would like to take a very long view and end on a speculative note. Most people are no doubt familiar with the "feral child" phenomenon, where children who are kept in isolation for prolonged periods or raised by animals are rendered severely retarded and/or autistic (Bettelheim, 1967; Curtis, 1981). Had those isolated children had access to television, a computer, and copies of the 100 most popular computer programs, they would have entered society as geniuses, not retardates.

Notes

1. This paper is excerpted from a longer work presented at a Symposium on Play and Cognitive Development in Cross-Cultural Perspective at the Eighth Biennial Meeting of the International Society for the Study of Behavioral Development, Tours, France, July 1985.

2. Chess originated in India more than 1,500 years ago and was modified as it traveled over time and distance from India to Persia to North Africa to Europe. The game in its essentials as we now know it has been around at least since 1100 A.D. (Bell, 1969).
3. These games included Mystery at Pinecrest Manor, Dragon's Keep, Troll's Tale, Death in the Caribbean, Dark Crystal, and Ulysses and the Golden Fleece.
4. This study is being conducted with Al Forsyth and Bernie Hayes. In addition to the fantasy adventures used in the previous two studies, we are now using Alpine Encounter, Mystery Master: Murder by the Dozen, Mask of the Sun, Transylvania, Swiss Family Robinson, Treasure Island, Alice in Wonderland, Wizard of Oz, Wizard and the Princess, The Sands of Egypt, Wishbringer, Seastalker, Ultima I & II, Jenny of the Prairie, and Adventure Master.

Acknowledgments

We are grateful to Merrill Harlan and his staff at Bicentennial School in Glendale, Arizona; Drs. Ted Williams and Eyre Turner and the staff of the Edith Bowen Laboratory School at Utah State University; Lee Colston; and the staff of Hillcrest Elementary School, Logan, UT for hosting these projects. We are grateful to Rick Moore and Chris Cangelosi for their assistance and to the many fine companies that donated hardware or software to support these projects, including Atari, Inc., Commodore, Inc., Electronic Arts, Micro Learn, Sierra Inc., CBS, and Sunburst.

References

Adams, S. (1985a). Wander into Wonderland! Adventure games take you on a vacation to a place as vivid as your imagination. *Family Computing,* **6**, 37–41.

Adams, S. (1985b). Without learning to program, you can now create your own adventure games. *A+ Magazine,* **3**(6), 42–47.

Ardai, C. (1985). Do it yourself software. *Computer Entertainment,* **3**(6), 22–25, 79–80.

Barry, H.A., II, & Roberts, J.M. (1972). Infant socialization and games of chance. *Ethnology,* **11**(2), 296–308.

Bell, R.C. (1969). *Board and table games, from many civilizations* (2nd ed.). London: Oxford University Press.

Bettelheim, B. (1967). *The empty fortress: Infantile autism and the birth of the self.* New York: Free Press.

Block, J.M. (1984). Making school learning more playlike: Flow and mastery learning. *The Elementary School Journal,* **85**(1), 65–75.

Brooks, B.D. (1983). A survey of youth between ten and eighteen years of age who frequent video game arcades and other locations with video games. In S.S. Baughman & P.D. Clagett (Eds.), *Video games and human development: A research agenda for the '80s* (pp. 14–16). Cambridge, MA: Gutman Library.

Burbules, N.C., & Reese, P. (1984, April). *Teaching logic to children: An exploratory study of Rocky's boots.* Paper presented at the annual meeting of the American Educational Research Association, New Orleans, LA.

Burghardt, G.M. (1985). On the origin of play. In P.K. Smith (Ed.), *Play in animals and humans* (pp. 5–42). Oxford: Basil Blackwell.

Burns, S.M., & Brainerd, C.J. (1979). Effects of constructive and dramatic play on perspective taking in very young children. *Developmental Psychology,* **15**(3), 512–521.

Chaffin, J. (1983). Motivational features of video arcade games. In S.S. Baughman & P.D. Clagett (Eds.), *Video games and human development: A research agenda for the '80s* (pp. 54–56). Cambridge, MA: Gutman Library.

Cheyne, J.A., & Rubin, K.H. (1983). Playful precursors of problem-solving in preschoolers. *Developmental Psychology,* **19**(3), 577–584.

Christie, J.F., & Johnsen, E.P. (1983). The role of play in social-intellectual development. *Review of Educational Research,* **53**(1), 93–116.

Curtis, S. (1981). Dissociations between language and cognition: Cases and implications. *Journal of Autism and Developmental Disorders,* **11**(1), 15–30.

Dansky, J.L., & Silverman, I.W. (1973). Effect of play on associative fluency in preschool-aged children. *Developmental Psychology,* **9**(1), 38–43.

Dansky, J.L., & Silverman, I.W. (1975). Play: A general facilitator of associative fluency. *Developmental Psychology,* **11**(1), 104.

Dunne, J.J. (1984, April). *Gaming approaches in educational software: An analysis of their use and effectiveness.* Paper presented at the annual meeting of the American Educational Research Association, New Orleans, LA.

Egli, E.A., & Meyers, L.S. (1984). The role of video game playing in adolescent life: Is there a reason to be concerned? *Bulletin of the Psychonomic Society,* **22**(2), 309–312.

Fink, R.S. (1976). Role of imaginative play in cognitive development. *Psychological Reports,* **39**, 895–906.

Forsyth, A.S., Jr. (1986). *A microcomputer search type adventure game and place-location learning in fourth grade students: Effects of map type and player gender.* Unpublished doctoral dissertation, Utah State University, Logan.

Greenfield, P.M. (1983). Video games and cognitive skills. In S.S. Baughman & P.D. Clagett (Eds.), *Video games and human development: A research agenda for the '80s* (pp. 19–25). Cambridge, MA: Gutman Library.

Groos, K. (1898). *The play of animals* (E.L. Baldwin, Trans.). New York: Appleton.

Hayes, B.L., Lancy, D.F., & Evans, B. (1985). Computer adventure games and the development of information processing skills. In G.H. McNinch (Ed.), *Comprehension, computers, and communication*. Athens: The University of Georgia Press.

Hutt, C. (1966). Exploration and play in children. In P.A. Jewell & C. Loizos (Eds.), *Play, exploration and territoriality in mammals* (pp. 231–251). New York: Academic Press.

Johnson, J.E. (1976). Relations of divergent thinking and intelligence test scores with social and nonsocial make-believe play of preschool children. *Child Development, 47*(4), 1200–1203.

Koehler, W. (1927). *The mentality of apes* (2nd ed.). London: Routledge.

Krasnor, L.R., & Pepler, D.J. (1980). The study of children's play. Some suggested future directions. *New Directions for Child Development, 9*, 85–96.

Lancy, D.F. (1974). *Work, play and learning in a Kpelle town*. Unpublished doctoral dissertation, University of Pittsburgh, Pittsburgh, PA.

Lancy, D.F. (1977). Studies of memory in culture. *Annals of the New York Academy of Sciences, 285*, 297–307.

Lancy, D.F. (1983a). *Cross-cultural studies in cognition and mathematics*. New York: Academic Press.

Lancy, D.F. (1983b). Sociodramatic play and the acquisition of occupational roles. *Review Journal of Philosophy and Social Science, 7*(1–2), 285–295.

Lancy, D.F. (1985). Play in anthropological perspective. In P.K. Smith (Ed.), *Play in animals and humans* (pp. 298–304). Oxford, England: Basil Blackwell.

Lancy, D.F., Cohen, H.C., Evans, B., Levine, N., & Nevin, M.L. (1985). Using the joystick as a tool to promote intellectual growth and social interaction. *Quarterly Newsletter of the Laboratory of Comparative Human Cognition, 7*(4), 119–125.

Lancy, D.F., Evans, B., & Forsyth, A. (1985, July). *Five models for using computers in schools: Perspectives from the United States of America*. Paper presented at the 12th Comparative Education Society—Europe Conference, Antwerp, Belgium.

Lepper, M.R. (1985). Microcomputers in education: Motivational and social issues. *American Psychologist, 40*(1), 1–18.

Lepper, M.R., & Malone, T.W. (1985). Making learning fun: A taxonomy of intrinsic motivations for learning. In R.E. Snow & M.J. Farr (Eds.), *Aptitude, learning and instruction. III. Cognitive and affective process analysis*. Hillsdale, NJ: Lawrence Erlbaum.

Liebert, J.N., Sprafkin, J.N., & Davidson, E. (1982). *The early window: Effects of television on children and youth* (2nd ed.). Elmhurst, NY: Pergamon.

Loftus, G.R., & Loftus, E.F. (1983). *Mind at play*. New York: Basic Books.

Malone, T.W. (1981). Toward a theory of intrinsically motivating instruction. *Cognitive Science, 4*(2), 333–369.

Maxwell, W. (1983). Games children play: Powerful tools that teach some thinking skills. In W. Maxwell (Ed.), *Thinking: The expanding frontier* (pp. 43–78). Philadelphia: Franklin Institute Press.

Mitchell, E. (1983). The effects of home video games on children and families. In S.S. Baughman & P.D. Clagett (Eds.), *Video games and human development: A research agenda for the '80s* (pp. 11–14). Cambridge, MA: Gutman Library.

Piaget, J. (1962). *Play, dreams and imitation in childhood* (G. Gategno & F.M. Hodgson, Trans.). New York: Norton. (Original work published 1951)

Piaget, J. (1965). *The moral judgement of the child*. New York: Free Press. (Original work published 1932)

Roberts, J.M., & Sutton-Smith, B. (1962). Child training and game involvement. *Ethnology, 2*(1), 166–185.

Simon, H.A., & Chase, W.G. (1973). Skill in chess. *American Scientist, 61*(3), 394–403.

Simon, T., & Smith, P.K. (1983). The study of play and problem solving in pre-school children: Have experimenter effects been responsible for previous results? *British Journal of Developmental Psychology, 1*, 289–297.

Smilansky, S. (1968). *The effects of sociodramatic play on disadvantaged preschool children*. New York: J. Wiley.

Smith, P.K. (1982). Does play matter? Functional and evolutionary aspects of animal and human play. *Behavioral and Brain Sciences, 5*(1), 139–184.

Smith, P.K. (1985, July). *Experimental studies of play: Are the problems just methodological?* Paper presented at the biennial meeting of the International Society for the Study of Behavioral Development, Tours, France.

Stewart, D.M., Kamm, K., Allen, J., & Miles, P.J. (1973). *The Wisconsin test of reading skill development: Test administrator's manual*. Minneapolis, MN: National Computer Systems.

Strehlo, K. (1984). Getting into adventure games. *Personal Software, 2*(2), 94–99.

Sudnow, D. (1982). *Pilgrim in the microworld*. New York: Warner Books.

Surrey, D. (1982). It's like good training for life. *Natural History, 91*(11), 71–83.

Sutton-Smith, B. (1967). The role of play in cognitive development. *Young Children, 6*, 361–370.

Sutton-Smith, B. (1976). A structural grammar of games and sports. *International Review of Sport Sociology*, **2**(1), 117–137.

Sutton-Smith, B. (1980). Children's play: Some sources of play theorizing. *New Directions for Child Development*, **9**, 1–16.

Sutton-Smith, B. (1983). Piaget, play and cognition, revisited. In W.F. Overton (Ed.), *The relationship between social and cognitive development* (pp. 229–249). Hillsdale, NJ: Lawrence Erlbaum.

Sylva, K. (1977). Play and learning. In B. Tizard & D. Harvey (Eds.), *Biology of play* (pp. 126–134). London: Heinemann.

Unwin, G. (1983, October). Adventures in education. *Creative Computing*, pp. 149–152.

A New Environment for Communication Play: On-Line Play

David Myers

Bulletin board systems (BBS) allow direct connection between any two appropriately equipped computers through the public telephone system. These computers can share files, information, and software. BBS software transfers control, within limits, of a "host" computer (one running the BBS program) to a "remote" computer (which initiates the connection). (Table 1 defines these and other terms common to on-line activity; see also Hiltz & Turoff, 1978.)

The limits of control of the host by the remote computer vary according to the particular BBS program in use and the modifications to that program made by the BBS system operator (SysOp). Typically, BBS allows non-real-time communication among callers in a manner similar to true bulletin boards. That is, messages (bulletins) are left within the system that can be read and replied to by subsequent callers.

According to most published lists (Besston & Tucker, 1984; *The On-Line Computer Telephone Directory*, 1984), fewer than 1,500 individually operated BBS are in the United States. However, published figures of BBS use are grossly underestimated. To give one example, the January, 1984 listing of BBS within *The On-Line Computer Telephone Directory* totaled less than 700 systems; only three BBS listings were given for Austin, Texas. During a 3-month observation period in the first months of 1984, 26 public electronic bulletin boards were discovered that could be reached by a local telephone call from the Austin area.

If all cities are as poorly represented in "official" figures, then these figures must be increased by at least a factor of five.

A major difficulty in gaining accurate estimates of BBS activity nationwide is the transient and underground nature of these systems. Yet, despite the inability of listing services to maintain an accurate directory of BBS, no doubt exists that their numbers are on the increase. This trend is evident in the published listings alone. The very first BBS for personal computer users, a remote CP/M system, was begun in Chicago during the early months of 1978. In late 1983 more than 100 RCP/M systems were in operation in the U.S. (Besston & Tucker, 1984:26).

Table 1   Terms Used in BBS Communications

BBS:	Bulletin Board System(s)
CMC:	Computer-Mediated Communications
CP/M:	first wide-spread operating system for microcomputers
download:	transfer files from host to remote computer memory
handle:	BBS user alias
Host computer:	computer that contains BBS software and system files
menu:	list of user options within a BBS
mods:	modifications and changes made to software/hardware
networks:	commercial BBS program for Apple][and][e systems
pirate system:	BBS devoted to duplicating and distributing commercial software
RCP/M:	remote CP/M system, a BBS using the CP/M operating system
Remote computer:	computer that connects (through telephone) to host computer
SysOp:	Bulletin Board System Operator
TBBS:	commercial BBS program for TRS-80 Models I/II, CP/M, and MS-DOS systems
T-net:	commercial BBS program for Apple][and][e systems
trading:	exchanging pirated software
upload:	transfer files from remote to host computer memory
wares/warez:	illegally copied (pirated) commercial software

Goals and Method

The goals of this study were to characterize the BBS environment as a context for public communication behavior and to discover representative patterns of individual communication behavior, particularly communication play, within BBS. To this end, several types of BBS were observed in the Austin area. These BBS differed according to the important contextual variables of hardware configuration, communications software, and system operator.

All 26 BBS in Austin were contacted at least once during a 3-month period (January to March, 1984). Three primary methods of data collection were used: participant-observation in Austin BBS activities; analysis of records kept within the host BBS computers; and in-depth interviews with system operators.

Participant-observation was conducted primarily at three of the most popular and longest-lived Austin BBS: TBBS#1 (described at some length later), the Austin Party Board (an Apple-based system), and the Armadillo (an Atari-based system). During the 3-month period, more than 100 on-line hours were logged on these three boards.

On-line records of system use (including messages and caller lists) were downloaded at regular intervals from each of the three systems so that an intact 3-month sequence of messages was available for each system. Messages were also downloaded randomly from other Austin BBS and indicated that the communication activity observed within TBBS#1, the Party Board, and the Armadillo was well representative of BBS communication activity elsewhere. In all, more than 1,000 messages were recorded for analysis.

In-depth, unstructured interviews with seven system operators were used to clarify and interpret message content and to access BBS user files not available to the general public. Other interviews with frequent BBS users were also conducted sporadically during the 3-month observation period. The SysOp interviews were particularly valuable in gaining an accurate estimate of the number of Austin area callers involved in frequent (at least once a week) BBS communications. Although many BBS user logs listed more than 500 registered callers, many of these names were duplicates and aliases. Fewer than 1,500 Austin area residents called the 26 local BBS and, of this number, less than 20% were likely to call any one system more than once a week.

Results

The BBS Environment: Play Contexts

The greatest similarity among BBS was found in their hardware configurations. Thus of the 26 Austin area boards, only five different types of computers were used as hosts. Nine Apple-based boards were found, the single largest category.

However, BBS software was found to be more crucial than computer hardware in determining specific characteristics of the on-line communication context. In this category a bit more variety existed. Of the nine Apple-based Austin BBS, five used Networks software, three used T-Net software, and one system used communication software designed and written ("home-brewed") by its system operator. And, even in the case of commercial software packages such as Networks, there were many instances of system operators rewriting code and customizing the software according to their own needs and desires, so that no two BBS communication contexts were exactly alike.

Nevertheless, enough similarities were observed among boards to classify user behavior within a common and relatively stable (during the observation period) BBS SOFTWARE-determined context. User behavior fell into distinct user "roles" within this context.

In order to better clarify these two representative characteristics—software organizational structures (macrocontexts) and user roles (microcontexts)—of the BBS environment, it is useful to look closely at one of the longest-lived Austin area boards: TBBS#1.

TBBS#1 was one of the first Austin-area bulletin board systems. It was begun in the late summer of 1982 by Tom Dougherty, an Air Force serviceman who had recently been transferred from Denver to Bergstrom Air Force

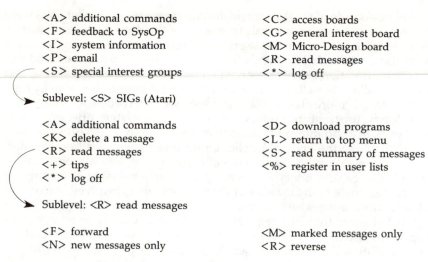

<A> additional commands   <C> access boards
<F> feedback to SysOp   <G> general interest board
<I> system information   <M> Micro-Design board
<P> email   <R> read messages
<S> special interest groups   <*> log off

Sublevel: <S> SIGs (Atari)

<A> additional commands   <D> download programs
<K> delete a message   <L> return to top menu
<R> read messages   <S> read summary of messages
<+> tips   <%> register in user lists
<*> log off

Sublevel: <R> read messages

<F> forward   <M> marked messages only
<N> new messages only   <R> reverse

Figure 1   TBBS#1 main menu.

Base in Austin. Tom Dougherty had first learned of bulletin boards in Denver, where he had been a member of the local TRS-80 computer club.

On coming to Austin, Tom Dougherty decided to start his own board "to meet people and become a part of the community." He began a board he called "Austin" soon after arriving. Within a couple of months he had switched to a newly developed, more sophisticated communications software package, The Bread Board System (TBBS). "Austin" became "TBBS#1" in September 1982.

In the course of bringing TBBS#1 on-line, Tom Dougherty created a menu structure that guided use of his BBS and that, due to the technological characteristics of the medium, had certain structural similarities with all other BBS menus. The TBBS#1 main menu is shown in Figure 1.

Branching off from the main menu results in the caller being presented with successive sublevel menus until he reaches either the information or communication function desired. For instance, to read messages concerning Atari computers on TBBS#1 requires that a user presented with the main menu select <S> to reach the Special Interest Groups (SIGs) sublevel; then <A> to reach the Atari SIG sublevel; and, finally, <R> to read messages within the Atari SIG.

Just as the SysOp determines the menu selections available at each sublevel, so too he determines who can choose among those selections and access different levels within the BBS. Thus a special password might be required to enter the Atari SIG within TBBS#1.

By determining the users within each BBS sublevel, and by restricting access to certain users, the SysOp can adapt the BBS software to serve his own interests and needs, resulting in a customized communications environment.

Tom Dougherty, motivated by his goal of meeting a large number of Austin-area computer users, established few restricted areas within TBBS#1. In fact, he designed the SIG sublevels to appeal to the widest possible BBS user population.

> When TBBS began there were already two other Apple boards and one other TRS-80 board in Austin. What I tried to do was give the other computer owners a place to go. We were the first BBS in Austin to devote sections to Atari and Commodore computers. And we're still the only bulletin board in Austin that has its own Timex-Sinclair SIG. (personal interview, Tom Dougherty)

TBBS#1 stands at one extreme in the BBS community as a very "open" system, allowing any user to log on and have immediate access to files and functions within the BBS. Other systems are, to a greater or lesser degree, "closed." Access may be restricted to certain sublevels (as mentioned earlier), or access may be restricted to ALL sublevels, or access may be restricted to the BBS as a whole (by use of an unpublished telephone number).

In this sort of environment, a BBS user hierarchy has developed, characterized by the amount of access a user has to the system. The SysOp stands at the apex of this system-access pyramid. Not only does the SysOp have access to all system functions, he also has complete control over those functions; he can create, manipulate, or destroy them at his leisure.

Slightly less control is given to BBS remote SysOps. Remote SysOps are a way of dividing the SysOp's singular burden of monitoring and maintaining the BBS. The overworked SysOp will grant knowledgeable and trusted callers increased system access and control in return for help in keeping the system up-to-date and functioning properly. TBBS#1, for instance, had remote SysOps charged with maintaining each of the separate SIG sublevels; outside their small SIG fiefdoms, however, the remote SysOps have only normal user-access privileges. In all cases, the remote SysOp does not have access to the BBS computer hardware, but plays his BBS role, as the name implies, from a remote location.

As many as 256 different access levels are allowed callers by some commercial BBS software; in practice, only two basic types of regular user access exist: high and low.

These divisions are more common on closed than open systems such as TBBS#1 and are usually indicative of something secretive and (perhaps) illegal going on among the high-access users. Pirate BBS involved in the free exchange of commercial software invariably have some (usually extended) form of high- and low-access user levels.

Within pirate BBS, high-access users can download pirated software from the BBS; low-access users cannot. Low-access users become high-access users either by being friends with other high-access users (connections) or by uploading pirate software for others to use (performance).

At the lowest access level is the new caller. Most BBS require user verification of some kind, if only to insert the proper information into an on-line file of callers. TBBS#1 requires that all users sign on with their real names, not handles. Users refusing to give their real names (along with their telephone numbers) are denied access to the system; they cannot even log on TBBS#1 and get to the main menu level: The system hangs up in their faces. Most other BBS require new callers to leave a telephone number and address, which is then verified by the SysOp, a process taking 2 or 3 days.

In summary, two general characteristics of BBS are common across boards and are especially pertinent to our discussion of user communication behavior:

1. Information and functions are layered within BBS "menus," much like the successive layers of an onion. This data organization scheme is commonly known as a tree structure.
2. Clear user hierarchies exist (corresponding to user "roles") within a BBS, based on the users' ability to manipulate and control BBS software structures. At the top of this hierarchy is the system operator; at the bottom is the new caller. The SysOp maintains his position at the top of the user hierarchy by limiting other users' access to the information and functions of his BBS. This is most often accomplished through personal adaptation of BBS software structures.

BBS User Behavior: Play Texts

Play within BBS begins with the creation of a BBS by its SysOp. Bringing the system up requires a goodly amount of conceptual architecture and is not unlike writing an autobiographical short story or sketching a self-portrait. Schwartzman defines play as a similar process: "creative and spontaneous metaphor construction and identity communication" (1982:25).

However, not only does the SysOp-determined content of a BBS immediately communicate its SysOp's personality, but that content also transforms and vitalizes that personality in subjectively important ways. Creating a BBS is a naming process both for the system and its creator.

Nor are the SysOp's motivations unique among the BBS user population. Virtually every regular user of BBS interviewed, certainly all heavy users, expressed a desire to become a SysOp and operate his own BBS in the future. All users wished to create their own unique, personalized, computer-mediated communication environment. Their actions within the BBS environment lent credence to this assertion.

A communication system consists of three basic elements: (a) messages, (b) senders/receivers of messages, and (c) network configuration(s) formed by interactions among message senders and receivers through message exchange.

Personalizing a communication system requires that individuals manipulate one or all of these basic elements. All BBS play observed can be classified according to its effect on one or more of these three basic communication system elements, if we are allowed to immediately add a fourth. The communication system context (the BBS software) is also an element to be manipulated and controlled. Such system-level play qualifies as metaplay and might be either creative (writing program code) or destructive (system crashing).

Figure 2 shows how play within each user role (microcontext) affects the four different communication system elements.

Note that each user role on the right side of the figure is a subset of the user role to its immediate left. Thus the SysOp has the ability to play at all levels within the BBS with all communication system elements.

Play is most limited for a user in the new caller role. Here, all behavior must be ordered by an extrinsic goal: obtaining access to the BBS environment. Usually this requires acquiescing to the rules of play laid down by the local SysOp. The personal naming process, which we are using as a central metaphor for BBS play, is limited to the simple, nominal act of submitting a handle (along with real world identification) to the SysOp for approval. Play occurs either in the creative choice of a handle or the destruction of a real world identity (through giving SysOp false information) or both.

At the next highest user role—the regular user with low access—a rather rapid accommodation period (Piaget, 1962) occurs in which play is more of a learning than a creative process. However, this period passes quickly for the experienced BBS participant due to the similarity among BBS software structures; in other words, one can apply information learned in the BBS environment as a whole within each local board. Working from

Play transforms . . .

these elements through these roles

	SysOp	Remote SysOp	High-access user	Low-acess user	New caller
Communication messages (content)	creates content	enforces content	tests content	learns content	
		semantic play		syntactic play	
Message senders/rcvrs. (identity)	defines others functionally	defines others nominally	defines self functionally	defines self nominally	
Network configuration (form)	receives messages	shares messages	exchanges messages	sends messages	NO ACCESS
Point of view:	hub of wheel	family member	dyad member	spoke of wheel	
Context (BBS software)	CREATES	ASSIMILATES/ maintains	MANIPULATES/ rearranges	ACCOMMODATES/ recognizes	

Figure 2 Play behavior within BBS.

common cues within computer-mediated communication environments, the low-access user soon learns the local system rules: how to travel among BBS sublevels and how to identify and use communication system functions. Because these sublevels and functions are the result of earlier SysOp choices, the low-access user is simultaneously learning something of the SysOp's own motivations and interests.

Play among users with low access levels is largely exploratory in determining system parameters and limits. At first, messages consist of simple requests for information about the system from the SysOp. Gradually, low-access users extend broader requests for information to broader segments of users.

Should the low-access user, during this feeling-out process, find the local system environment amenable to his personal communication patterns and interests (and the SysOp finds his behavior appropriate within the system), then he is likely to become a high-access user and redirect his play behavior to more personal goals. Exploratory play and information requests are replaced by more creative, expressive, and intrinsically motivated play behavior. The naming process becomes more difficult and more gratifying; it now must be accomplished through actions as well as words.

High-access regular users are most likely to rearrange communication system elements in an attempt to personalize the communication environment. Play within this user role is well representative of the majority of on-line play. Therefore, high-access user play is examined in the section that follows with specific examples from the Austin BBS environment. These examples are arranged in three categories: (a) play with message content, (b) play with on-line identities (senders/receivers), and (c) play with network relationships (configurations). Finally, a brief discussion of play with system (context) is presented, which, as can be seen from Figure 2, is at the upper limit of the high-access user's capabilities.

Play with objects: Message content.   The following message within the Austin Party Board, a local Apple-based system run by a University of Texas student, displays most of the results of play with message content.

MESSAGE #65: OHHHHHH
peachy keen ultra meato mega-fine new
warezezesszzzszzszszsszzezszszsz . . .
pooyan (kool)
it's the pits, mugshot, spud
(the last 3 really sux deluxe)
hard-worx (awesum bbs package) all mods!
questron sorceror (enchantor ii or zork iv,
what-ever u wanna call it . . .)
messiah
disk rigger 1.1 (atom rulez like a mo)
all older shit like a mo . . .

later daze in the haze!!!
be cool, don't drool!
live fast, blast a bast!
live slow, hoe a mo!
/__\ hardcore /__\
[pi/ratz]-npg/dos-hackin' hell-raisers]
raisers . . .
// if ya got anything new drop a trade note . . . \\

Content play includes personalized punctuation and spelling patterns, which most often tend to shorten words and expressions ("awesum," "u," etc.). These manipulations of the normal rules of grammar are conscious and intentional in that they are motivated by the desire to send and receive messages spontaneously, according to individual initiative and desire (and ability), without regard to any predetermined style or structure. The easiest way to do this is to write messages off the top of one's head, and most messages are composed, written, and sent in a single on-line session—letters that are truly "dashed off."

The jargon of the message consists of terms common within a computer software environment ("mods"), a computer communications environment ("bbs"), a computer game-playing environment ("zork iv"), and, of course, a computer software pirate environment ("warez"). This last example is particularly useful in explaining the on-line transformation of common words and meanings.

"Warez" is a transformation of "wares," which is in turn a clipped version of "software." A pirate's "warez" are those commercial software programs he has copied and can distribute to other BBS users. These copied programs are used both as money and as status symbols within the pirate community. And the final "z" is frequently attached to other words to indicate their use within a pirate context. Thus "atom rulez . . ." indicates that Atom is very proficient at copying commercial software.

Another, more localized example of the transformation process can be seen in the use of the phrase "like a mo." Originally referring to the zaniest member of The Three Stooges, this phrase was, for a time, sprinkled liberally throughout messages within Austin BBS to indicate the power of a free and playful context. Thus "atom rulez like a mo" adds both emphasis and attitude to Atom's skills.

Other common manipulations of message content found within the example are the almost obligatory obscenity ("shit") and the use of graphic embellishments ("/__\").

Play with self: Sender identity.   Play begins with users choosing (frequently colorful) BBS names/handles. Whether the name chosen is the same as that used in other communication environments is immaterial. Even when the name is superficially the same, it has one important difference: It has indeed, in its new incarnation, been chosen by its owner. Off-line ("real") names are often given unique stylistic embellishments by their creators in order to more clearly distinguish the new from the old. The name might always be placed at the same odd position within a message, or always typed in capital letters, or always written with some other distinguishing feature or mark. Thus "Brad Donnell" becomes "--BRAD DONNELL--" and "Phil Putnam" becomes "Phil!" These names have each been transformed into trademarks, distinctive individual smells by which their users are recognized as either friends or enemies within an otherwise vague and anonymous BBS communication environment.

Users rarely embellish real names with formal titles (Mr., Ms., MD, etc.). Regular users of systems that forbid the use of handles are known by either their two given names (such as Tom Dougherty) or, more commonly, by their first name only.

However, informal titles and extended embellishments of user handles are common. Three prominent BBS users observed in the Austin area were: "THE //CORELLIAN//," "= = = => Hacker #25," and

J
O
S
H
U
FALKEN

The Corellian's name was always signed with the preceding and succeeding slashes and always positioned at the lower right-hand corner of a message. The number of equal signs in Hacker #25's arrow varied, but the arrow design was always a part of the signature. "Joshua Falken" was always written in crossword-puzzle style, perhaps to distinguish it from the character in the popular movie *War Games*, which was its inspiration.

Several users interviewed confessed (and user files documented) that they often used multiple handles within BBS. The different handles were indicative of separate user personalities. The off-line name was almost always used as a front man, one who obeyed all the local rules and, if need arose, dealt with the local officials (SysOps) for information or higher level access. Most regular users were also known by a single handle within the BBS environment as a whole. They used this handle at one time or another within all Austin area BBS.

However, anonymity was called for at times (during play), and newly created handles were required. During these times, users would create as many identities as necessary (or that they could get away with).

The user files of most BBS are filled to overflowing with such temporary handles, and the practice of creating multiple handles is generally frowned upon by SysOps due to lack of memory space in the host computer. The prevalence of multiple handles indicates that the BBS user role is not simply a one-to-one replacement for a real world communication role lacking subjective meaning. Even BBS user roles are transformed; even self-created handles grow tiresome and must be replaced.

The attraction of the BBS communication environment is not that unappealing communication roles are transformed into better ones so much as it is that these changes can be made whenever the individual user feels the need. Play is often both the means to and end of this transformation process.

Play with others: Network relationships. Although handles are first chosen outside the BBS environment (by new callers), they gain meaning and significance only inside that environment in the user-to-user relationships that develop during sending and receiving messages. Occasionally, these relationships extend beyond the BBS and into other media, but more often they are restricted to the BBS environment.

The first relationship formed is between the new caller and the SysOp. Indeed, the BBS network is primarily a private network of the SysOp and his BBS friends (Myers, 1985).

But, whereas SysOp play within the user network tends to nurture and strengthen network relationships, high-access users frequently exert whatever manipulative power they possess in the opposite direction during play and attempt to destroy relationships.

In fact, regular users malign one another frequently in messages carrying threats of, among other things, quick and violent deaths. Subsections within Austin BBS are devoted to nothing but "ranking" messages of this kind. Sometimes these insults are based on a disagreement over which computer or political candidate is best; but, whatever the original motivation, the message contents quickly become secondary to a chest-thumping display of on-line egos.

Relationships quickly form and dissolve within such a context. Here, quoted verbatim, is one user's description of that context.

MESSAGE #56: THE DEATH ALLIANCE
Msg Left By: D-DAY DAN
I invite you to be a member of the Death Alliance on the Texas Leprechaun Insult board (9) [:B9 ; B9:R+ ; <cr>].
Read all the messages on this board and decide if you want to make a new personality. It is lots of fun to insult each other but don't get involved (?).
There are 3 groups, roughly on this board, I should say 4.
1. This is the group that consists of:
> THE Mysterious One
> Caliban
> Capt. Crunch
> The Assassin
> Fag Killer
> > and
> Blade
2. This group consists of people who don't (or rarely) insult each other:
> Luca Brasi
> Michael Corleone
> The Militant Boatman*

> Bad Cats Mahoogan
>
> *one-timers
>
> 3. These are the people that only have characters which last a short while or are not part of any alliance:
>
>> James Arthur Strohm
>>
>> Tom. T
>>
>> J-----
>>
>> Etc.
>
> 4. The Death Alliance
>
> I am the leader of this group, and we want to get rid of everyone who we dislike. (this is fun to do!)
>
> Members:
>
>> D-Day Dan
>>
>> Adamn the Anarchist
>>
>> Tapyr (may be kicked out)
>
> New insulters are welcome.
>
> Please consider joining, for that matter, my group needs good insulters.
>
> Leave me a message on one of these BBS's . . .

As can be seen from this message, character defamation is a self-conscious and playful activity but not without its serious overtones. Messages left within this "Insult Board" on the Texas Leprechaun BBS would probably be forbidden and deleted by the SysOp should they appear anywhere else.

Also important to note are the complex alliances that have formed within the Leprechaun's insult board. Actions within these alliances, that is, actions manipulating alliance relationships, form the basis for extending the BBS naming process and creating a more detailed on-line identity. A large number of messages within BBS end with a plea for responses and added participants in on-line communication play. Thus although the play process is individually motivated and performed, it requires multiple participants.

Network relationships formed within a BBS are frequently included in a user's handle, as in the following case:

> perfidious pirate
> 202 alliance

This user handle, left as a signature at the end of an on-line message, is indicative both of an on-line personality and an on-line network relationship; in this case, membership in a local pirate club that exchanges commercial software among its members.

Occasionally, such signatures take on the air of a royal decree.

> one eye on the a.p.b.
> on the diner its one eye
> on the t-net its one eye
> on the lep its one eye
> on the wacker board its one eye

on the treasure island its one eye
on the trove its one eye
one eye
member of the life alliance and
the black chevy cult and
the d-day dan fan club

Such extended network relationships seldom persevere, however. Like BBS message content, they are spontaneous and free-form with well-established rules for their creation but not for their sustenance.

Play with the system: Metaplay. Ultimately, the individual finds relationships begun within BBS more easily sustained in other, more "intimate" communication media (voice telephone, face-to-face). However, playing within these other media is not as easy; social and moral barriers inhibit off-line identity manipulation, character defamation, and "real" (as opposed to on-line/"play") theft of computer software.

Communications play within BBS remains, in its purest form, an individual activity. Groups bring with them rules and common goals that are broken and destroyed through individual transformations. Therefore, individuals who truly wish to build their own communication environment are motivated to build their own bulletin board systems and become SysOps. System play within the SysOp role must be balanced against the time, cost, and skill that BBS manipulation and maintenance require.

Conclusions and Implications

The first important conclusion of this study is that its observations support a view of play as a transformational process (Bamberg, 1983; Schwartzman, 1978). This definition of play allows for certain important similarities in play behavior to be found among all BBS user roles, leading naturally to the interpretation of these roles as an expanding set of microcontexts, each determined more by independent, extrinsic (system hardware/software) variables than by the relatively constant intrinsic desire among all users to manipulate, transform, and ultimately control the local communication environment, that is, to *play*.

The second major conclusion of the study is that the computer-mediated communication environment has unique characteristics that make it an environment well suited to free communication play and, accordingly, communication play research. These characteristics are

- user anonymity,
- user interactivity (both with other users and with the system itself), and
- user hierarchies (determined by system software structures).

The last characteristic is something of a surprise in that a hierarchical structure of user roles serves to motivate on-line play more often than inhibit play. This does not imply that the software-imposed hierarchical relationships were necessarily adhered to during play; in fact, exactly the opposite often occurred. However, without the presence of a user hierarchy or some sort of rudimentary social structure to "play off," BBS users frequently created their own straw-man versions (such as the D-Day Dan Death Alliance).

The third major conclusion of this study is that on-line play has adapted on-line communication systems (BBS) according to the desires of users and is an important and necessary part of the overall BBS design process. The most immediate implication of this conclusion is that public communications software is more properly a public activity than a private design. National commercial networks must recognize this characteristic in planning for mass market systems of the future.

Unfortunately, local BBS offer only one model for computer-mediated communication systems—a model in which system structures are subject to trial and transformation through user play. National commercial systems are currently based on another model, one in which system structures (predetermined by system designers) are given first priority, and individual play behavior that might transform or undermine these structures is restricted and curtailed (De Sola Pool, 1983; Marvin, 1983; Vallee, 1982).

If we are to evaluate these two models on the basis of how much individual "fun" each provides, then surely the local BBS model has an edge. What is unclear at present is how well group goals are served by allowing individual users unrestricted opportunities for play. Play will likely continue to be restricted within national commercial home computer networks until both the constructive and destructive aspects of play are recognized as integral to computer-mediated communications evolution and (re)design.

References

Bamberg, M. (1983). Metaphor and play interaction. In F.E. Manning (Ed.), *The world of play* (pp. 127–143). Champaign, IL: Leisure Press.

Besston, T., & Tucker, T. (1984). *Hooking in: The underground computer bulletin board workbook and guide*. Westlake Village, CA: ComputerFood Press.

De Sola Pool, I. (1983). *Technologies of freedom*. Cambridge, MA: Belknap Press.

Hiltz, S.R., & Turoff, M. (1978). *The network nation: Human communication via computer*. Reading, MA: Addison-Wesley.

Marvin, C. (1983). Telecommunications policy and the pleasure principle. *Telecommunications Policy*, **7**, 43–52.

Myers, D. (1985). *Home computer communication networks: A first look at BBS*. Unpublished manuscript.

The on-line computer telephone directory (pp. 5–9). (1984, January).

Piaget, J. (1962). *Play, dreams and imitation in childhood.* New York: W.W. Norton.

Schwartzman, H.B. (1978). *Transformations: The anthropology of children's play.* New York: Plenum Press.

Schwartzman, H.B. (1982). Play and metaphor. In J. Loy (Ed.), *The paradoxes of play* (pp. 25–33). Champaign, IL: Leisure Press.

Vallee, J. (1982). *The network revolution.* Berkeley, CA: And/Or Press.